What previewers said.

◆ "I loved the chapter with the three-way sex scene. It seemed very familiar. Was I there?" *–Name withheld by request*

◆ With a bit of 'Portnoy's Complaint' and lots of Woody Allen moments, Michael's book is a hilarious trip down memory lane – sometimes poignant, mostly hysterically funny, bawdy, and delightful for anyone with a kooky sense of humor. This book provides one of the best descriptions of what we all go through in adolescence as we make at least a feeble effort to become "grown-ups." Although the author writes about our generation — the '60s — this book is really for anyone and everyone who wants to roll on the floor, laughing until the tears come. *–Sheila M. Clark*

◆ "I was laughing my ass off reading the excerpt from your book, and I can't wait to read the rest of it." *–Jim Flick*

◆ "I knew the lesbian painter. She was a lousy painter but an excellent lesbian. When does the movie come out?" *–Wendy Liu*

◆ "Marcus has been threatening to publish this for years. When you read it, you'll remember when you were young and insane and you won't stop laughing. Don't write to Marcus to share your similar experiences. He's going to be put away where he can't get email." *–Ted Foti*

◆ "A perfect combination of silliness and seriousness. I worked with you in '72. You remember everything. I'm glad you didn't see me doing anything illegal or stupid." *–Susan Weiss*

◆ "I didn't realize what an A-hole I was back then. If this book wasn't so funny, I'd sue you for libel. I'll settle for an autographed copy. Thanks for changing my name." *–Marty Gilbert*

◆ "Every time I start laughing, there's my husband peering over my shoulder wanting to know what's so funny. This book is! Michael, your wife is a saint!" *–Deborah Slutsky Samuels*

PLEASE NOTE: Some comments on the previous page are printed exactly as submitted by readers. Some comments have been slightly edited. A few are complete fabrications written by the author in an effort to entice people to buy books. Please don't feel deceived. He only promises that the book is at least 80% true. If you do the math, you'll know that up to 20% could be bullshit. ALSO: If you're surprised not to see Roman numerals in the beginning of the book, please see page 316 for an explanation.

The author's blogs:

♦**For The First Time (or the last time)** talks about changes in society and technology: first toilet paper, last country to get TV, first voice-mail, last Automat, first female Boy Scout leader, etc. http://4TheFirstTime.blogspot.com

♦**Oh How Stupid** provides an occasional look at some of the stupidest things done by human beings. http://OhHowStupid.blogspot.com

♦**Gotta Get One** recommends and criticizes electronics, cars, cameras, tools, movies, food, books and more. http://GottaGet1.blogspot.com

♦**911 Wackos.** Some folks call 911 for strange reasons. Sometimes they get into trouble after the call. Sometimes the 911 operators get into trouble. http://911Wackos.blogspot.com

♦**Dial Zero** provides a look at what's silly, stupid or surprising in telecom. http://DialZero.blogspot.com

♦**Book Making** is where Michael discusses writing, editing and publishing — for writers and readers. http://BookMakingBlog.blogspot.com

♦**Become a Real Self-Publisher** is the online companion to the book by the same name. It's the repository for additions, corrections, and comments. http://Real-Self-Publisher.blogspot.com

His other books:

♦CB Bible (co-author, 1976)
♦What Phone System Should I Buy? (1996)
♦I Only Flunk My Brightest Students (2008)
♦Phone Systems & Phones for Small Business & Home (2009)
♦The AbleComm Guide to Phone Systems (2009)
♦Telecom Reference eBook (2009)
♦Become a Real Self-Publisher (2010)

Stories I'd Tell My Children

(but maybe not until they're adults)

◆

Michael N. Marcus

SILVER SANDS BOOKS

www.SilverSandsBooks.com
230 Woodmont Road, Suite 15
Milford CT 06460
books@ablecomm.com
203.878.8383

ISBN-13: 978-0-9816617-5-9
Library of Congress Control Number: 2009909686
Version 1.41 (LS-6)

Portions of this book were published in the *New Haven Register* and are published here with permission. Portions were published online. Portions were published in *I Only Flunk My Brightest Students: stories from school and real life.*

For corrections, questions or comments. please use the address on the previous page.

This book is distributed by Ingram Book Group, Baker & Taylor, and NACSCORP.

♦Editor: Sheila M. Clark (Her comment on the first page was
made before she became editor.)

♦Cover artist: Carina Ruotolo

♦Front cover photographer: Michael Kempf

Contents

Foreplay, to get you in the mood:

"Laugh, and the world laughs with you. Weep and you weep alone."
 -Ella Wheeler Wilcox (author and poet)

"Laugh alone and the world thinks you're an idiot."
 -Alfred E. Neuman (gap-toothed symbol of *MAD* magazine)

"Over? Did you say 'over'? Nothing is over until we decide it is! Was it over when the Germans bombed Pearl Harbor? Hell no!"
 -John Belushi as Bluto Blutarsky in *Animal House*

"Women need a reason to have sex. Men just need a place."
 -Billy Crystal as Mitch Robbins in *City Slickers*

"Foul-mouthed? Fuck you!"
 -Eddie Murphy as Axel Foley in *Beverly Hills Cop*

"Opinions are like assholes. Everybody has one."
 -Clint Eastwood as "Dirty" Harry Callahan in *The Dead Pool*

"She thinks I'm a pervert because I drank our water bed." "Stop whining and eat your shiksa."
 -Woody Allen as Miles Monroe in *Sleeper*

"There was a moment last night, when she was sandwiched between the two Finnish dwarves and the Maori tribesmen, where I thought, wow, I could really spend the rest of my life with this woman."
 -Ben Stiller as Derek Zoolander in *Zoolander*

"I have a penis and a brain and only enough blood to run one at a time."
 -Robin Williams on the *Tonight Show*

"Listen, let's get one thing straight. In the hours you're here taking care of my mother, no ganja."
 -James Gandolfini as Tony Soprano in *The Sopranos*

"Fuck 'em if they can't take a joke."
 -Many people, including Michael N. Marcus

My only child, Hunter J. Marcus
He licks himself and he licks me, but he can't laugh.

Introduction

This book's title may seem strange. You might wonder why I didn't name the book, *Stories I Told My Children*, or *Stories I'll Tell My Children*.

I can't use those titles because I don't have any human children that I know of, and I'm not likely to have any.

Unless some unknown offspring shows up to claim a percentage of my income, the closest I'll get to parenting is with Hunter, my Golden Retriever.

Though he's not human, Hunter is a pretty good substitute. He receives and returns a lot of love. He's a good communicator. He's empathetic. I don't pay for college. I just pick up poop.

He listens while I tell him my stories. He smiles, holds my hand, licks his weenie and licks my face. But he can't laugh.

I need an audience which laughs. So I write.

I don't often dwell on my lack of human children. My wife Marilyn and I tried, but it didn't happen, and neither of us felt like adopting. It just seemed like too much of a gamble. Hunter, however, was adopted, and he's just fine. If I had to be a dog, I'd like to be like him. But I'd want parents like us, to spoil me.

Sometimes I feel that by not reproducing, by not fully participating in the human continuum, I've never really grown up. *Maybe I became my own kid*— and that's why I do some silly stuff (like this book?) and buy myself so many big boys' toys. Maybe I'm like Peter Pan ("I *won't* grow up. I don't want to wear a tie. I will stay a boy forever").

OK. That's all the serious stuff I plan for the book. Now we can move on to the fun and the filth.

This book could be considered a "coming-of-age" book, with young male silliness and horniness in the tradition of *Animal House* and *Porky's*. It is that, but there's more to it.

It's a collection of more than 100 stories that span 55 years starting at age six. The stories are mostly short and funny. One is long and funny, and weird and chilling. Culture clash is a frequent theme. So are food, phoniness and incompetence. There's lots of sex, drugs and rock & roll. Even the sex and drug stories are funny. Some stories were written as revenge for bad teachers and evil bosses. I also talk about some wacky relatives.

There are stories about the women I thought about marrying and the one woman I did marry (and what she had to do in bed to defeat the competition). And there are stories about painful encounters with Macy's and Walmart, and an excruciating report on a software upgrade.

The stories took place in New York, Connecticut and Pennsylvania There are four murders. If I get killed for writing this, there will be five and someone else will write the sequel.

Different parts of this book were written for different reasons.

The teacher stories started out as a warning, and later evolved into entertainment and revenge. People have said that living well — or looking good, or success, or just surviving — is the best revenge. Telling stories works best for me.

In 1963, when a guidance counselor asked what I most wanted to get out of high school, I shouted, "ME!" I've had a few wonderful teachers, but they're not much fun to read about. My strongest memories are of the bad ones and nutty ones. Some were amusingly inept. But others hurt.

In the 1950s and 60s, there was no notion of "student rights." Parents insisted that teachers should never be criticized, and must be respected no matter how evil, incompetent or deranged they were.

When I was in the sixth grade, way back in 1958, I was the victim of the first of those shitty teachers. I promised myself that someday I would tell the world what most of the kids' parents refused to listen to. It took me over 50 years, but I've kept the promise.

I can still visualize exactly where I was standing when I made the decision to write about a sadistic egomaniacal lazy ignorant bitch named Julia Quinn. I'm calling her a bitch because I decided not to use the "c-word" in this book. If people enjoy this book, it may be the only good thing that the evil horrible despicable cu — sorry, bitch — ever accomplished.

If I go to hell I'm going find Quinn and beat the crap out of her. But I may have to wait in line for my turn. If you think I didn't like her, you're underestimating my passion. I hated her fucking guts. And I still do.

The rest of the stories were written because I like to tell stories. I like to make people smile and laugh. I don't perform on the stage, just on paper.

How do I know the book is funny?

❶ I just know it.

❷ My "previewers" said it's funny.

❸ Even my serious wife laughed at the few parts I let her see.

For comparison, Marilyn also laughs at *I Love Lucy, Boston Legal* and *Curb Your Enthusiasm*. I, too, think Lucy is extremely funny, but I think the Larry David character on *Curb Your Enthusiasm* is an asshole. I can't stand watching him, so Marilyn watches him with the dog. However, Larry is a good writer.

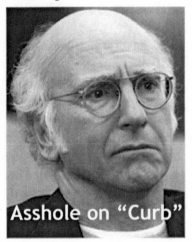

Asshole on "Curb"

No foreword. No preface. A **foreword** is usually a short section at the beginning of a book that's written by someone other than the author.

The person who knows me best is Marilyn, my wife. I don't want her to read the book until *after* it's been printed so she can't nag me to change it.

Another reason not to have a foreword is because some people would think I spelled it wrong, and that it should really be "forward."

Furthermore, unless a foreword has only one word in it, like "Hi," it should be "fore<u>words</u>."

A **preface** is written by the author and it tells the story of the book's origin and development. I put that here, in what I've called the **introduction**. Everyone knows what it means and how to pronounce it.

I don't want to hear dumb hillbillies saying "pree-face" instead of "pref-iss."

Autobiographies usually start at the beginning and progress in chronological order, but this is not an autobiography. It's a bunch of stories, meant to be entertainment, not history. I'm over 60. I can't remember exactly when things happened (or where I put my keys), but it shouldn't matter.

Readers can simply choose any chapters that sound interesting, and **I made it easy to find the DIRTY PARTS.** The many short chapters make this book good for reading on planes or while waiting for one. It's also good for reading during TV commercials or while on the toilet.

I hope it won't be used as toilet paper.

I don't want to get in trouble like the "Oprah authors" who were lying, so I say **the book is at least 80% true.** That's a better guarantee than you get on the Internet or with restaurant menus.

There's a good chance that the "Maine" lobsters were trapped in Massachusetts and that the "French" dressing was really made in the Wish-Bone factory in Kansas City— not in Paris or Bordeaux. It tastes fine anyway.

Actually, I merely *assume* it tastes fine. To be 100% truthful (or at least 80% truthful), I really don't like French dressing and I *never* eat it. But I do like Italian, Japanese and Russian dressings. Even if they're made right here in the good old U.S.A.

There's a good reason why there's no English salad dressing eaten in America. English food sucks. Steak and kidney pie? Bleccchhh. No fucking way!

The Brits use something called "salad cream." It's sort of like mayonnaise, and is so disgusting that it's illegal to eat in the United States.

The venerable and authoritative British

"Rule, Britannia!"

Broadcasting Corporation recommends putting the yellow glop on cold pizza and mashed potatoes.

It's no wonder the Brits lost the Empire and have bad teeth.

Where'd I get my sense of humor? It might be genetic. My father was very funny and my grandfathers, Walter Marcus and Dr. Jay N. Jacobs, were like George Burns and Jack Benny. Grandpa Jay could juggle while telling jokes. There was a lot of laughter in my house even before we got a television, and we were one of the first families to get a television. Pop introduced me to *MAD* magazine. All fathers should do that. It's as important as teaching about the birds and the bees.

My old man messed up that lesson. He skipped the fun part. He never told me how the "pollen" got from the daddy to the mommy. I first thought it flew through the air and I couldn't figure out how it reached the right mommy and got inside her. Now schools teach sex— probably a better idea.

Are the names real? I changed the names of some nice people to maintain their privacy. I changed names of some bad people if I'm no longer as pissed off as I used to be and I don't want to embarrass them or their descendents. Or if I think someone might sue me or beat me up.

I'm a writer, not a fighter.

The names of some *very* bad people have not been changed, and I'm not afraid to "say ill about the dead," especially if they pissed me off.

Dead people can't sue me. Fuck 'em.

What's so funny? My wife often complains that I have a reckless sense of humor and I "go too far." She's afraid that I'm going to get into trouble like Lenny Bruce and George Carlin. I think artistic expression outranks domestic tranquility. In my domicile, we have much more expression than tranquility.

Like Penn and Teller, Bart Simpson and the folks on *Jackass*, I'll do almost anything for a joke.

Other people have occasionally described my humor as sick, tasteless or black humor. That's because I can find humor in 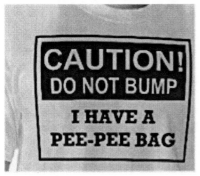 almost any situation, and that can make people uncomfortable. I designed and wore this shirt when I went to the hospital to be treated for a kidney stone. It made people laugh. Laughter is the best medicine. Most people are too serious most of the time. Fuck 'em if they can't take a joke. And fuck the horses they rode in on, too!

I'm *almost* embarrassed to say this, but back in 1963 I came up with a joke about President Kennedy's assassination within a few minutes of the shooting. I don't remember the joke, and it wasn't as grotesque as the necrophilia satire that Paul Krassner published in *The Realist* with Lyndon Johnson copulating with JFK's bullet hole because he was so happy to become president.

But I'm frequently able to find humor where others can't, like that pee-pee shirt.

My day job is running a company that sells phone equipment. Other companies describe the color of a certain kind of wire simply as "blue and yellow." I decided to use flavors instead of colors and call it "blueberry-banana." Even the straitlaced Pentagon procurement officers order many thousands of feet of our blueberry-banana wire.

It's good for bureaucrats to lighten up. One of my basic rules is, "if it's not fun, don't do it," and I'm often able to make dull things amusing. More people should try it.

General William Tecumseh Sherman said, "War is hell," but *Hogan's Heroes, McHale's Navy* and *MASH* made war funny. Some day the war in Iraq will seem funny.

I enjoy finding bloopers, errors and inconsistencies. I love typos on book covers and in ads and on big expensive signs that were checked dozens of times. In movies, I look for cavemen wearing watches and shoes.

Even menus make me laugh. In a typical Greek diner, the price of a slice of ordinary cheese can range from a dime to a dollar or more, depending on what it's attached to. In a Chinese restaurant you can pay $3.95 for a small order of fried rice, or $2.95 for four chicken wings *with* the same rice.

Most recent TV sitcoms do nothing for me. I watched exactly one episode of *Seinfeld* and hated it. I never watched *Cheers*. Nothing done in recent decades seems to equal *Lucy* or the *Honeymooners* or *Bilko* or *The Beverly Hillbillies*. Among latter-day sitcoms, my favorite is *Married, With Children*. I miss early *SNL* and Johnny Carson, but I enjoy Leno, Letterman and *30 Rock*.

Boston Legal and *The Sopranos* can be hilarious, but they're not full-time comedies. *The Simpsons* is. And so are *South Park* and *Family Guy*. I wish I had time to watch every episode. Like most males and unlike most females, I like the *Three Stooges* and Howard Stern. I love Jay Leno's *Jay Walking* segments and when Dave Letterman dropped stuff off the roof to smash in the street below.

I think this picture is funny. You first notice her hair and the hand on his mouth— but count the hands.

I don't like it when comedians pick on nice people, but I do like taking funny pictures of friends and relatives. (Those are my sister's kids.)

I also like elaborate pranks, spoofs and put-ons. I'm very good at manipulating the media and circulating believable phony news— a talent I inherited from my very funny father.

I try to make enforcers realize the absurdity of the rules they are enforcing. Logic is good. Illogic is funny.

I sometimes obey the letter of the law but not the spirit. In high school we had to wear ties, but there was no rule against wearing extremely ugly ties.

I like deflating pompous people and institutions.

When I was an editor at *Rolling Stone*, I went to press conferences at the fancy-shmancy 21 Club in Manhattan with friends from other magazines. The 21's dress code required that men wear jackets and ties, but three of us were noticeably informal.

Our corporate hosts had paid big bucks for 21 to feed us, so despite our scruffy appearance, we were too important to be rejected by the stuffy *maître d* in the tuxedo.

Other customers wore $200 "power ties," but *we* had real power and dined *sans cravate*. The restaurant was lucky we didn't decide to dine *sans pantalon*.

Thanks

I thank my parents **Rita and Bud Marcus** for putting up with a lot of crap, providing material for me to write about, exposing me to many things and inspiring me in many ways.

I thank my wife **Marilyn Marcus** for loving me, encouraging me and tolerating me. She used to be jealous, but now she knows that if I'm not in bed at 3 a.m., I'm with a computer, not with another woman. Marilyn is a worrier and thinks I should have changed *every* name in this book. I'm betting she's wrong. We'll see what happens.

In ancient Greek mythology, the "muses" were beautiful goddesses who inspired the creation of literature and art. I've had several muses, and they are all beautiful and smart women.

For most of my 40-year writing career I've written about things, and about how people related to them. In 2004 I started writing about people without the things. In 2009 I finally became comfortable writing about emotions.

This most recent and perhaps most important evolutionary development coincided with my reconnecting with **Rosemary Garcia**. We dated in high school and college. In 2009, after no contact for 43 years, Rosemary emailed me from 1,300 miles away. She helped me to become a more complete writer, and a happier, more tolerant and less cynical person.

Deborah Lurie Edery was my first muse. She put me in the mood to write more stories after she said she liked the first one in 2005. Deb is a very important former girlfriend from college, who reconnected with me via email from 15 miles away, after about 40 years. Deb activated my memory and pushed me to turn thoughts into pages. This book would not exist without her.

Phyllis Caplow Helfand put me in the mood to finish writing the stories after I stalled and got out of the mood. Phyllis was one of the first females I was attracted to, when we were in the second grade in 1953. In 2007 Phyllis became my second email muse, reconnecting after 43 years from 3,000 miles away. Her unintentional but powerful push was a nice payback for the cookies I gave her 55 years earlier. Phyllis remembered things about me that I forgot. This book would not exist without her.

Dedication

Bertram "Bud" Marcus
1922 – 2009

My father died while I was writing this book. I'm sorry he did not get to read it. Pop introduced me to most of the things I care about, including technology, humor, collecting, traveling, building things, languages and history. My father was one of the world's greatest storytellers and is a major influence on my writing. I miss him a lot.

Acknowledgments

Sally Cafarelli (1915-1986) is my wife's late mother. Sally said she worried double to make up for my refusal to worry at all. Who knows? Maybe it helped.

Gerald Light (1919-2004) was my first boss in advertising, at the Kane Light Gladney ad agency in Manhattan. Gerry taught me a lot about the ad business. After the SOB fired me, I used what he taught me, to take business away from him. **Fuck him, and the horse he rode in on.**

Dave Evans is a friend and former housemate and business partner. He shared some of the great college-era adventures. I still use the hair brush Dave left behind when he graduated from Lehigh and moved out over 40 years ago. I don't need to use it as much as I did back then, and it will probably outlast me.

Skip Foti is my wife's cousin, a kindred spirit, and occasional dance partner whom I didn't meet until after the great adventures. If I knew him back then, Skip would definitely have been part of the fun. We might even have shared a jail cell.

Ralph-The-Navigator Romaniello spent some long nights strapped into in the right seat of my 1974 Fiat and kept us heading in the right direction— most of the time.

Morris Rosenthal and **Aaron Shepard** are the two mavens of modern publishing. They saved me time and money and provided excellent advice. Anyone planning to write a book should read their books.

The beginning of the Baby Boom and the fabulous Hillhouse High School Class of 1964, "the last great class." The guys: best buddies Howie Shrobe and Marty Kravitt, fellow Foofum Kevin McKeown, fellow Finster Barry Tenin, unindicted co-conspirator Alan Disler, honorary Jew Billy Priestly, world-class wit Harry Whitney, dead fish depositor Howie Krosnick, neighbor from across the swamp Ed Cohen, ultra-creative writer Mike Baldinger, favorite phantoms Steve Schmuck and John Quimby. Girl friends (but not girlfriends): Janet Braverman, Phyllis Caplow, Carol Cherkis, Linda Howard, Annie Iwanciwsky, Cynthia Lynes, Patty Miller, Rocky Myers, Il-leine Saslafsky, Carrie Setlow, Marilyn Winokur. They made the bad times feel better, even decades later.

Chapter 1
Runaway

While in college in the late 1960s and for several years thereafter, I was involved in a number of unpleasant romantic relationships.

They all started out fine, of course, with young women who were beautiful, smart, sexy, funny and good cooks; and — much to my amazement — they somehow perceived me as handsome, smart, sexy, funny and a good cook.

Invariably, the women turned out to be less than perfect.

Two were heavily into drugs. One of them was a drug dealer who was contemplating suicide.

One was a thief. She even stole a concert poster from the wall of my apartment.

One decided she wanted to try being a lesbian for a year. I was scheduled to be her last man. That was a big burden. Would it be my fault if she didn't come back?

Another thought she could finance college through prostitution and wanted me to be her pimp.

And another wanted me to help her make bombs.

Although the sex, food and conversations were good, there was clearly something missing in the stability department; and I wondered if it was my fault.

Did I make them this way?

Do I attract nutty women, or do I drive women nuts?

These days I don't remember which alternative I thought was better.

And I'm not even sure that one *is* better.

23

Back then, though, I wanted to find out.

It was time for an experiment.

I abruptly ended the relationship I was in, and decided that for 30 days I would become socially passive. If Sophia Loren was standing naked next to me in the supermarket checkout line, I resolved to not look or speak, unless spoken to first.

I planned to just go through life, minding my own business for a month. I'd keep my mouth shut, and see who'd show up.

The first few weeks were boring but tempting. I never saw naked Sophia at Stop & Shop or Ursula Andress in a wet white bikini at the Post Office, but there were a few hot babes I would have at least spoken to under normal circumstances.

Late one night I was on a bus operated by Public Service Coordinated Transport, somewhere in the middle of New Jersey. The bus stopped at a rural convenience store. I was sleepy and there wasn't much light, but I saw two people get off the bus, and then an absolutely gorgeous red-haired woman got on, carrying a small suitcase.

The bus was nearly empty. The redhead could have had two seats for herself, or sat behind the driver or next to a jock or a priest, but somehow she decided to sit next to me. I was flattered, curious, horny and hopeful.

Even if I didn't complete my research project, maybe I'd get lucky.

We immediately started talking and laughing and touching. It was wonderful. We were soul mates. This was the match made in heaven. After ten minutes I thought we'd known each other for years. I was ready to spend the rest of my life with her.

We had some long kisses in the moonlit bus, and eventually got around to learning each other's names, biographies, and travel plans.

She told me her name was Cheryl, she was 24, born in Hackensack, and had graduated from Montclair State University with a BA in anthropology.

She also told me she had killed her husband, was running away from the Greystone Park State Psychiatric Hospital in Parsippany, and would perform oral on me if I gave her enough money to get to Pittsburgh.

How did she know to sit next to me?

Chapter 2
Love can kill

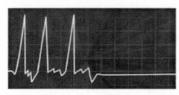 In the 1959-60 school year I was in eighth grade in the Dr. Susan S. Sheridan Junior High School in New Haven, Connecticut. Our curriculum included a course called "Core" that combined English and history.

Our Core teacher was Winnifred, an elderly spinster with a name and personality that belonged in the 1600s. She was a prude to the extreme and equally stern. If she was Catholic and not Protestant, she would probably have been a knuckle-whacking nun in a parochial school.

Her sole concession to levity in our classroom was a life-size cardboard stand-up Santa Claus that advertised Coca-Cola.

When Fidel Castro was in the U.S. to visit the United Nations, "Winnie" wore a black armband to protest his pres-ence. Politically, she was slightly to the right of Attila the Hun. Sexually, she had probably never seen a penis except in a picture, and the horror of potential penetration undoubtedly traumatized her.

Much of our class time was spent diagramming sentences and copying what Winnie wrote on the blackboard.

She explained that her words would make a stronger im-pression on our young minds if we had to write them down than if we merely heard them or read them on a mimeographed handout sheet. The real reason was probably that if we were busy copying from the blackboard, she wouldn't have to teach.

In one blackboard lecture, Winnie warned us that "any writer who uses writing as a source of income is unworthy of being read." Better cross Shakespeare, Dickens, Melville, Fitzgerald and

Hemingway off our reading list. The list of potentially worthy writers was made smaller still, because Winnie declared that any writer who mentioned sex or love was off-limits to young teenagers. There go Aristophanes, King Solomon, Charlotte Brontë and me.

When the young teenagers in our class giggled at the two dirty words in the line, "Stand like harpers hoar, with beards that rest on their bosoms" in Longfellow's *Evangeline*, Winnie barked at us, with orders to "get your minds out of the gutter," and a reminder that "the body is a temple."

One time while walking around the classroom, Winnie spied a paperback book on Alan's desk. It was a copy of *The Untouchables,* the basis for the TV series starring Robert Stack as FBI agent Elliot Ness.

Curious, Winnie picked up the book, and flipped through the pages. When she realized that the cover illustration showed an FBI raid on a whorehouse, she dropped it as if it was on fire and ran to the sink to purify her hands and soul. The next day, Winnie was absent from school.

Our substitute teacher was Elizabeth Krick, an equally old, old lady, but Winnie's polar opposite in personality, politics and prudery.

Winnie was out for a long time, and the months when Mrs. Krick replaced her were a trip to an intellectual Disneyland. The dreaded sentence diagramming sessions were gone, there were no notes to copy from the blackboard, and we were encouraged to read ANYTHING we wanted to.

I found a strange paperback book entitled *The Wayward Comrade and the Commissars*, by Yurii Karlovich Olesha, definitely not a book that commie-hating Winnie would approve of.

It contained one novelette and three short stories; and Mrs. Krick agreed that Alan would report on the novelette *Envy*, and I'd cover the short stories.

Alan got the best part which included the memorable line, "How pleasant my life is. Ta-ra. Ta-ra. My bowels are elastic. Ra-ta-ta. Ta-ra-ree. My juices flow within me. Ra-tee-ta. Doo-da-da. Con-tract, guts, contract. Tram-ba-ba-boom!"

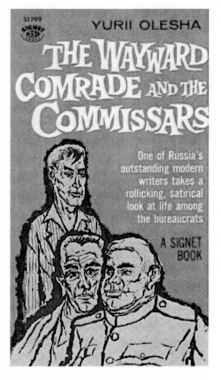

YURII OLESHA

THE WAYWARD COMRADE AND THE COMMISSARS

One of Russia's outstanding modern writers takes a rollicking, satirical look at life among the bureaucrats

A SIGNET BOOK

My part of the book was not as stimulating, but a deal is a deal, so I started reading and writing.

On the day we were to deliver our book reports, the sky was dark, Mrs. Krick was gone, Winnie was back, and I was in shock.

There was no way in hell that Winnie would accept a "book report" on three short stories, especially if the three short stories were written by a detested Russian.

I had to do some quick improvising. I decided to verb-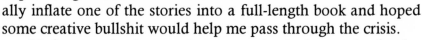ally inflate one of the stories into a full-length book and hoped some creative bullshit would help me pass through the crisis.

Unfortunately, the one short story that had enough of a plot to support my embellishment was titled *Love*.

When it was time for me to deliver my report, I quivered at the front of the classroom, put a hand in front of my mouth, and mumbled something like "I am reporting on Grphshnrf Moknop Cribnuk by Hrebdrop P. Fnarp."

Winnie asked me to repeat it, and I mumbled something like "I am reporting on Klapfnak Heebdump by Fligglediggle Nark-nark."

That didn't satisfy Winnie either, and she demanded that I speak CLEARLY AND LOUDLY.

The jig was up. I was caught with pants down. There was no turning back. I couldn't claim that my dog ate my homework.

So, I looked down at the floor and inhaled deeply, then raised my head, stared straight at the back of the classroom, and proudly announced to the world that "I am reporting on LOVE, by YURII KARLOVICH OLESHA."

Winnie clutched her chest, screamed, and ran from the classroom.

Love gave Winnie a heart attack.

The next day the sun shined brightly, and Mrs. Krick was back at the desk in the front of the room.

Chapter 3
The attack of the killer sunfish

In the early 1970s, while I was an advertising copywriter, the ad agency I worked for sent me to Bermuda. It wasn't truly a vacation because I had to attend a few meetings with clients of the agency, but the trip didn't cost me a penny and I had ample spare time to explore, swim and sail.

The hotel where we stayed had free sailboats for use by guests. They weren't big, or complicated. They were Sunfish, weighing about 150 pounds and measuring about 14 feet long. They were intended to be sailed by just one person, and all that the single sailor had to handle were a few ropes and the rudder.

Designed in 1951, the Sunfish is both simple and durable, basically a VW Beetle with a sail instead of an engine, that moves on a liquid highway.

The guy who was in charge of the hotel's fleet asked me if I had sailed before, and I quickly answered, "Yes Admiral" and gave him a fake Navy salute. He said the Sunfish was "a cute little boat and shouldn't give you any trouble at all."

Fortunately, the admiral of the fleet did not ask me for details and there was no written application, test or oath. I did not have to supply dates, details or references.

I did not lie when I said I had sailed, but most of my sailing was in motorized vessels that had no sails. I also rowed some rowboats and paddled some canoes and I had once been a passenger on a 24-foot sailboat. When asked or commanded by the real sailor, I willingly moved from port to starboard or from starboard to port. I also coiled up some ropes and hung bumpers over the side when we neared the pier.

My major achievements were staying out of the way, not falling overboard, and getting a good tan. I knew that the bow was up front, the stern in the back, a john is a head, a rope is a line, and food is in the galley. I know a bit about halyards and clevis pins and cleats and I even know that "forecastle" is pronounced "foc'sle." I also like to swim in and drink water, and if drafted to serve my country, Aye Aye Sir, I'd choose the Navy.

Despite my only-partially-impressive resume, I felt up to the task. A Sunfish is an itty-bitty boat — not much bigger than a canoe — and I was sure I could handle it. Sunfish advertising talks about simplicity, stability and a "forgiving feel" that's "suitable for beginners." That's my kind of boat.

And since my mother didn't have any stupid kids, I was sure I could teach myself to sail in Bermuda's beautiful protected harbor, where Spanish sailor Juan de Bermudez arrived in 1503. Bermuda was named after him.

I quickly figured out how to get the mast vertical and unfurl the sail. A convenient puff of air took me gently away from the pier, and I felt ready to skip right from raw recruit to admiral.

Had I attended Annapolis like an actual admiral, or even read the *Boy Scout Manual* chapter on water safety, I would have known to check the weather forecast before venturing out.

It turned out that the little puff of air that kindly and conveniently propelled me away from shore was actually an advance sign of THE BIGGEST FUCKING WIND STORM TO HIT BERMUDA IN 68 YEARS.

That initial puff was very quickly followed by a breeze, and then a wind, and then a squall. The wind speed hit 52MPH— the fastest non-hurricane wind on record.

I was never so busy in my life. I was simultaneously trying to learn how to sail, keep the boat upright, keep it from taking me out into the Atlantic Ocean, and trying to avoid being decapitated by the boom that kept swinging from port to starboard and back to port, and back to starboard.

I longed for an outboard motor, or a simple rowboat, and gained new appreciation for the HMS Bounty mutineers.

I was wrestling with the Sunfish, and it was both wrestling *and* boxing with me, and karate-chopping, too.

The "cute little boat" was beating the crap out of me.

Every time I got up, I got knocked down or knocked overboard. My arms and legs were abraded raw and red from the sandpaper-like surface of the deck.

I was clearly no match for the Sunfish or the squall.

I suddenly realized that my worst prospect for the formerly sunny day had progressed from merely having a lousy time to actually *dying* from a concussion by swinging boom or drowning or being lost at sea and becoming fish food.

There was no way I could control the "cute little boat."

Applying some very basic nautical analysis, I realized that the wind — normally a source of ventilation and propulsion — might actually kill me.

The only way to minimize the effect of the wind was to minimize the size of the wind catcher— my sail. I had hoped to lower the sail and just use the Sunfish as a giant surfboard or kickboard and slowly move it back to the beach. Unfortunately, the ropes were so snarled that there was no way to lower the sail.

Reluctant to abandon ship, I wrestled with the mast and tipped the boat over. With mast submerged and keel facing the sky, I was able to both kick and paddle it back toward shore. After a while I noticed that the mast, boom and sail had become detached from the hull socket, but they were still tethered to the Sunfish by rope and were following me to the distant shore

Despite the much smaller profile without the sail, I still had to fight the wind, and the waves were growing. It seemed to take forever to reach land. When I got close, I saw an ambulance with flashing lights on the beach, and two men in white shirts with red crosses and white Bermuda shorts and knee-high socks running toward where they thought I would come ashore.

As soon as the boat stopped moving, I crawled away from it through the shallow water and onto the sand. I collapsed and tried to spit out the salt water, seaweed and sand in my mouth. The two medics kneeled in the sand next to me, and seemed to be examining me. They spoke, but their words didn't register.

I either rolled over on my back or was rolled over by them, and eventually I sat with their support. I felt like I was still bouncing on the waves. One of them opened a medical kit and took out bandages. Then the two of them started swabbing me, and I saw that the bandages were quickly turning from white to red. There were even red spots on their white Bermuda shorts.

When my head stopped spinning and my breathing returned to normal, they helped me to slowly stand up. They supported me under each of my arms. I looked down and saw that I was covered with blood from shoulders to fingers and toes. Even my nose was bleeding. I was told I had a black eye and that I should be X-rayed. My sunglasses were gone. My diver's watch was gone. So were my waterproof camera and most of my bathing suit. Every part of me that had feeling, felt really bad.

One of the medics asked me if I was attacked by just one shark or by several, and if I lost a passenger. I said that I was sailing alone, but it took a while before I could admit that I had been attacked by a cute little Sunfish.

Chapter 4
Cat Woman

When my best friend Howie learned that my junior-year English teacher was Bertha K. Frehse (appropriately her last name rhymes with "crazy"), he told me that his mother and brother were in her classes previously, and that Frehse was NUTS then and NUTS now.

"Crazy Frazy" had day-glow complexion, and orange hair like Clarabell the clown on *Howdy Doody*. She had been torturing students for decades before it was my turn to be a victim.

It was alleged that she had held onto her job despite countless criticisms because she provided excellent investment advice to the school principal. Apparently they bought Texas Gulf Sulphur just before a big spike in the share price.

Frehse was crazy about (among other things) cats.

Her house was filled with long-clawed felines that hissed and leaped from floor to furniture to the shoulders of unfortunate visitors. Her classroom was filled with pictures of cats. Frehse even purred like a damned cat.

When she wasn't purring, this teacher of English often talked baby-talk.

Favored cats, and favored students, were called "foofums." Frehse rewarded the most favored human foofums by showing them cat books, page by page by interminable page.

When she wanted to point out something that impressed her, she'd murmur like a two-year-old, "Saaay, look uh nat."

When she was enthusiastic about a book with words, not just pictures, she'd tell us that's she'd "crawl barefoot on bloody stumps over broken glass" to read it. She had a very strange obsession with the Civil War Battle of Chickamauga, and often read about it and talked about it.

Hillhouse High School had a central courtyard with a few benches, bushes and scraggly trees. One tree, the foof-tree, was favored by Frehse. A lot of our class time was spent looking at, and at Frehse's command, waving at, purring to, and talking to the damned tree.

Some students were punished by Frehse and commanded to water the foof-tree. Some students kissed Frehse's ass by voluntarily watering the foof-tree. Many students wanted to chop down or burn down the fucking foof-tree.

We never knew what to expect when we entered foof-land.

Sometimes as we marched in, a student would be pinched on the shoulder and commanded to go to the blackboard and "write ten beautiful words," or "write 200 words about tobogganing," or "explain why striped cats are superior to spotted dogs" or "list 500 reasons why Elvis should be president."

Our English teacher used her classroom power to defend "The King" from showbiz competition. Frehse once caught a girl with a picture of singer Pat Boone in her notebook, and gave her *double F's* on a homework assignment. The quick-thinking girl instantly flipped the page to reveal a picture of Elvis, and the lunatic changed her mark from abject failure to *double A's*.

One time a class was ordered to write 500 words on "how Capri pants have been the downfall of western civilization." (Girls couldn't wear pants to our school.)

As we sat at our desks writing either ludicrous compositions or serious exams, Frehse would scurry around the room, purring like a damned cat, and sticking a pin into our arms and shoulders. Fortunately, this was before HIV.

One regular classroom activity was centered on a grammar workbook developed at Manter Hall School in Cambridge, Massachusetts.

Frehse's "Manter Hall Day" was like a perverted TV game show, and could have been invented by Monty Hall. Or Monty Python.

One third of the class would be seated in chairs spread in an arc across the front of the room, with titles like Number Boy, Card Girl, Question Girl, and Third Assistant Alternate Score Keeper; and they administered the quiz to the rest of the class.

Frehse was emcee, seated in the middle of the stage.

She'd shout "Number Boy!," "Card Girl!," and so on; and if any Vanna White prototype missed a cue, she lost the job and

joined the less-lucky classmates who had to answer the questions.

The only relief was to sneak into Frehse's classroom, and steal the card with your name on it. Yes, I confess that I did it. I was also half of a two-man commando team that stole the door knocker from her house. Alan Disler was the other half.

Our exploit was too good a story to keep to ourselves, and we could not resist displaying our shiny trophy at school. Word traveled fast and we were quickly confronted by the indignant cat lady. We went back to her house and replaced the knocker. At least we weren't arrested.

Getting a bad mark from Frehse was no reason to be upset, unless you wanted to satisfy your parents or get into college.

In a strange effort to make failures feel better, she claimed that "**an F is the mark of true genius**," and often said, "**I only flunk my brightest students**." Unfortunately, very few college admissions officers knew that Frehse's F was the equivalent of another teacher's A.

The girl who got *double F's* for liking Pat Boone must have been a future Nobel Prize winner.

Frehse lost an exam of mine during the first marking period. Despite contrary attendance documentation, she accused me of playing hooky that day and failed me for several months' work.

The next term I earned an apparently indisputable A average, but Frehse gave me a C.

The orange-haired cat lady said that she knew I deserved an A, but it was "too great a jump to go from an F to an A," so I was stuck with the mediocre C.

This was during our vital junior year in high school, when our marks would affect college admissions and influence the course of the rest of our lives.

In my yearbook, the crazy cat lady wrote that I was "a wonderful person," and maybe I should be pleased that I had an F on my report card to prove that I was one of her brightest students.

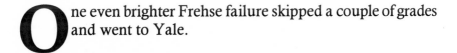

One even brighter Frehse failure skipped a couple of grades and went to Yale.

Chapter 5
Drugging Miss Daisy

One summer while I was in college I needed a job and the Pennsylvania state employment office directed me to the PairAway ShoeCenter in Bethlehem.

It was a huge self-service store with a huge sign that proudly proclaimed "2 Pairs for $5."

If you only needed one pair, you paid $2.99, but hardly anyone ever bought just one.

If someone did need just one, she'd hang around the store and partner with someone else who needed one, so they could share the five-buck deal.

Five bucks paid for style, but not much quality.

These shoes were made of plastic, cardboard, glue and staples. If you wanted footwear constructed with thread and the skin of a cow or a pig, you had to shell out the big bucks at PairAway, at least $5.99 for a pair. Few of the expensive shoes were sold, mostly prom shoes, and the $8.99 steel-toe work shoes that were necessary to protect steelworkers' lower extremities.

I was vastly over-qualified for a self-service shoe joint because I had experience working in a real shoe store and actually knew how to measure feet and could judge if shoes fit. But they needed an employee and I needed a job, so a deal was done.

The store manager was Davey, who had recently returned from a few years soldiering in Viet Nam. He was aware of my anti-war politics and agreed with them.

Second in command was Daisy, the wife of a Marine then in Viet Nam. Daisy was still in the "my country, right or wrong" state of mind, but never argued about the war with Davey or me, She just wanted her husband to come back whole and healthy.

Miss Daisy drove a bright red fastback Chevy Impala with a USMC decal on the rear window and a noisy exhaust system. The car looked like it was 40 feet long. She drove it very fast and got a lot of tickets. The cops couldn't miss a loud and long bright red Impala.

Daisy's sister Janie worked at the nearby Just Born candy factory, and often brought Daisy bags of chocolate-and-molasses coated Peanut Chews, which Daisy eagerly scarfed down, apparently to compensate for the absence of her husband and high school sweetheart, Gary.

Thanks to the Peanut Chews, and a daily Whopper-With-Cheese from the nearby Burger King, Daisy put on about 20 pounds in two months. Then she panicked when she learned that Gary would be coming home for some unanticipated "R&R" (rest and recreation.)

Not wanting to scare him away, she determined to quickly shed the effects of the excess eating and regain the body she had on their honeymoon. She made an appointment with a "diet doctor," who sent her home with a supply of Dexedrine brand amphetamine diet pills, known outside the doctor's office as *speed*. "Dex" is a powerful psycho-stimulant that increases wakefulness, energy and confidence while decreasing fatigue and appetite.

Davey and I were amazed at the effect the Dexedrine had on Daisy. Not only were the pounds evaporating, but she was absolutely energized. She started coming to work earlier than she had to, and working later than she had to, and was actually waiting on our customers instead of just sitting behind the cash register. The combination of drugs and increased physical activity gave Daisy an amazing body sculpting, and she was HOT. Male customers ogled her and tried ineffective pickup lines. Daisy looked so good that Davey said he would have tried to take her to bed if she was not his employee, and if her husband was not a massively muscled Marine who was coming home soon.

39

He did seem to give her many more hugs than before the transformation and he admitted to me that she had become the subject of his masturbatory fantasies. It was apparent that if she gave him the slightest encouragement, the ex-Army man would make a move to temporarily replace Daisy's Marine.

I, too, was attracted to the new Daisy, and I wasn't her boss or afraid of her husband. However, I had a girlfriend at the time, and wasn't interested in an affair with someone else's wife.

Just as Daisy's sister Janie had shared her supply of Peanut Chews, Daisy offered to share her speed. Davey readily agreed. I was not a good pill-taker, having only recently made the transition from rectal aspirin to oral, but I had tried LSD and marijuana, and this was the 60s, so why not?

The next day, after sampling Daisy's supply, Davey and I met with her doctor. This was a time when doctors could actually *sell* medication to their patients — not merely write prescriptions for pharmacists to sell to the sickly — and he did not demand much proof of the need for speed.

Soon there were three pill-popping amphetamine-addicted idiots working at PairAway.

We were excellent employees. We were hyper, hyped-up employees. The store looked GREAT. I made beautiful window displays. Davey made beautiful signs. Daisy kept the store clean. As soon as a speck of dirt appeared on the carpet, out came the vacuum cleaner. As soon as a fleck of dust or a fingerprint appeared on the front counter, out came the spray bottle of Windex glass cleaner.

When a pair of shoes was sold, leaving a gap on the shelves, we'd immediately start shifting the stock to fill in the space, so it looked perfect. There were times when we three stayed in the store for days at a time, only going home for a quick shower and a change of clothes.

We seldom ate, seldom stopped working, and never stopped talking, We drank gallons of Pepsi to lubricate our perpetually dry mouths.

One day my parents drove to Bethlehem with my brother and sister for a surprise visit and they took me out to a nice restaurant for lunch.

I was whacked on speed and would not shut up.

During a brief moment of sanity, I was able to step outside my body and observe the sick scene.

I realized I was acting like an asshole.

After lunch, I went back to PairAway and gave my remaining speed to Daisy. She gave me a bag of Peanut Chews. I think I came out way ahead on the deal.

Unfortunately, Daisy's husband Gary's Marine platoon was ambushed in Chu Lai. Sadly, when he returned to Bethlehem, it was for his funeral, not for R&R.

 few months later, the still slim widow Daisy quit her job at PairAway and married her former boss.

Chapter 6
Freedom for the Phantom Schmuck

If you've ever spent any time wandering around airports or municipal buildings, you've probably passed by a *Freedom Shrine*.

The shrine can be a spotless and spotlighted room, a few feet of hallway, or a dust-shrouded basement corner. It displays framed replicas of historical documents provided by and possibly maintained by the local Exchange Club.

The documents range from obscure articles of surrender and presidential correspondence, to the Bill of Rights and the Declaration of Independence.

Several dozen different pieces are usually displayed. There is seldom any discernable order, sequence or pattern; but the unmistakable themes are rebellion against tyranny, and FREEDOM.

Hillhouse High School had a Freedom Shrine *Room*. It measured about eight by eight by 12 feet, had bright and hot lights, a glass wall and no ventilation.

In the ultimate perverse irony, our shrine to freedom was our *detention room* — the place where the bad kids were kept and freedom was denied.

The shrine was not quite as inhospitable as a Viet Cong "tiger cage," or a prison cell in Abu Ghraib, but the temperature was often above 100. And of course, boys in Hillhouse — a public school — were required to wear ties and either sportcoats or sweaters.

Each morning during homeroom period, crew cut Assistant Principal and Gestapo Kommandant George Kennedy's voice would boom over the PA system: "The following students will please report to the Freedom Shrine Room," and we'd hear the names of hooky-players, class-skippers, test-cheaters, glue-sniffers, toilet-stuffers, library-smokers, fire-alarm-yankers and sundry suspected terrorists.

There was a regular group of hard-core Shriners.

Camille, John and Gus made the list almost every day. Occasionally there'd be a new name, but it wasn't always a real name.

In an effort to free the Freedom Shrine, the class of '64 took the "Who's Dick Hertz?" joke to a new level.

(When a substitute teacher circulated an attendance sheet for students to write their names on, someone would write "Dick Hertz." The next day, the substitute would use that sheet for roll call, and if no one responded to the false name, the naïve teacher would inevitably ask "Who's Dick Hertz?" All of the guys in the class would immediately raise their hands and yell "Mine does!" This was particularly effective with young female subs.)

Our school had a nice swimming pool, and we went swimming each week, with instruction available for those who needed it. At the first class in September, teacher James J. ("JJ") Davin distributed index cards for us to record our name, homeroom, division number, swimming ability, next-of-kin, etc.

Someone got an extra card and signed up a phantom student named Steve Schmuck. ("Schmuck" is the Jewish term for a penis or a fool.) Steve became part of the official class roster, and JJ read his name when he took attendance at the beginning of each class.

For the first few weeks, one of the co-conspirators would yell out "yo" or "here" to establish credibility for our invisible classmate. But there was no way we could come up with an extra body to take the upcoming swimming test, so we stopped answering when Steve's name was called.

After Steve seemed to miss a few classes, JJ inquired about his welfare and whereabouts, and some of the guys said that they had seen Steve earlier in the day in English or algebra. JJ reported Steve for skipping class, and the next morning our phantom friend achieved a new level of legitimacy and fame.

More than 3,000 students and teachers heard official tough guy George Kennedy announce through the loudspeakers in every classroom, hallway and other place of habitation, "**Steve Schmuck, please report to the Freedom Shrine Room.**"

That was the only time our Freedom Shrine ever deserved its name.

The Shrine was freed by the Schmuck.

I still hear the cheering, the applause and the laughter.

YAY, STEVE!

Chapter 7
What's a nice word for "fart?"

Eleanor Browne taught junior high English. She was a vicious and sadistic misandrist — a man-hater — and our class had 31 men-to-be, and not even one young lady.

Browne made our lives MISERABLE around 1960. She tortured us at test time ("What five adjectives did Dickens use to describe the horse pulling the cart up the hill in *A Tale of Two Cities*?"), and she had a strange aversion to basic bodily functions.

Except when in medical school, few people like to discuss excretion and secretion, and perspiration is certainly unpleasant. But Browne found even nasal emissions offensive, and she demanded that we ask her permission to leave the room to sneeze or blow our noses.

If she was in a particularly sadistic mood (which happened often), she'd ignore a franticly waving hand until the unfortunate penis-bearer turned bright red or pale white and finally yanked his hanky without permission.

The punishment for unauthorized use of a human nose was temporary banishment to the hallway outside the classroom, where the male malefactor could wheeze and sneeze in peace.

Browne had a particularly low, gravelly voice.

One time she was talking in the front of the room, and I farted in the back of the room.

She escorted me to the office of the assistant principal Lou Rubano, but she did not accuse me of committing the offensive anal act.

She told Mr. Rubano that I was MIMICKING HER VOICE.

45

Browne left me with Mr. Rubano, who took me into his private office to get my side of the story.

I was momentarily speechless. I was afraid to say "fart," had not yet learned "break wind" or "pass gas," and was embarrassed to use the family word, "boompsie."

I thought for a while, and then told Mr. Rubano that I had "involuntarily generated anal gaseous emissions that produced simultaneous aural and nasal stimuli."

He looked at me, and looked at me, and looked at me. And then started laughing hysterically.

"Oh, you FARTED," Mr. Rubano shouted. "I guess there's no good reason to punish you merely because her mouth sounds like your ass."

He said he'd tell Browne that he took care of me, and he informed me that "flatulate" is the nice word for "fart."

Chapter 8
You can't always get what you want, or what the doctor ordered

Although my parents were commoners (in the British sense) and I'm not a prince, I was born in the Royal Hospital in 1946. The hospital was on the Grand Concourse in the Bronx, back when the Bronx was grand.

I was scheduled for a return visit to have my tonsils removed in 1952. Royal Hospital was overbooked, and I was instead sent farther west to Mother Cabrini Hospital.

Not only was it not Royal, but it provided my first exposure to nuns. I had never seen nuns before, and these were not like Singing Nun Debbie Reynolds or Flying Nun Sally Fields. They had scary black clothing — like witches — and stern demeanors, and they poked needles in my ass.

I endured the horror and pain however, by focusing on my future sweet reward.

I was less than happy about the prospect of being cut open to have part of my body removed. But Dr. Casson, our family physician, had assured me that the surgery wouldn't hurt, and that when it was over, I could have any flavor of ice cream that I wanted.

That was a deal I could live with, and Dr. Casson wrote in his notebook that I was to get *fudge ripple*, my favorite.

Had I known when I was led to my hospital bed that his promised prescription applied to Royal but not to Cabrini, I probably would have tied bed sheets together and gone out a window and hitchhiked home.

In blissful ignorance, I kept my eyes on the prize.

I endured the anesthesia and surgery, and awoke in the recovery room happily anticipating a pint of fudge ripple.

Then scary Sister Evil appeared, carrying a bowl. She reminded me of the wicked witch who stirred the boiling cauldron in *Snow White and the Seven Dwarfs*. That scene had scared the shit out of me a few months earlier and I made my grandmother take me out of the movie theater.

The nun-witch put a bowl of reddish glop in front of me.

I thought she was showing me the bloody tonsils that the surgeon had cut out of me. Timidly, I asked what the stuff was. She said that it was my *strawberry* ice cream.

With a very hoarse voice, but as forcefully as a frightened six-year-old who had just endured surgery could be, I tried to explain that there must be a mistake. "Please lady. Dr. Casson said I could have fudge ripple," I pleaded.

With much more force, Sister Evil then replied, "You get what you get or you don't get any!"

I've remembered her exact words for nearly 60 years, and in all those years, I have never eaten strawberry ice cream.

I don't care much for nuns, either.

Chapter 9
Of course cops and teachers lie.
They're human.

Around 1998 I got a ticket for making an illegal right turn in Queens, New York. It was late in the afternoon, when the sun was low, and the sun caused so much glare that it was impossible to read a sign that said that right turns were not permitted between 4 and 6.

I pointed this out to the cop, and he said, "That's what everyone tells me." My nephew was with me, and I thought he could be a good witness for me in traffic court.

I did some research before going to court. I checked the printed regulations, and spoke to a *traffic device maintainer* who worked for the city. I determined that in situations where sun glare is a known problem, cities are supposed to provide additional signs farther from the intersection and/or large shields around the affected signs.

I went to court and cited chapter and verse to the judge. I also asked the cop if others had complained about difficulty in seeing the sign, and the lying SOB denied it.

My 14-year-old witness disagreed with the cop, but was deemed to have less credibility. Or maybe truth just doesn't matter when the city needs to grab every buck it can.

The judge admired my research and said he'd give me an "A for effort," but I still had to pay the fine. My nephew learned that cops can be liars, even in court, and even under oath. That's an important lesson. I'm glad he learned it when he was just 14.

When we were in high school, my best friend Howie drove a Triumph Herald. It wasn't a real sports car, but it was close enough: a cute little convertible, made in England, with Britsh Racing Green paint, a wood dashboard and a 4-speed manual transmission.

Howie drove me to school in it most days, and we parked in the student lot next to the school. On one winter day, I slipped on some ice in the parking lot, dropping my book bag and scattering my notebook, texts and papers.

I briefly perched on the rear of Howie's car to put my things in order, and then we both went into the school.

A little while later, during homeroom period, assistant principal George Kennedy summoned the two of us to the "Freedom Shrine" detention room.

Apparently someone saw what happened in the parking lot, and told someone else, who told someone else. Eventually the story reached Herman Cherman, a busybody history teacher cursed by his parents with a dumb rhyming name. Cherman found it necessary to add a bit of embellishment and he told Kennedy that we had driven to school with me *sitting up on the convertible top*!

Not only would it have been very cold up there and hard to keep my balance, but I would probably have broken the top and fallen in on Howie and caused us to crash.

Fortunately the school cop Joe Manna came to our defense. He told Kennedy, "These are good boys; they would never do anything like that."

In the one time he was ever nice to me in three years, Kennedy said, "I wish Cherman would mind his own damn business. I have enough real problems to deal with without him making up fake problems."

Chapter 10
An unauthorized elevator operator

My wife's cousin's late husband Artie Stepanian (who was also my best friend during many important years) was a Navy-trained electrician with an unusual innate understanding of architecture.

He could build anything, fix anything, and seemed to have X-ray vision. Artie could look at a wall or a building and instantly sense the path of least resistance for slithering a wire through it from point A to point B. Some of Artie's admirers, especially me, called him the "Super Snake."

In the 1980s, Artie frequently helped me to install phone systems in Manhattan. One night we rendezvoused in a parking lot on East 30th Street that gained valuable space by using individual mini-elevators to raise cars up in the air, so other cars could park beneath them.

We left our vehicles around 8 p.m., and went into a nearby building to do our work. We came out around 2 a.m. and learned to our horror that the office had closed at midnight. Our keys were locked in the office, our transportation was eight feet up in the air, and no one answered the emergency phone number shown on the sign in the office window.

Artie was not one to panic, and there was some good news. In his wallet, he had a spare key to his van.

All we had to do was drive his van off the elevator, or build a ramp up to the van, and then drive to my house, get my spare key, and come back and rescue my car. Unfortunately, the chance of Artie's aging van surviving an eight-foot drop was not very good, and we could not find any suitable ramp-building supplies.

Artie was a "Seabee" in the Navy. The term comes from the abbreviation for "Construction Battalion." Their motto is "We Build, We Fight," and a lack of lumber would not stop Artie from defeating the parking lot.

Super Seabee Artie analyzed the Manhattan battlefield. He saw that the elevators were operated with an electric-hydraulic pump, controlled by a master power switch inside the office, with individual levers at each elevator. The obvious solution was to go into the office and flip the pump switch, but the office was locked.

Artie was unable to pick the lock, and smashing the window would have been noisy and messy. Lots of people were walking nearby. Some of those people were cops.

Artie analyzed more, and spotted an electrical panel on the back outside wall of the office. He opened his tool bag, opened the panel, traced the circuits, bypassed the master switch, and soon a motor hummed and lights came on.

He went to "his" elevator and brought down and liberated the van, and then he put the elevator back up. Next we drove to my house in Westchester, got my spare key, went back to Manhattan, rescued my car, restored the second elevator, and closed up the electrical panel.

While closing the panel, Artie was wounded in battle.

He got a bad cut on his finger, and closed the wound with black electrical tape. Then we went for hotdogs at Gray's Papaya at 72nd and Broadway, and drove home.

I would have loved to have been at the parking lot at 7 a.m. when the manager came in and opened the office, and saw two sets of keys hanging on the wall, and two empty elevators up in the air.

Chapter 11
Health can be unhealthy

In the early 1960s Patrick J. Leone taught health and science at the Dr. Susan S. Sheridan Junior High School in New Haven, Connecticut.

Leone preferred that his name be pronounced as a two-syllable anglicized "Leon," and he was obviously shaken if anyone acknowledged his Italian ancestry and pronounced the final vowel.

This seemed strange, because New Haven was a very Italian city and there were many Italian-American teachers and students in the schools. Another Italian-American teacher would deliberately piss him off by calling him "Pasquale" or "Patsy Lay-o-nay."

Leone would squirm and blush.

Unfortunately, Leone had lower standards for his own verbalizations than for others, pronouncing health as "helt" and science as "sines."

His speech defect was complemented by a persistent memory problem. Every time my class entered his room — three times a week for ten months — he'd look at us plaintively and ask, "Division Eight, helt or sines?"

He didn't know which subject he was supposed to teach us; and even when we confirmed that we were in his classroom to learn about helt, he sometimes tried to teach us sines.

Leone sure knew a lot about sines. He once told a class that "Det (death) kills instantly."

Unlike our friends who had other teachers for helt, or health, we had no textbooks. Leone blamed the problem on the "Board of Ett," and for months he assured us that the texts would be arriving soon.

Leone gave no lectures. There were no discussions, and few quizzes. Most of our class time consisted of laboriously copying into our notebooks, the words that he had laboriously written onto the blackboard.

Sometimes one of us would notice an error on the board, such as a "to" that should have been a "too." Usually Leone would blame "juvenile delinquents" who'd sneak into his room during lunch period and change his words. Other times he'd try to justify his writing and deliver a long dissertation on grammar with parts of speech we never heard of in our English classes ("subdulated abominative"). A few times he blamed defective chalk that twisted in his hand.

Leone was a frustrated performer/producer/director, and parents' visiting day was SHOWTIME.

Parents would be welcomed by the class singing the *Brusha Brusha Brusha* song from the Ipana toothpaste commercial (starring Bucky Beaver), and then he sailed an embalmed bat around the room like a balsawood model airplane. For his grand finale, he squirted the children with water from a hypodermic syringe.

I was not the only Michael in our seventh-grade health class. The other Michael, whose last name Leone always mispronounced, got sick early in the school year and was out for several months. Leone confused the two Michaels, and frequently reported me for skipping class.

Throughout the year, there was a mysterious stack of cardboard boxes gathering dust in a corner of the classroom.

In June, with summer approaching, the kids were feeling frisky, and one of them dared to sneak into the unoccupied classroom during lunch period. He cut open the cartons and found our missing textbooks, which had been in the room since September and had *not* been delayed by the inefficient bureaucrats downtown.

The burglar noticed that one carton had been opened previously. And after flipping through some pages of one of the texts, the familiar words soon made it obvious that Leone had removed one of our books for personal use.

Each week he secretly copied a chapter onto the blackboard, and then we'd spend three days copying those same words from the blackboard into our notebooks.

The kids in our class had assumed that Leone, and not some wise medical authority hired by Houghton Mifflin or Prentice Hall, was the author of those words we were ordered to copy each day, while Leone sat and stared out the window and hummed for 45 minutes.

We were never allowed to see "our" books because Patsy Leone found it much easier to copy and have us copy, than to learn and to teach.

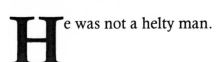e was not a helty man.

Chapter 12
Medical care makes me sick

What they don't teach at medical school

In the 1980s I had a severe pain in my foot. I no longer remember which foot it was or what caused the pain, but it hurt so bad that I went to a hospital.

I was interviewed, tested and X-rayed and given a bill to sign. I was also given one crutch that was adjusted to the right length for my height and a prescription for a few weeks of pain killers.

The crutch is a simple device, and it comes without a user's manual, and it wasn't hard to figure out how to use it. I raised my bad foot off the ground and let the tip of the crutch serve as a substitute foot, and headed for the exit.

The orthopedic surgeon who had examined me yelled at me to STOP and come back. He explained to me that the crutch is "supposed to be used on the good side, not the bad side." That didn't make much sense, but I'm not a doctor.

Then the orthopedic nurse who had assisted the orthopedic surgeon, yelled at him. She said that the crutch is "supposed to be used on the bad side, not the good side." That did make sense, but I'm not a doctor.

The two medical experts then started a lengthy and spirited debate, each citing appropriate arguments for their divergent opinions. I stood around for a while, and then I

56

plopped into a chair. The audience grew, with supporters for each side cheering and kibitzing.

After 10 minutes it became apparent that neither one was going to surrender, and no higher authority was likely to intervene. My wife was waiting in the parking lot and I had to get out of there so I came up with a solution.

I grabbed a second crutch off a rack, grasped it with my other hand, raised my bad foot off the ground, and hopped out of there without looking back.

What they should teach at medical school

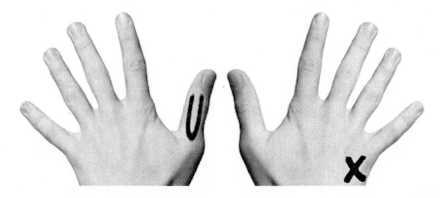

In 1999, to help a busy storekeeper I knew, I went behind the front counter to answer his ringing phone.

I looked ahead toward the phone and didn't notice a step. I fell forward. Reflexively, I put both hands out to break my fall.

My left hand impacted the sharp edge of a metal electrical box. A long flap of skin peeled away from my left thumb and I was quickly bleeding like the proverbial stuck pig. An ambulance rushed me to the hospital and a hand surgeon was summoned from the golf course and the ugly gash was stitched up.

I still have a faded U-shaped scar and limited motion. The precisely calculated permanent disability paid me not nearly enough money to retire to Monaco. I was instructed to see my own doctor in a week to have the dressing changed.

When I did, I mentioned that my right hand — not the one with the cut — was swollen and hurt a lot, and I was X-rayed. The film revealed that I broke the fifth metacarpal bone, a bone midway in the hand that connects to the pinky. A week earlier, when I was in the emergency room, I had complained about pain in both hands and the E. R. staff knew I had landed on both hands, and my right hand was obviously red and swollen. But all they cared about was the hand that was gushing blood all over their nice clean floor.

I think it would have been logical to examine both of my hands, but I never went to medical school.

What doctors don't tell patients

The pinky is a small and not particularly useful finger, but an orthopedic assistant constructed a monstrous cast to contain, protect and immobilize it.

My pinky and fourth finger of my right hand were wrapped in gauze and encased in plaster and frozen in a curl, pointed at my palm. The cast covered all of my hand except for three fingers and extended beyond my wrist to just below my elbow.

You might think that still having three functioning fingers meant life was OK, but life actually sucked.

I'm right-handed and the cast weighed so much and restricted me so much that I could hardly use the hand. I couldn't even dress myself. It took so long to unzip my fly that I often peed in my pants.

I've saved a Post-it note I wrote a few words on at that time. It's hard to read.

Using a computer keyboard and mouse was extremely difficult. I ultimately hung a wire from the ceiling

58

over my desk with a loop that could support my arm while I tried to type. My typing was a little bit neater than my handwriting.

When I got the cast, I was told to come back in eight weeks to have it removed.

It was a miserable eight weeks. I gained new sympathy for amputees. I couldn't drive, and I had to learn how to urinate lefty if I had the need to pee while out of the house.

At home it was easier to just "drop trou" and then pee hands-free in the shower. (I hope my wife isn't reading this.) Wiping my ass was difficult, uncomfortable and unsanitary.

I'll spare you the gruesome details and just say the cast got dirty.

Eating was sloppy, too, and sleeping was never restful. I went in the swimming pool with plastic bags over both arms, as instructed. I perspired inside the bags so the cast and bandages got wet anyway. I had created my own personal enclosed weather systems, and there was a danger of softening the plaster so I gave up on water sports for awhile.

When I had a mid-arm itch, I shoved a chopstick into the cast to scratch it.

Love-making was possible but dangerous and required caution. Casts are great for S&M fans.

Life goes on.

When the eagerly anticipated date finally arrived I went back to the orthopedic surgeon's office expecting but not receiving quick relief.

A nurse X-rayed me and looked at my cast and told me I was doing fine and should come back in a month. I protested, saying that I had been told that the cast would be removed after two months and my time was up.

She smiled and said, "I know. We lied to you. We always lie about the time casts stay on. If we told patients the truth, they'd get depressed and cut the casts off."

Chapter 13
Pee in your pants and beat the crap out of your friends

Our sixth grade teacher at Davis Street School was Julia Quinn. I'm not sure what her political orientation was, but she unintentionally provided a perfect introductory course on the evils of bureaucracy and socialism.

She also thought that Jews worshipped Jesus.

Despite her abundant ignorance, Quinn viewed herself as a superstar, more of an executive than a mere instructor. She spent a lot of time in the principal's office when she should have been teaching.

Quinn demanded that the parents of the kids in our class chip in to buy her an expensive Wollensak tape recorder that was seldom used in the classroom. Parents also felt obligated to give her much more lavish Christmas gifts than were given to other teachers.

On the first day of school, Quinn was out of our classroom for about an hour. The kids were bored. The only book in the room was a dictionary, so kids started flipping pages, looking for dirty words. Someone found "stinkbug," and started laughing.

The page was bookmarked and the book was passed around the room. When Quinn came back, she found about 30 kids giggling hysterically. No one would admit to discovering the bug, so we were all made to stand on the "baby line" for punishment before entering school in the morning.

The classroom was divided into groups of five children, each commanded by an 11-year-old future commissar.

In order to address our Most Exalted Comrade Teacher, we had to ask permission from our Highly Revered Group Leader.

If she or he wasn't a friend, a kid could have wet pants before getting permission to ask Quinn for permission to go to the boys' room or girls' room to urinate.

Normal teachers gave spelling tests to encourage children to learn to spell. Quinn gave spelling tests to build group loyalty and destroy friendships.

She wasn't satisfied by our learning to spell new words each week; we had to memorize them in alphabetical order. On quiz day, each group had to recite and spell the new words. The first child did the first word, the second child did the second word, and so on.

But if anyone said a word out of order — even if it was spelled correctly — the whole group failed.

child who goofed up in class was often beaten up after class.

Chapter 14
My one cool teacher

 Cullen S. Hodge had been an aeronautical engineer, a guy who designed airplanes.

The way he explained it, one day while sitting at his drafting table, he looked out of the window and saw a plane flying by. He was suddenly stunned, suffering with paralysis of the pencil. He realized that if he specified the wrong size screw, a plane could crash and hundreds might die.

He changed career paths, becoming an excellent high school physics teacher. He was dignified, scholarly and extremely knowledgeable. Mr. Hodge seemed overqualified, perhaps more suited to be a professor, not just a high school teacher.

His class was difficult, but he was fair; and if he was not liked by all of his students, Mr. Hodge was respected. He's one of the few teachers in this book who gets a "Mr." before his last name. I didn't think about it. It happened automatically.

In addition to teaching physics, Mr. Hodge was advisor to the philosophy club, math club and chess club, and to the pompous and short-lived Committee for Research into Existential Metaphysics and Ethics.

Despite his often aloof demeanor, our class was not without laughs. He made coffee in a calorimeter and taught us to cook hot dogs by swinging them from a pendulum through the flame of a Bunsen burner.

One day a messenger came to our classroom from the principal's office. He gave Mr. Hodge a square flat package from the Columbia Record Club.

Mr. Hodge paused his lecture on the brachistochrone curve to carefully slit open the container.

He removed, held up, and smiled at Mussorgsky's *A Night on Bald Mountain*, and carefully slid the package across the front counter until it fell off the end and precisely dropped into the waste basket.

Stephanie Abeshouse, the one girl in our class, started frantically waving her hand, and said "Mr. Hodge, Mr. Hodge, your bill is in the package you threw away."

Mr. Hodge calmly replied, "Do not worry, Miss Abeshouse; they will surely send me another."

ool.

Chapter 15
The last girl on Earth
(and hiding hard-ons, and nipple hunting)

Suzanne was a petite seventh-grader with an enormous ego better suited to someone twice her size with greater beauty, brains and talent. So great was her opinion of herself, and so low the opinion that others had of her, that there seemed to be permanent graffiti in the street in front of her house proclaiming that "SUZANNE IS CONCEITED."

She and I attended Cotillion, a dancing school that also attempted to teach the social graces to young teenagers on Friday nights. One Friday night was also Halloween night, and Cotillion management wisely realized that the only way they could get 12-year-olds to forsake trick-or-treating for dancing school was to have a costume party with prizes.

For me, this was the second best reason to go to Cotillion. The best reason was to dance with the 18-year-old female dance instructors who had breasts and hips.

Halloween was my favorite holiday. I started preparing costumes in mid-summer and consistently won prizes for my efforts.

I don't remember what I wore that year, but as I expected, I won "Best Boy," and my peers applauded. My prize, unexpectedly, was not a trophy or even a big bag of candy.

I got to choose to dance with any girl I wanted to.

Conceited Suzanne assumed she was the leading candidate, and aware of my rock-bottom social status, she tried to hide behind some taller friends. She wasn't completely hidden, however. I moved close to the microphone, looked at her and announced in a deep voice, "Don't worry, Suzanne, I wouldn't pick you if you were the last girl on earth!" There was thunderous applause, especially from the other girls.

Then, instead of skinny flat-chested conceited Suzanne, I picked Gloria, one of the 18-year-old dance instructors who had breasts and hips.

Gloria was much nicer than Suzanne and gave me a kiss on the lips to congratulate me, and then we did a slow Foxtrot in the spotlight. We danced *much* closer than normal for 12-year-olds, but probably normal for 18-year-olds.

I can still remember the Foxtrot steps from 50 years ago: Forward. Sidestep. Back. Feet together. Slow. Cross that foot.

Gloria grinded against me and gave me a woody.

It lasted for a long time and fortunately I didn't dance close with the next girl or I might have been banished from Cotillion for being a pervert or a potential rapist.

♦ ♦ ♦ ♦

In seventh and eighth grade as our female classmates were starting to "develop," and male hormones were also raging, schoolboys often had wet dreams in bed at night and inflated pants in school during the day.

One time I was called to the blackboard in Spanish class while aroused. I walked bent over at the waist to avoid revealing my erection and then practically buried my dick in the wall at the front of the room.

I suppose in the 21st century, teenage boys are proud to wave their flagpoles in the classroom, but back then we were advised to wear jockstraps every day and to take a lot of cold showers and to stop thinking about breasts. It's impossible for heterosexual teenage boys to not think about breasts. (See chapter 67.)

Summer times were great for breast watching. At our beach club, the 14-year-old boys in Titty Club would float in the deep end of the pool with diving masks and snorkels, facing the diving board, ogling females who'd dive off the board. When they'd plunge down to the bottom of the pool and quickly reverse direction to swim up to the surface, sometimes their bathing suit tops would pull back and we'd actually spot a NIPPLE.

A few times we got really lucky. Some girls had not tied their bikini tops tight enough before diving and they lost them in the water, and we got to see TWO COMPLETE BREASTS. Our diving masks made them look even bigger.

For a change of pace, the horny divers would swim around the pool to try to spot pubic hairs popping out from teenage girls' bathing suits, or head for the shower shows.

There were undetectable peep holes under the benches in the individual shower rooms. Whenever a hot female went into a shower room, one of us would go into the adjacent room. Sometimes our view was blocked by a towel, but we saw a lot.

We gave our subjects nicknames based on their physical characteristics, just like an anthropologist studying apes in Africa. A woman with oversize areolas came to be known as "Helmet Nipples" and was one of our favorites. So was her young teenage daughter, "Helmet Nipples Junior." Years earlier I had played doctor with HNJ and we got naked and wrapped each other with gauze. Later I was her first date.

◆ ◆ ◆ ◆

Before I was old enough to have a real job, I "worked" Saturdays in the toy department of my father's store. Once I was telling an attractive woman about a toy and could not avoid noticing her breasts. I said that the toy was made by "Playtex" (the bra brand) instead of "Playskool" (the toy brand).

◆ ◆ ◆ ◆

➜ **ADOLESCENT MALE SECRET REVEALED**: Elvis Presley and my friends and I had nicknames for our penises. The King called his "Little Elvis." Ours were called Rover, Fido, Schnick-enflritzer, Joe, Max and Axolotl. We even had a song about them. I no longer remember my dick's name.

Chapter 16
Not the phonophonopheneloscope

Tom Dolan was a sadistic and egomaniacal junior high science teacher who made us polish our shoes before entering his classroom and forbade us to laugh in his presence.

Before a much-needed winter vacation in 1959 or 1960, he gave us an assignment to write reports on the phonophonophenelo-scope, due for the first class in January.

About 140 miserable children missed sledding, skating and family trips, and spent their vacations pestering librarians with consistently negative results.

Back at school after New Years, Dolan announced, "I'm sorry kids. I made a mistake. It's not the phonophoNophen-eloscope, it's the phonophoTopheneloscope."

We wanted to lynch the bastard!

One student, it must be noted, surmised Dolan's error and reported on the proper device.

Phyllis later skipped a grade, earned a PhD degree at Harvard, and became a professor at Yale.

Chapter 17
Irreparable typing, irremediable reading, and an offer I couldn't refuse

Eighth grade was decision time. Fourteen-year-old children were supposed to choose their life's path. Would they wear blue collars, or would they wear white, or maybe pink?

Inherent to the decision-making process was exposure to basic training in three directions.

To try out a life in house-building, factory-working, or car-fixing, we (boys only, of course) had brief courses in mechanical drawing, printing, and woodworking. Our white collar life sample was a short "Language Exploratory" course in an arbitrarily selected foreign language. After studying Spanish, French or Latin for five months, we were supposed to know if we wanted to go to college. For the other five months of the school year, all eighth-graders had typing class, to prepare for a career in an office or beauty salon or maybe the military. It was confusing.

I had started sort-of-typing around age 10, on a very old Remington with sticky keys that my father had brought home from his office. Like most beginners, I began with the basic index-finger hunt-and-peck method, and had advanced to pretty quick two-fingered typing when I was given my very own Royal portable at age 13.

By the time we started "Business Exploratory" (a.k.a typing), I was a very fast six-fingered typist. I didn't always use the same fingers for the same keys, and had no idea where the "home position" was or why it existed, but I typed well, and seldom peeked at the keys.

My teacher (a nice lady whose name is lost to history) was faced with a major dilemma. Even though I did everything the wrong way, on the first day of class I was already typing faster and more accurately than my class was expected to type after five months of instruction.

To make it worse, she knew that if she tried to force me to type correctly, I would inevitably type more slowly, make more errors, and maybe sprain a wrist. Maybe I'd even sprain two wrists.

Since she recognized that I was heading for college, not a career in business or hairdressing, and would probably never need to touch a keyboard after eighth grade (HAH!), my enlightened teacher gave me an easy "A," and let me sit and read a book propped up on the typewriter until the course ended.

Four years later, in my senior year in high school I was again misplaced, but unfortunately this time the teacher was not nearly so enlightened.

I had always been an avid reader, and a good reader. I routinely scored at the 99th percentile in reading speed, comprehension and retention.

Despite my superstar reading status, in September of 1963 I inexplicably found myself in a *special education* remedial reading class surrounded by kids who could be charitably described as "slow learners."

Less charitably, their intellectual superiors called these classmates "hoods" and "greasers" and "retards."

This class made the Sweathogs on *Welcome Back, Kotter* seem like Rhodes Scholars. They probably traveled to school on the half-size yellow school bus and even in high school they had their mittens clipped to their jacket sleeves.

I knew there was a mistake, and as soon as the teacher came in, I went to his desk to attempt to arrange for my prompt exit. But before I could speak, the teacher held up his hand between his

DIRTY WORD

face and mine, and commanded me to "shut the fuck up and sit the fuck down."

Our relationship got worse after that.

The first classroom assignment was intended to assess our degree of reading retardation. The reading teacher distributed neatly printed pages, bearing four simple paragraphs with short words printed in large type.

It was more like an eye chart than literature.

We were instructed to read the paragraphs, and then turn over the paper and answer the questions on the back of the page. We were not supposed to turn the page over again to the front once we started writing our answers.

The stories were only slightly more complex than the "Oh, Sally, see Dick" adventures we read in first grade. I finished the assignment in approximately 14 seconds and then noticed that my classmates were laboriously sounding out each syll-a-ble.

The teacher noticed I had stopped reading, and said, "What's the matter, dumbass, too tough for you?"

If there had been a stack of lumber in the room I would have been tempted to whack the SOB over the head with a two-by-four.

But we were not in woodworking class.

I meekly said that I had finished the test but he refused to believe me. Eventually, he looked at my paper and saw that I had answered the questions, and answered them all correctly.

At this point, most of the kids had flipped over their papers, and were trying to copy answers from each other.

Seeing their overt and clumsy cheating led our teacher to the only logical conclusion: I must have stolen a teacher's copy of the test and had copied the answers onto my paper.

I was escorted to the principal's office, and then I eventually got to see my guidance counselor, and she uncovered a scheduling error. I was given three free periods a week to swim or hang around the library, and someone else got a chance to "shut the fuck up and sit the fuck down."

א In my junior year, I was taking Hebrew as a foreign language. I'm Jewish and had studied Hebrew before, but the public school course was very different from the religious school version, and getting a good mark would have required much more work than I was willing to do.

Most days my major academic accomplishment when Mrs. Samson asked me a question was to reply with the Hebrew equivalent of "I don't know." I had a lot of practice saying that particular phrase. I said it better than anyone.

Because of a strange anatomical quirk, I had a very sensitive nose. If she gave us a "pop quiz" I could just tap my nose and in seconds a red river would be gushing from my right nostril. I'd soon be heading to the nurse's office for a nice 30-minute nap until the hemorrhage subsided.

After a while Mrs. Samson realized that I was a hopeless case. She was friendly with my parents and didn't want to flunk me. So just like Don Vito Corleone in *The Godfather*, Frances Samson made me an offer I couldn't refuse. She said, "I know you're not doing any work, but I want you to get into a good college, so I'll give you a B."

Mrs. Samson didn't have to put a gun to my head to convince me to take the deal. It was a better deal than I deserved, and I owe her a lot.

Chapter 18
Grandma, the lesbian painter, and arroz con caca
(Where were you when the shit hit the floor?)

After numerous changes of curricula and colleges, I pulled the plug on my formal education at the end of 1969 and moved to New York to become a magazine editor.

I spent the first week living in the Bronx with my grandmother, but we were the *Odd Couple*.

Grandma Del was like a fastidious female Felix Unger. She

was a neat freak who ironed shoelaces and wrapping paper (I'm not kidding) and had floors that were clean enough to eat off of (not kidding about that either). I was more like Oscar Madison. I was a 23-year-old male who had been living unsupervised since graduating from high school, and my standards were different from my grandmother's.

We loved each other, but as with a lot of marriages, we could not live with each other. I had to move out.

Although I had the title of Assistant Editor, my salary was only $115 per week, and even in 1970, that didn't pay for much real estate.

I schlepped my suitcases downtown and checked into the Grand Central YMCA, where I could afford a cell-size cubicle within walking distance of my office. I spent weekends wandering the streets of Manhattan looking for a more permanent and pleasant residence where I could bend over in the shower if I dropped my soap without attracting a new boyfriend.

I quickly found out that I was about 20 years too late for a $100-per-month loft in Greenwich Village, so I looked at the East Village. There, I found places that I could afford, but didn't like, and places that I liked, but couldn't afford. There were novel architectural touches, like bathtubs in the kitchens, roaches in the bathtubs, and drunks and drug dealers in the hallways.

Then I had a revelation.

If I did somehow find a suitable place in the East or West Village, I'd have to take the subway to and from work, which would probably take about 20 minutes in each direction. Since I had to be on the train anyway, why not consider living in one of the "outer boroughs," outside Manhattan, with a slightly longer commute?

I could have gone to Staten Island, Brooklyn or Queens, but I was born in the Bronx. It was familiar turf. That's where Grandma Del's familiar cooking was, I knew the stores and the restaurants, and it would be an easy train ride.

I went to a real estate agency that specialized in apartment rentals, and was directed to a potential home on Walton Avenue, near both the number four train that goes down Lexington Avenue in Manhattan, and the D train that runs on Sixth Avenue. (Tourists say "Avenue of the Americas.")

The apartment was no palace, but it was affordable ($66.21 per month, thanks to New York's weird rent control laws), convenient, and good enough. It was considered to be a "professional apartment," the type of dwelling often rented by a doctor, on ground level with its own private entrance. My front hallway turned out to be the perfect place to park my Vespa motor scooter.

The law required the landlord to paint the apartment for each new tenant, but he refused and wasn't worried about prosecution. He was, however, willing to give me a free month's rent and six gallons of white paint and some brushes, rollers, trays and drop cloths if I agreed to take care of the painting.

I had recently met a beautiful, smart and very funny girl named Laurel at a mutual friend's party. It was a terrific party.

One of the guests had a copy of a studio master tape of what would turn out to be Elton John's *11-17-70* album.

Laurel, too, had recently moved into New York and she offered to help me paint. I liked her a lot and hoped for a weekend of painting plus passion. After we painted and had sandwiches and beer I embraced her, and kissed her romantically. She kissed me back sisterly. Then she told me she was a lesbian.

Anyway, I got the place painted and furnished and began my life as a New Yorker. I enjoyed exploring and taking pictures and seeing how much had changed — and not changed — since I had moved from the Bronx to Connecticut in 1952. For a while I thought I'd write a book about my discoveries. Its tentative title: *In the Bronx, Boys Still Piss in the Street.*

At about 4 a.m. on a Sunday morning, about a year after I moved in, I heard a strange gurgling sound. I got out of bed, checked my bathroom and kitchen and found nothing abnormal, and went back to sleep.

Around 7 a.m., I heard much more gurgling, and much louder gurgling, and got out of bed. I was horrified to see a stinking slimy mixture of RICE AND SHIT ("arroz con caca" in the common Bronx vernacular) oozing out of my bathtub, sink and toilet and rapidly coating the floors of my apartment!

I remembered the old joke about someone falling into a septic tank and yelling "FIRE," because no one would come to help if he yelled "SHIT." I called the fire department, and asked them to pump me out. They wouldn't, but they did arrange for the city's Emergency Services Department to clean up and find out what caused the disaster.

DISGUSTING

Apartment buildings have vertical waste "stacks" — pipes that run from the basement to the roof and connect to the drains in each apartment.

Typically, there is a stack for all of the bathrooms in the "A" apartments, all of the "B" apartments, etc. and other stacks for the kitchens in each apartment line. At the top, the stack is open to the air on the roof to help the waste to flow downward. At the very bottom, below my ground-floor apartment, the stack made a turn to run almost horizontally through the basement and then go underground to the sewage pipe in the street.

Investigators found that some wise-ass kid had gone up on the roof and dropped a 7-Up can down the waste stack. It passed through six floors to the basement below my apartment, but couldn't make the turn to the street, and it blocked the path for the flowing crud.

As people in the building awoke and started cooking, eating and flushing, whatever should have gone outside, backed up, squirted out, and ended up in my carpeting.

Two months later, it happened again and I moved out.

Chapter 19
The food chapter: stalactite spaghetti, sink spaghetti, barbecued spaghetti, cat lasagna, too-famous lasagna, fried dicks

Stalactite spaghetti

The lunches served in our high school cafeteria cost us 35 cents a day. And as you might expect of food supplied by the lowest bidder, it usually sucked.

As an alternative, sometimes we'd bring brown bags of mommy food, or go to nearby Chuck's or Al's restaurants after school. Sometimes we'd go to one of the kids' houses and raid the refrigerator.

My mother was getting pissed-off about the fridge raids. She didn't mind us eating the leftovers, but she didn't like the mess we usually left on the stove and in the sink. Mom gave me specific instructions to terminate the after-school cooking.

One day some friends were at my house, and of course we were hungry. I didn't expect my mother to get home for a couple of hours, so I thought we could safely reheat some spaghetti, eat it, and clean up any trace of it before she came home.

Unfortunately, Mom's plans changed and she walked in while the pot of pasta and sauce was still on the stove. She got REALLY pissed-off. She grabbed the pot, and flung it at us.

Mom was no Tom Seaver, Cy Young or Sandy Koufax. She'd never be a major league pitcher. She missed us, and the spaghetti hit the ceiling. The individual noodles hung like stalactites on the ceiling of a damp limestone cave.

Every so often a noodle would wriggle out of its saucy adhesive and go "bloop" and hit the floor.

Mom didn't laugh. We did.

Sink spaghetti

Years earlier, before I was allowed to use the stove, I tried to cook spaghetti by putting it in the bathroom sink and running hot water over it for about 15 minutes. After it softened up, I dumped in a jar of sauce and stirred the glop. It was terrible, but I ate some of it. I didn't realize that boiling was a critical part of the pasta preparation process.

I also failed in my effort to store ice cream sandwiches in my toy chest by loading up the big maple box with ice cubes. **I'm sorry about the mess on the floor, Mom.**

Barbecued spaghetti

Many years later, while waiting for the kitchen to be completed in my new house, we did most of our cooking on a barbecue grill on our rear deck. We even tried to make spaghetti. The water *almost* boiled. That mushy meal tasted almost as bad as sink spaghetti.

Cat lasagna

One Saturday while we were in junior high school, best friend Howie and I went to Pepe's, a neighborhood Italian restaurant, for lunch. It was not glamorous. It was a dingy, long and narrow place with tables against two walls, and a center aisle that ran from the front door to the counter and kitchen in the back of the joint.

Instead of our usual pizza, we both ordered lasagna, and we waited. We waited for a very long time. Periodically, our waitress would come out from the kitchen and apologize for the delay, refill our water glasses, and promise that our meals would be out "soon."

At some point, a bedraggled alley cat came in through the open front doorway, and quickly walked down the center aisle, made a quick jog around the counter, and went into the kitchen.

A moment later, we heard a clatter and squealing that sounded like an episode of Itchy and Scratchy on *The Simpsons*. Or maybe the velociraptors in the *Jurassic Park* kitchen.

After a little while, the waitress brought out two plates of lasagna. Howie and I turned pale, got up and walked out, without eating or paying.

Too-famous lasagna

Another time Howie and I were wandering around Greenwich Village. We were hungry and almost out of money and were looking for an inexpensive way to fill our bellies.

We were relieved and pleased to find a really crappy looking restaurant with grease-encrusted windows, a door with cracked glass, tufts of litter swirling near that door, a drunk sleeping under the torn awning, and a suitably unimpressive name.

"Joe's Italian" seemed to be a likely source of cheap two-buck lasagna.

When we went inside and sat down and started looking around we sensed that we might be wrong.

78

This Joe was not merely some anonymous Joe. He was Giuseppe Marcello Bacciagaluppe, an award-winning chef who apparently had no need to pay anything to enhance the exterior décor of his famous establishment.

Photographs on the wall showed Joe with Frank Sinatra, Dean Martin, Tony Bennett, Perry Como, Annette Funicello Connie Francis, a pope, two mayors, a governor, two presidents and a capo de tutti capi from the Mafia.

Joe's lasagna would have cost $14.95 each.

We quickly sneaked out before the waiter put water on the table and we found a Sabrett's hotdog cart that better suited our budget.

The Sabrett's cart had a picture of just one president, and Jack Kennedy was not shown shaking the hand of the Greek hotdog man.

Sautéed piscatorial penises

Steve was hired to teach biology, but he wasn't much of a teacher. He read each textbook chapter just before the students, misassembled a human skeleton and had trouble pronouncing words — even one-syllable words.

Steve's first love was music, and hardly a day went by without him demonstrating some newly discovered sound that would emanate from one of the major orifices of the ventral or dorsal surfaces of his body.

But even if he had insufficient gas to belch or to fart, the show would still go on. Steve would treat our class to a mangled recitation of the cafeteria menu. He loved to announce "fried fish dicks" instead of fish sticks.

Chapter 20
Do you really want to know what goes into the world's greatest coleslaw?

Around age six, a favorite restaurant in Yonkers, New York, not far from where we lived in the Bronx, was demolished to make room for a huge shopping center, and I stopped eating ketchup and coleslaw.

Nearly two decades passed before I again painted my fries red, but at age 16 I tasted some extremely good coleslaw, and got hooked.

It was not at a gourmet restaurant, or even at a kosher deli, but at the lowly lunch counter of a W. T. Grant's five-and-dime, next to a store where I had my first summer job.

It was perfect. It was crunchy, not slushy, with cabbage shredded, not chopped. It had just the right bite of vinegar, and I got a decent size portion with a 75-cent roast beef sandwich that fit my $1 lunch budget.

I had tried other coleslaws since The Adventurers Inn closed to make way for the Cross County Shopping Center in Yonkers, but nothing impressed me until I tried the coleslaw at Grant's.

I was curious about what made it so great, but since I had no interest in making it myself, I was not sufficiently curious to ask for the recipe.

One morning around 10, I was sent to Grant's to pick up coffee and a toasted corn muffin for Mike, my boss. While waiting for the muffin to be toasted, I learned the secret of the slaw.

There was a huge stainless steel vat on the back counter, filled with the coleslaw ingredients.

Elizabeth, the tiny chief cook who was maybe four feet, eight inches tall, was standing on a stool, and she was arm-pit-deep into the vat — violently stirring, squishing, mashing and mixing by hand.

The little lady was wrestling with and almost strangling the cabbage and the carrots.

She then withdrew her ungloved hands, and wiped each arm off into the vat, with the opposing hand.

After she cleaned herself, I could see that Elizabeth's little Barbie-Doll-size arms had a resemblance to King Kong's giant-gorilla-size arms.

The secret ingredients in the world's greatest coleslaw were *arm hair and sweat.*

It was many years before I tried coleslaw again. Even nearly a half century later, it was tough to write about Elizabeth without barfing on my keyboard.

Chapter 21
French, fried

On TV's *Saturday Night Live*, Beldar Conehead feared that his family would be harassed or harmed if the Earthlings in his new suburban neighborhood knew that they were aliens from the planet Remulak.

The Coneheads couldn't conceal their strangeness, so they tried to explain it by claiming to be from France rather than from a different planet.

Our strange high school principal capitalized a letter in the middle of his last name so we'd think he was French like the Coneheads.

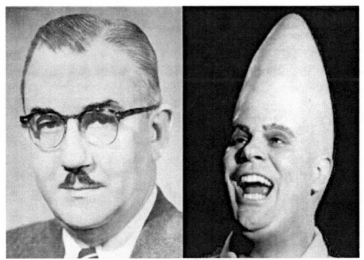

Phony Frenchmen Bob and Beldar

Little Bobby Levine grew up to be Mister (or maybe Monsieur) Robert T. LeVine, with the "vine" rhyming with "wine." He had a smarmy mustache and reminded me of Sergeant Schultz on *Hogan's Heroes*.

LeVine was obsessed with IMAGE.

Although many of his students aspired no higher than a life of soldiering or hairstyling, LeVine ran our Hillhouse High School like a pretentious prep school. In fact, he once proudly informed us that a magazine described Hillhouse as a "public prep school for Yale."

Young ladies could not wear pants to school. Young gentlemen could wear dark blue pants only if they were not made out of denim, and denim pants only if they were not dark blue. The fatal combination of dark blue *and* denim marked the wearer as a juvenile delinquent, right out of *Blackboard Jungle* or *Rumble on the Docks*.

Each young gentleman had to wear a necktie plus a sweater or sportcoat to prepare us for college, where we would wear inside-out sweatshirts with the sleeves cut off.

Because of cost-cutting dumb designs, classroom temperatures were often above 90 degrees, and the only air conditioner in the building was, of course, in LeVine's office. Only LeVine was important enough to be comfortable in hot weather. And he could loosen his tie and remove his jacket when his door was closed.

In June, our final exam papers were often soaked with perspiration.

Kids rebelled by dressing like Bowery bums for "Clash Days," or wore high-neck sweaters and no ties, or pulled fire alarms to cool off outdoors. LeVine would not let boys leave the apparently burning building until he yanked down sweaters to check for ties.

Purely by chance, Elliot, Arthur and I owned a shirt, a tie and a jacket made of the same batik cloth. Periodically, we'd loan apparel to each other so one lucky guy could wear all three matching items and appear to be tie-less from a few feet away— just to make a fool of and piss-off math teach-er Harry Levitin.

Harry was a nasty prick who resembled Frank Perdue, and was LeVine's chief tie inspector. The horrid henchman would stand in the hallway and yank down boys' high-neck sweater collars to catch cheaters who tried to get through the day *sans cravate*.

Sometimes we'd wear ties made of a single strand of thread, or a ribbon, or nearly invisible Saran Wrap ties. We were legal because there was no official definition of a tie.

In our yearbook, LeVine was quoted as saying that "the ability to express ideas, to think and to question, is of the utmost importance." But our questions about ties and blue denim went unanswered.

LeVine's invitation to free thinking and expression came back to haunt him on our graduation day.

About eight hundred blue-gowned seniors marched one-by-one onto the stage of Yale University's ornate Woolsey Hall to receive their diplomas.

As he shook our hands, some dignified and proper students said, "Thank you very much, Mr. LeVine." Some kids just grabbed their diplomas, said nothing and skipped gleefully across the stage. Some kids needled him with "Thanks Bobby" or called him Leveeeen, not LeVine.

A few tried to high-five him, but he didn't know how to respond. Others looked him in the eye and said slowly and very distinctly, "Fuck you very much, Mr. LeVine." The diplomas had already been issued. The class graduation list had been sent to the newspaper. Colleges had already said "yes." There was nothing LeVine could do but squirm.

In the 1964 yearbook, LeVine wrote that "our nation must have intellectual superiority so our kind of society will survive." But the *image* of intellectual superiority was easier to attain than the real thing.

He was suspended for "gross incompetence" in handling school transcripts. Following complaints from colleges, investigators found some 1,300 grading discrepancies. One student received grades of D+, D-, and D from his biology teacher. The official transcript showed a C for the year.

Someone who was on the school staff back then told me, "All the principals did it. He's the one who got caught."

In 1965 *Time* magazine said "a lot of kids got a break they did not deserve, and others, perhaps, lost out as a result." LeVine was forced to retire early, and the hated neckties went with him. Eventually girls were permitted to wear pants to school, and blue Levi jeans were not automatically assumed to mark the wearer as a criminal.

In the ultimate irony, when you type "LeVine" using Microsoft Word, the software wants to change our principal's phony French name back to his actual birth name, "Levine."

Bill Gates knows what's right.

YAY, BILL!

Chapter 22
Spooky story

Wendy's family paralleled mine. She was my age. Her younger brother was the same age as my sister. Our parents were friends.

Wendy and I were often in the same class. She sat next to me in first grade, where she once dropped a milk bottle. It smashed on the floor at our feet, and then she peed into the milk puddle and the vile mixture splashed on my shoes.

I got even with Wendy in third grade when I was drinking milk in class. I started laughing at something and I sneezed some milk at her.

When we were young teenagers, we belonged to the same beach club. At that time, her father had a terminal illness. One night I was at a teen dance at the club, and my mind kept repeating a horrible phrase, "Hi, Wendy, is your father dead yet?" "Hi, Wendy, is your father dead yet?" "Hi, Wendy, is your father dead yet?" Those words — which I could never, ever, say — were haunting me. My mouth was closed, but my brain kept speaking.

At some point in the evening, I saw Jean approaching me. She was my friend and also Wendy's friend.

Jean was crying, and when she got close to me, her face turned fiery red and she started pounding my chest with her fists, screaming and calling me horrible names.

When she eventually calmed down, Jean said that she had seen Wendy a few minutes earlier, and that Wendy's father had died two weeks earlier, and that Wendy told her that I had just said, "Hi, Wendy, is your father dead yet?"

I had not even seen Wendy that day, but she read my mind. Years later, Wendy was killed by her husband.

Chapter 23
The weirdest experience in my life

One summer, my wife and I were in Maine, driving south from Quebec to Bar Harbor. Beautiful mountain vistas surrounded us and beckoned us, but we wanted to reach our hotel before dark.

Besides, I'm a water boy more than a mountain man, and it seemed that every 500 feet we'd encounter a sign indicating that the next turn would take us to beautiful Lake Bigfish, Lake WeWeHaHa or Lake Dip-yer-toes.

It was becoming increasingly difficult to ignore the water pressure. I took the next turn with an appropriate sign and salivated over the prospects of getting wet in the cool clear waters of some random but authentic Maine lake.

While looking for the lake, I thought my eyes were playing tricks on me. Perhaps the weird Canadian food had warped my brain. *Poutine* is a disgusting Quebec snack consisting of French fries topped with slimy cheese and gravy.

I thought I saw a sign that said *Telephone Museum.*

This made no sense because there was no reason for any museum to be in this area. It also made no sense because I collect telephones and would love to see a telephone museum.

I looked again and saw that the sign was real, not an illusion. I thought I had made a random turn, but maybe I had made an involuntary response to something my wife did. Maybe she poked me at the intersection. Maybe she also made advance arrangements for some Maine woodsman to hang up a phony sign to mess with my mind. We drove a few minutes deeper into the woods, and then on my left appeared The Telephone Museum. Really. I'm not kidding. I swear it happened.

Chapter 24
Electrocution experimentation

Although practices vary around the world, and even within individual countries, in those places where the electric chair is used to carry out the death sentence, 2000 volts seems to be the right number.

When I was in the eighth grade, we were assigned to do "research" for Anthony Accurso's science class, and I was curious to see if it was possible to build up immunity to electric shocks. I had no expectation of being tried for murder and facing two kilovolts in the chair in the big house, but I wanted to see how much juice I could take.

I knew that even the puny 90 volts that ring a phone could provide a nasty jolt. On the other hand, I knew that the 12 volts that powered a doorbell was not even noticeable. I figured my limit was somewhere between 12 and 90; but perhaps with training, I might be able to go higher. Like a golfer I hoped to break 100, but in the opposite direction.

I had heard that if you put a live frog in a pot of cool water on the stove, and then turn on the burner, the water would heat so gradually that the frog would just cook, rather than notice a sudden high heat and try to jump away.

But this story is not about heating or eating frogs.

I was curious to see if I, acting as a somewhat larger and perhaps smarter frog, could apply a gradually increasing voltage to electrodes on my forehead — and remain comfortable and alive.

88

I attached a couple of screws with washers and nuts to a headband, and used wires to connect the screws to a variable transformer with a voltmeter that showed how much juice it was putting out. I wet my forehead where the screws would touch me to decrease resistance and improve the connection, put a chart on my clipboard, and went to work. I did not tell my parents or write a will. I did not have an ambulance standing by.

I started rotating the big black knob and was surprised that I felt nothing as I passed through the 20s, 30s, 40s, 50s and even the 60s.

But at around 70 volts something strange happened.

I still didn't feel a shock. At most, it was a tingle.

But the tingle was accompanied by a *sizzle*.

The water that I had put on my forehead to improve electrical conductivity, mixed with my own perspiration from nervous anticipation, was starting to boil and bubble.

HOLY SHIT! I was cooking myself.

I remembered the dead frog story and quickly unplugged the transformer. After I cooled down and wiped off, I thought up a new science experiment that could use the same equipment.

The next day I removed the wires from the headband, and attached them to two nails that I hammered through a pine board, about six inches apart.

Instead of cooking me, I then took a Hebrew National hotdog and stuck it onto the nails, cranked up the transformer to 250 volts, and in about a minute it was *chow time*.

I submitted a beautiful graph to Mr. Accurso showing Heeb-Nat cooking time versus voltage. I got an "A" for my experiment, and apparently have had no lasting damage from either eating the electrocuted hotdogs or zapping my head.

But, on the other hand, maybe people with brain damage just can't tell if they have brain damage damage damage damage.

Chapter 25
Fearing Mother Nature, gender equality, and seeing the beauty in pup poop

When I was a little kid in the Bronx, from 1946 to 1952, we lived near a really nice park. It was a great place at any time of year. I remember three things about the park:

One winter when I was around four or five, I was sledding down a hill, and my sled crashed into a tree. I thought I was in big trouble for hurting Mother Nature, who was God's wife. I started chanting, "I love God. I like God. I love God. I like God." I wasn't struck by lightning or by the tree, so apparently my penance was effective.

In the Bronx, it was (and probably still is) perfectly normal for boys and men to urinate outdoors, usually seeking some privacy between parked cars, or in a dark shadow. One time my three-year-old sister Meryl and I were playing in the park, and she knew she couldn't "hold it in" until she could get back to our apartment, so she went to the side of the road and dropped her pants and acted like one of the boys.

A UPS driver watched her.

Another day my mother was talking with a friend on a park bench while I was collecting twigs and rocks. The nicest specimen I found was a shiny, slightly curved, speckled gray stone about five inches long and an inch in diameter. I showed it to my mother, who said it was nice, and then she resumed her conversation. I walked away. Then she yelled at me to "DROP IT NOW." It was petrified dog shit.

Chapter 26
Clams and Klingons

YUCKY or YUMMY?

It's been said that the bravest man in the history of the world was the first guy who ate a raw clam. Or maybe it was really a raw oyster. Or a lobster. It doesn't matter much. The principle is the same. Some delicacies are best devoured in the dark, at least for the first time.

As a kid I loved fried clam strips.

I naively thought that frying was the only way that clams could be prepared for eating. (I now know better, and I even operate a website called <u>WeLoveClams.com</u> devoted to the many ways of preparing and eating the beloved bivalve.)

One time I was waiting for a bus to take me back to college from the Port Authority Terminal on Eighth Avenue in Manhattan. I was hungry, and nearly broke, and went across the street to a sleazy neighborhood dive for a cheap meal.

I was relieved to see they had clams on the menu at a price I could afford, so I placed my order.

I expected a plate with familiar crunchy golden-brown fried clam strips on a roll with tartar sauce like I got at Howard Johnson's.

But I was presented with a dozen squiggly, slimy, quivering wet iridescent gray and purple things on the half shell.

They reminded me of a picture I had seen when a friend and I sneaked a look at his mother's obstetrical nursing text book.

Or maybe the inside of a cow's eye that we dissected in biology class.

I was also presented with a bottle of Frank's Louisiana Hot Sauce and two previously used pieces of lemon on a faded and scratched plate.

I was staring at the scariest food I had ever seen. This was before live Klingon food was shown on *Star Trek*.

Joe's Bar was not a place where a suburban college kid could survive sending a meal back to the kitchen, and I was hungry and now broke.

Somehow I got up the courage to stab and swallow one of the disgusting gray slime balls, and I liked it.

I still do.

Hunger and poverty can cause human beings to discover unknown courage.

Chapter 27
Silent Night: a story about sex, drugs, rock & roll, steel, food and murder (section 1)

◆The Bethlehem that I passed through, in west-central Connecticut, was serene and unsullied at Christmas.

◆The Bethlehem that I lived in, in east-central Pennsylvania, had loud noises and dirty snow.

Despite declining business and eventually a complete shut-down, Bethlehem Steel Corporation dominates the city.

In the mid-1960s, I spent my sophomore college year living with a local family. "Poppy George" Webster started working at "The Steel" at age 15 and he was close to retirement when I moved into his home. It was a suburban split-level, several miles northeast of the steel mill's noise, flames and filth.

I rented the master bedroom with a private bathroom. Mrs. Webster ("Annie-Love") slept in one of the children's bedrooms, and George slept downstairs in the family room.

He said that this was because he was Catholic and she was Episcopalian. They did have a child, so I assume they were once in the same bedroom for a few minutes.

The son, Wayne Webster, was 21 years old and could have been mistaken for Jethro Bodine on TV's *Beverly Hillbillies* — but Jethro was smarter.

A neighbor told me that the family had paid bills for a few of Wayne's teachers to get him promoted, but he was forced to leave junior high school on his 18th birthday.

Wayne volunteered for military service during the war in Viet Nam and was trained to drive a truck, but he confused oil and gasoline and couldn't shoot straight. Despite the Army's need for large quantities of warm bodies, Wayne was not permitted to re-enlist.

Wayne was working in a fabric store when I moved in with the family, but was soon fired because he confused inches and yards and couldn't cut straight. He spent a few weeks in a junk yard, and then found his true calling as a cab driver.

He awoke each morning a little after four, had breakfast, and was behind the wheel of a taxi from six to six. He then came home, had supper, watched TV, and nodded off before nine. The schedule never varied except for one weekend each month when he had Sunday free. That meant that he could stay up late the night before, and he often went to the burlesque (pronounced with three syllables) in neighboring Allentown to "look at the naked ladies."

Wayne loved his job and urged me to leave college and drive a cab because of all the ladies I'd get to meet.

Wayne never had a date or went to a disco or dance while I lived with the family, but he kept porn magazines under his bed. And whenever the Websters' dog Flower was in heat, she seemed particularly attentive to Wayne. Flower would often raise her tail and wiggle her rear end in his direction, and she spent an awful lot of time in his bedroom.

Mr. and Mrs. Webster were troubled by Wayne and they fretted about his future. Most childhood problems had been solved with cash and kisses; but adolescence, adulthood and aging were not so simple.

The Websters had long planned to retire to Florida when George stopped working at age 65. Unfortunately, Wayne assumed he would retire with them, at age 24, and they were afraid to tell him otherwise.

They were also afraid to die.

Mrs. Webster said she could never rest in peace knowing she had left Wayne behind "with no one to make him a home." Sometimes she and George darkly joked about suicide pacts and hired killers.

Annie had given birth to Wayne when she was 40, and was physically worn and emotionally drained from dealing with his problems for two decades. But she was a loving mother who remained compassionate and tried to appear cheerful and optimistic.

She'd kiss Wayne goodbye and look him over carefully before he left for work each morning, and made a point of complimenting Wayne whenever there was the remotest reason — even the disappearance of a pimple. She tried to help him make the most of his cabby career, advising him on grooming ("shine your shoes and zip your fly"), manners ("don't tell riders how much to tip you") and corporate politics ("be nice to the dispatcher even if he's not nice to you.")

Mr. Webster had little patience for Wayne; he avoided physical contact and hated it when Wayne called him "dad" or "poppy" in public.

He felt his son was a disgrace to the family, and regarded him with a combination of disgust and amusement, apparently much like the 16th-century Londoners who paid money to watch the lunatics in the Asylum of Our Lady of Bethlehem.

(In cockney speech, the Asylum of Our Lady of Bethlehem was called "Bedlam," and is the source of a synonym for "chaos." Bethlehem in Pennsylvania is going through similar pronunciation degeneration. Other than tourists and students, hardly anyone pronounces the name phonetically. Many Pennsylvania Dutch call the city "Bottleheim," and some of the locals prefer "Bethlem" or "Beth-lee-um." The most common pronunciation is "Betlem," and even "Bedlam" is sometimes heard.)

The tourist brochures proudly promoted Bethlehem's history of religious freedom, the nation's first municipal water system and cable TV system, a hotel where George Washington slept, concerts and colleges.

Residents talked about Christmas and Bethlehem Steel.

The company's best times were wartimes, and the periods when Washington spent heavily on public works.

Bethlehem Steel pioneered important technical advances and had a major role in the defense of the nation, employing more than 30,000 men and women during World War II. In 1885, it made the first modern fleet of warships for the American Navy, and was the largest ship builder and military steel supplier for many years. Its steel was used in the Empire State Building and the George Washington Bridge and countless other important structures.

Once a major industrial force, it suffered greatly from foreign and "mini-mill" competition, lack of diversification, pollution control costs, expensive executive perks, recurring strikes, crippling union contracts, and replacement of steel by plastic and aluminum in many products.

In a futile effort to survive, the company cut benefits (such as chauffeurs and security guards for executives), sold off expensive resources (including coal mines, jet planes and a country club) and reduced employment from 115,000 in 1975, to 48,500 in 1984.

But by the late 1990s, Bethlehem Steel made no steel in Bethlehem, ending a tradition that lasted about 140 years.

The huge factory site has been renamed "Bethlehem Works," and has a casino. Future plans include cultural, recreational, educational, entertainment and retail projects.

Back when steel was actually made in Bethlehem, the rust-colored and dust-covered factory snaked along the southern bank  of the Lehigh River for several miles, and the river was like a castle's moat, separating the relatively affluent, pleasant and picturesque north side of Bethlehem from the grim and grimy south.

Most of the level ground on the south side is in a corridor about three blocks deep. It held Bethlehem Steel's blast furnaces, coke dumps, slag heaps and offices and was bordered on one side by the river and on the other side by a broad hill that eventually becomes South Mountain.

Just beyond the plant was a rundown retail and residential section that's now getting gentrified. It literally lost ground for fifty years as the steel company expanded uphill and Lehigh University grew downhill.

In the 1960s, the south side had very few new homes other than low-income housing projects. These projects, and prewar single- and multi-family homes, were inhabited mostly by Slovak-, German- and Mexican-Americans; plus students, alcohol abusers and a variety of people who just didn't realize that the neighborhood had deteriorated.

The top ridge of South Mountain has a giant electric Star of Bethlehem and a futuristic-looking research center that resembles Auric Goldfinger's Alpine headquarters in the James Bond *Goldfinger* movie. It was Bethlehem Steel's pride and joy, but most of its buildings were sold to Lehigh.

Large segments of the river bank steel mill were also sold or demolished, as the company and city sought to replace heavy metal with high-tech. One particularly repulsive landmark, the "Merchant Mill," was transformed after years of idleness. The mill produced steel bars. Its replacement made plastics — the ultimate insult for a steel town.

All employees of Bethlehem Steel referred to the company as "The Steel." Blue-collar workers, regardless of the geographic direction of their commute, worked "down the steel" (just as people who live in New Jersey, vacation "down the shore").

On the day I moved into his home in September of 1965, George Webster asked if I liked to play pool. I said that I did, and the next day he spent nearly $1,000 on a table for the two of us. Son Wayne was disappointed, but not surprised, when he was forbidden to play. The pool table was sold a few days before I moved out the following June.

The family's main source of recreation was their new color television. It was the center of their lives and the envy of their neighbors.

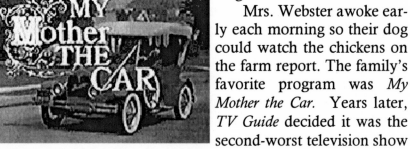

Mrs. Webster awoke early each morning so their dog could watch the chickens on the farm report. The family's favorite program was *My Mother the Car.* Years later, *TV Guide* decided it was the second-worst television show of all time, just behind *The Jerry Springer Show*.

The family felt that any color program was better than any black-and-white program. Mrs. Webster said, "I don't understand why you go out Saturday night when you could stay home with us and watch all the pretty colors on *Lawrence Welk.*"

The Websters had two pieces of "literature" in their home. One was the local newspaper. The other — which all three called THE BOOK — was not a holy bible, but *TV Guide.*

After the television, the Websters' most-prized possession was a European console stereo system with detachable speakers. The speaker for the right channel was kept in the living room near the console, and the left speaker was in the basement near the pool table. Mr. Webster complained about missing sounds, but never accepted my diagnosis or tried the obvious remedy.

I don't recall the Websters doing any entertaining. Most holidays were merely days to sleep late or investigate reports of cheap work pants in distant shopping malls. There was no talk about relatives and they never seemed to take vacations or go visiting. Mr. Webster went to a bar at the end of every Steel shift to meet his buddies to drink Four Roses with Rolling Rock chasers, but the men never got together on weekends.

Mrs. Webster was friendly with a neighbor lady of dubious evolution, who had only recently emerged from the swamp.

Lulu had an enormous repertoire of recipes based on various cuts of long-dead pig meat (which a sister would mail to her each week in not-very-securely-wrapped parcels from somewhere down south) combined with whatever she could pick, dig up, shoot or snare in her back yard. When Lulu started cooking, the whole neighborhood stunk; and if I spied her bringing over samples, I'd hide in the basement.

Lulu and her husband lived in a very small house, made still smaller because they shared it with a very-much-loved and very-much-blind pony. The pony was obviously not long for the world, and neighborhood opinion was divided as to why it was kept in the house: to be nursed or to be near the stove?

Chapter 28
Silent Night: a story about sex, drugs, rock & roll, steel, food and murder (section 2)

Although I was allowed to keep snacks in the Webster kitchen and occasionally joined them for a family meal, I usually ate on campus or at a local drugstore lunch counter. I was spending most of my money on books and records in those days, and was fortunate to be able to get a meal for ten cents: a small Coke and a pack of peanut butter crackers were a nickel apiece.

Bethlehem's cuisine was a massive culture shock. It borrowed a bit from Philadelphia and a bit from Lancaster and had touches of Atlantic City and Germany, but there was very little to make the saliva flow within the mouth of someone born in New York.

Cream soda was red instead of brown. Root beer was clear instead of brown. Corned beef was gray with iridescent green edges and came pre-sliced and laminated to a piece of cardboard that hung on a Pegboard hook between the olive loaf and the head cheese. You couldn't find an imported beer, and most of the domestic brews had names ending in "itz," "atz," and "utz." The big cheese store had 200 varieties, but no Munchee for me. Hotdogs were seldom all-beef and sauerkraut was unavailable.

One translation of the biblical name "Bethlehem" is "house of bread." To me, that means a *bakery*. But when I lived in Bethlehem you couldn't buy a fresh rye bread or even a frozen bagel.

Bethlehem's restaurants offered four ethnic foods: pizza, tacos, kielbasa and pierogies. The nearest Chinese food was in Allentown or across the New Jersey state line in Phillipsburg, and the city's one kosher delicatessen was replaced by a Steel parking lot between my freshman and sophomore years.

Lehigh's University Center snack bar specialized in the "California hamburger" (a normal burger with lettuce and to-mato) and Coca-Cola mixed with any flavor syrup you dared to order. Even chocolate.

A lot of local people seemed to get their total daily nutrition from Rolling Rock Beer and the juice of chewing tobacco, but Bethlehem's favorite "real" foods were hotdogs and scrapple (a dry, off-white granular sausage loaf made from skin, snouts, and other pig parts that were normally thrown out, plus cornmeal, flour and seasonings).

A Bethlehem Banquet

If you're thinking about trying scrapple, this description from Wikipedia may change your mind: "Scrapple is typically made of hog offal, such as the head, heart, liver, and other scraps, which are boiled with any bones attached (often the entire head), to make a broth. Once cooked, bones and fat are discarded, the meat is reserved, and cornmeal is boiled in the broth to make a mush. The meat, finely minced, is returned, and seasonings are added. The mush is cast into loaves and allowed to cool thoroughly until gelled. Scrapple is typically cut into quarter-inch to three-quarter-inch slices, and pan-fried until browned to form a crust. It is sometimes first coated with flour. It may be fried in butter or oil and is sometimes deep-fried." Sometimes it's fried in lard, to provide even more of the authentic pig taste.

In the 21st Century, Rolling Rock Beer has achieved almost cult status, and as part of the Anheuser Busch Empire is available in most parts of the country. Back when it was independent and bottled in Pennsylvania it was merely cheap beer. Some students called it "Rolling Piss," rating it just slightly above urine. We bought it only if we couldn't afford Bud or Colt 45, or as an end-of-binge beer to chug or swig after many bottles of better brews had been consumed.

The major hotdog brand was Yocco's, a simplified spelling of the family name of Lee Iacocca. Lee was an Allentown boy who shared my alma mater and later helped develop the Mustang, save Chrysler and refurbish the Statue of Liberty. The dogs were normally served with mustard or a red chili and onion mixture and washed down with some A-Treat soda in whatever color was currently in fashion. (Local folks ordered soda by color; visitors from outside picked actual flavors.)

When parents visited campus, it was traditional to get dressed up and go to the Hotel Bethlehem on the north side of town for the "Famous Sunday Roast Beef Buffet." Some of the students, particularly country hicks, thought it was a big deal, but two of Yocco's tube steaks tasted better to me, and could be eaten without a necktie.

If I had some serious money to spend (over four bucks), my favorite restaurants were the Grotto and the Tally Ho. The Grotto had great Italian food in a not-quite-Little-Italy atmosphere ("Joeeeey, I need two annie-passed-uhs!") It was fun to rearrange or swipe the beer tap handles when the bartender wasn't looking. I still have some of them.

The "Ho" was a traditional campus saloon with initials carved in the tables and four varieties of condoms in the men's room vending machine. Since contraception was opposed by the Catholic Church and no one challenged a church in a city named Bethlehem, rubbers were "Sold Only for Prevention of Disease" before anyone heard of AIDS.

The Tally Ho was a great place to go with friends or professors. You could sit forever, devouring steamed clams, grilled ham-and-cheese sandwiches, and juicy Ho-burgers with crisp raw onion.

Draft beer and talk both flowed endlessly. My friend Vicky and I once sat down around eleven in the morning and didn't leave until they locked up at 3 a.m. the next day. For low-budget meals, students visited Pete-the-Greek or Louie-the-Greek. Pete's place was known for hot dogs. Louie's Blue Anchor Steak Shop had the best cheese steak sandwiches, and Louie let me run up tabs between checks from home.

Louie worried a lot about Greek and American politics. He was a kind man with compassion for everyone but the dreaded communists. Louie complained about the old guy who'd spend all morning lingering over the same cup of coffee, but held off increasing the price from 10 to 15 cents a cup until he really had no choice. He regarded his customers as family and some of us felt the same way about him. I tutored his son and tended his fish tank. I got paid for the tutoring, but took care of the fish for free.

If we were really broke and too embarrassed to ask Lou-ie for more credit, we could fill up for free at Northampton County Area Community College. It was a new school, commonly called "nack-ack" or "C-squared," then in temporary quarters on farmland in the northeast section of town.

Its best features were open admission, tiny tuition, and — if you were creative with condiments — free lunch!

Vegetable soup was a cup of ketchup and relish diluted with hot water. Onion soup was made from onion slices and pepper in hot water with cracker crumbs, butter and grated cheese. Pizza was Saltines with ketchup, pepper and grated cheese. There was an unlimited supply of pickle slices, and we could make lemonade with lemons and sugar scrounged from the tea supplies.

Closer to Lehigh and right across the street from Louie-the-Greek, was the old New Merchants Hotel. Its first-floor bar did a

thriving business selling take-out beer to underage student drinkers.

In Pennsylvania, liquor stores are owned by the state, and Liquor Control Board agents had reputations like redneck sheriffs. But, de-facto, you could drink with impunity in Bethlehem if you were either 21 *or* a Lehigh student.

Lehigh had a well-deserved reputation as a big drinking school. Sunday dawn would reveal campus lawns strewn with empty kegs and cups, and roadways iridescent with beer, urine and vomit. The fine art of keg-tapping was the first lesson taught to new fraternity brothers, and there was a well-circulated story that Lehigh was banned from intercollegiate drinking competition because we had lost our amateur standing.

During the year I spent on the far side of town with the Websters, I was isolated from campus life before and after classes. There were few college students in my neighborhood, and if I required some minimal social stimulation, I'd hang out at the laundromat or McDonalds or the Two Guys pet department.

The local people didn't know what to make of an apparently healthy, apparently adult, male human being who was on the street at ten in the morning or three in the afternoon. As far as they were concerned, any man who wasn't crippled or retired should be shooting in Viet Nam or sweating "down the steel."

I tried explaining that college was like having a part-time job going to classes plus a full-time job doing homework. One guy said he knew what I meant because he had a cousin who took some courses in the Army.

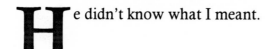 He didn't know what I meant.

Chapter 29
Silent Night: a story about sex, drugs, rock & roll, steel, food and murder (section 3)

The Lehigh campus and the rest of Bethlehem were solidly behind the American effort in Viet Nam. My "Make love, not war" bumper sticker was a frequent target for snowballs, rocks, feces, urine and other unpleasant substances.

A couple of students complained about ROTC and cam-pus recruiting by napalm-maker Dow Chemical, but peace rallies seemed to attract more FBI photographers than protesters.

One year, Pentagon biggie General Maxwell Taylor was invited to speak on campus, and there were six people on a picket line out of a university population of over 5,000.

Taylor thought that even six was too high a number, and tried to have us removed. Freedom of speech prevailed.

Taylor was obviously annoyed the next morning when some of the protesters turned up as invited guests at a press breakfast. We were on the student newspaper, proudly wearing anti-war pins with our press badges.

We had been given a list of questions compiled by several journalism classes. One query referred to "covert" operations in Viet Nam, but because of a typewriter problem, the letter "v" was missing. None of us bright college boys recognized the word and we couldn't figure out the missing letter. One student reporter favored "comert," and another suggested "cosert."

I was unsure, and it was *my* job to ask the question; but I avoided the problem by pronouncing the word "co-ert." Taylor's brain filled in the missing "v" and he answered the question.

I was in and out of college for five and a half years and often just a few steps ahead of the draft board. They wanted me to report to Wilkes-Barre for a physical, but I kept postponing it.

One day I was making a movie with some friends in a local park. I had to slide down a waterfall carrying my dog, "Sniffer," and then walk through a stream. I stepped on a concealed broken bottle, which nearly passed through my foot, and it took 54 stitches to close the wound.

As soon as I got home from the hospital I contacted the Federal marshal and said I was ready for my physical, but unfortunately Uncle Sam didn't want me just then. I spent months with a wheelchair and crutches and swallowed Darvon painkiller capsules like popcorn.

I was scheduled for a pre-induction exam nearly six months later and I hoped the foot would not heal too fast. By the time I had to report to Wilkes-Barre I was actually in pretty good shape and walking unassisted, but I used the crutches and limped and groaned and tried to look like I was in agony.

107

The Army's doctor was sharp. After looking up my asshole, he closely examined the scar on my foot and even checked my armpits for crutch calluses, but I did successfully fail my physical.

I also failed the mechanical aptitude test because I didn't know enough about carburetors, and I confessed to being a member of some international friendship league that labeled me as an Unwitting Dupe of the International Communist Conspiracy.

The final verdict was that if I really wanted to serve my country and had some political pull, I just might get an assignment as an orderly in a war zone hospital. I didn't pursue this option because I saw no reason to kill Viet Cong or haul bedpans for people who did; and compared to Saigon, even Bethlehem looked good.

Natives of Bethlehem did not know much about the rest of the world, but they were sure they lived in the best possible place. Gray skies, brown rain, ash-laden breezes and blackened snow were as reliable indications of prosperity as the crocus is a sign of spring.

The loyal citizens gladly tolerated perpetually dirty cars and speckled sheets and underwear on their clotheslines, and they inhaled soot like it was the finest cologne.

To someone in Bethlehem, adjacent Allentown was the BIG CITY. It boasted a population over 100,000, a Mack Truck factory, two newspapers, the burlesque, and both wonton soup and lox. (It had hard times, too, commemorated in Billy Joel's *Allentown* song.)

Allentown had a high-class department store, Hess's, and a big discount store, Almart. Locals were sure it was named in honor of Allentown, but it was really named for its owner, Allied Stores.

If someone who lived in the Lehigh Valley couldn't meet her shopping needs locally, she usually did without. For many, New York City, or even Philadelphia, was too frightening, too far, or too irrelevant to be alluring.

Mrs. Webster couldn't understand why I'd pay for *The New York Times* since I came from New Haven, and could read her *Bethlehem Globe-Times* for free.

High school kids planned graduation night trips to Manhattan and innocently vowed to "get drunk in every bar" in the borough.

A neighbor of the Websters once tried to drive to Manhattan, but ended up in Brooklyn by mistake. She didn't like it, and vowed never to return to the Big Apple.

Wayne Webster, however, was excited about New York City.

He wasn't interested in the traditional tales of streets paved with gold or even the abundant hookers.

What impressed him were the stories of sexy girls on street corners giving out free tickets to TV shows.

Chapter 30
Silent Night: a story about sex, drugs, rock & roll, steel, food and murder (section 4)

After one year imprisoned in a freshman dorm and one year bored with the Websters, I needed a change.

There was an old three-story peak-roofed house on the south side, one block from the movie, next door to a newsstand with pinball machines, and across the street from a pizza joint that sold joints.

The house was one block downhill from the campus. It was split down the middle, with different people owning each half. The western half was owned by a dentist, "Dr. Steve," who once lived in the building, but had moved to a nicer part of town.

He kept his dental office in the front of the first floor, and rented the rest of the building to students. He charged very little, just about enough to cover costs so the building would always be occupied and his office would be watched over.

Dr. Steve was a good man and a nice guy. He seemed to get some vicarious fun from his attachment to student life and never bothered his tenants, even if rent was months overdue, and sometimes provided us with discount-priced dental care, or even freebies. Dr. Steve really cared about us.

For some unknown reason, the building had traditionally housed students from India. They'd move in, stay for a year or two to earn a graduate degree, and then pass the rooms on to their countrymen. Dave was the only non-Indian who lived in the building. I had met him in my freshman year, and although we were not particularly friendly at the time, he introduced me to Dr. Steve and got me a place to live on very short notice.

The building was not divided into formal apartments, but had a setup resembling suites, each with one or two bedrooms and zero or one bathroom. There was one kitchen, in the rear of the first floor, which was shared by the three-to-five students who lived in the building at any given time.

The third floor, which was really an attic and had been unoccupied for several years, became my home for $35 per month. It had two bedrooms, a living room, and a bathroom. There was no kitchen, but the bathroom measured about eight by 16. I put up a partition between the sink half and the toilet-and-tub half, built a counter, found a cabinet, bought a $35 fridge, and settled in.

I cooked whatever could be made with a hot plate, toaster, electric broiler and electric skillet. I blew a lot of fuses, and washed dishes in the bathtub. We were less than immaculate; I once slipped on a ravioli pod while getting into the tub to take a bath.

I went to the supermarket by motor scooter, and often towed a shopping cart home.

We'd use the empty carts to hold empty beer cans, and more than one of them went down a flight of stairs, like us, fully loaded. Bethlehem was probably as great a culture shock to the Indians as it was to me. Their ideas of America were derived

111

from ancient sitcoms and stale movies. Kevin (a strange name for an Indian) arrived in the middle of the hippie era, wearing a skinny tie and shiny pointed-toe shoes, and he complimented me on my "keen pad."

The Indians were shocked by the size of Americans, particularly American women and American women's breasts. Blonde hair was a special source of amazement.

Two local girls, Joanne (commonly known as Jo-Fuck) and Kara, visited us one night. They were semi-drunk and got into a screaming match which quickly turned into a wrestling match. Joanne yanked Kara's long blonde hair, and it went flying. Ramah grabbed it before it hit the floor; he thought Kara had been scalped!

Even after we showed him there was no blood and told him it was polyester, Ramah was reluctant to return the hair, claiming it would bring good luck on his exams.

Townies like Joanne and Kara were called *Steelies*. They spent a lot of time chasing and being chased by Lehigh students but seldom married them. The intellectual and cultural gap was, with few exceptions, an unbridgeable chasm. Barbara became a long-term friend; but most of the girls were mere providers of favors, or part-time sex slaves.

Some Steelies would allow a student to dictate a term paper over the phone in the morning (while being paid by Bethlehem Steel). At noon, they'd bring the first draft, cook lunch and have a quickie. At the end of the day they'd deliver the final version, cook dinner, thank the student for the typing practice, and get back in bed. Life was good.

The Indians and Dave shared the first floor kitchen, and I did my own cooking in the attic. The Indians were vegetarians when they moved into the building, but soon gave into temptation, usually starting with Campbell's Noodles with Ground Beef soup. It didn't take long to move on to pepperoni pizza, spare ribs and Burger King.

The kitchen was by no means state-of-the-art, but it seemed very advanced to most of the Indians. Somehow, they just could not understand what went where.

Butter was often left out on the counter all day. Milk could be found in the top of the broom closet. Eggs were kept in the breadbox. The refrigerator often contained napkins, spoons, paper cups and Rice Krispies. At least the bugs couldn't get at them.

At the top of the stairs, just outside the door to my living room, was a six-foot stack of pizza boxes containing leftover crusts that we ate like breadsticks when they were sufficiently hardened. Strangely, bugs never bothered them.

At the point where the diagonal banister met the horizontal stairwell railing, there were two wooden decorations shaped like the pointed domes of an Eastern Orthodox church. They wore my girlfriend Anita's bra.

Anita was physically different from most other girls I was attracted to. My standard set of fetishes included dark hair and deep cleavage. Anita was one of the very few blondes I dated, and had what she described as *French tits*, (just big enough to fill a Champaign glass, and separated by several inches.)

She was a very smart, sexy, precocious and pretty girl whom I probably should not have gotten involved with. But I lacked the information that would have kept me away.

When we met, she told me she was a "sophomore at Moravian." I assumed she meant that she attended nearby Moravian College, which would have made her probably 19 years old, a year younger than I was at the time.

Boy was I wrong.

It was only after several months — several months of frequent and recklessly unprotected sex — that I found out that

SEX AND BLOOD

Anita was a sophomore at Moravian *Preparatory Academy* (a high school) and was only 15 years old!

For some unknown reason Anita had trouble losing her virginity both with previous boyfriends and with me. She had remained a "technical virgin" with an intact hymen much longer than she wanted to.

One time the two of us were in my bedroom during a whole-house party and we were trying unsuccessfully to break down the barrier. We were humping so hard that *I* — not Anita — started bleeding. I got a nosebleed for my efforts to break her hymen. I guess the blood pressure was very high throughout my entire circulatory system.

That night Anita really wanted to show her best friend that she finally "became a woman" so she faked the evidence. She used some blood from my nose to redden the sheet to show off.

A few days later, after she got advice from her older sister, we tried a new position and 15-year-old Anita became a woman, though still not an adult.

Sex was almost a toy for Anita and we tried it in strange places, including the garden just below her parents' bedroom window and in the deep end of the swimming pool while treading water. (It doesn't work. The leg motions that keep you from drowning are not the motions you want to be making.)

We once followed the Beatles' suggestion, "Why Don't We Do It In The Road?" and were chased away by the farmer who owned the road. If you want to do it in the woods, make sure there are no park rangers, hikers or hunters in the area. Air mattresses floating in the pool flex too much, and it's easy to fall off. Water beds don't provide enough support and the sloshing is distracting. Don't have sex in a room with a dog, because the pooch may want to sniff or hump. Cars are cramped. Vans are fine. Couches and big chairs work well. All in all, a conventional bed is probably best, but a deserted beach can be nice, especially at a fresh water lake where you can rinse off.

(but maybe not until they're adults)

Strangely, Anita's parents didn't object to her dating a man five years her senior. Perhaps it was because her father and I shared interests in cars and electronics, and I seemed "respectable." Or perhaps it was because they knew it was simply impossible to control Anita.

Her parents had a big house with a pool, horses and snowmobiles. They fed me well and treated me very well.

Anita treated me very well, too. She had a key to my apartment and stopped by on her way to school to give me an oral awakening five days a week. She often saw me on the way home, too. And of course on the weekends.

We were horny enough and foolish enough to shun contraception. Fortunately we beat the odds. Anita thought that postcoital urination would flush out the sperm. We tested her theory a lot and she also tested it with others before me and after me and didn't get pregnant.

Young Americans and Asians were dying daily in Viet Nam, but life was grand in Pennsylvania.

Chapter 31
Silent Night: a story about sex, drugs, rock & roll, steel, food and murder (section 5)

We had good times in Dr. Steve's building. They were probably the best times of my life. If I ever manage to build a time machine, that's where I'm going first. We had sex, drugs and rock & roll, nearly 24/7/365.

Dave and I formed a company to manage and book local rock bands that played at fraternity parties, discos and bars. We named the company *Positively Fourth Street* after the Dylan song and the street where we lived.

That's us in the old picture. We didn't play any instruments, but we did smoke pipes. We even had groupies.

Our house quickly became a hangout for musicians and their groupies, plus sundry camp followers including a gay hippie who was thrown out of high school for refusing to cut his hair, a bisexual college instructor and his student lovers, two dope dealers and a cop.

The cop was also a part-time dealer *and* a part-time pizza maker, so there was a danger of paying him for marijuana and receiving overpriced oregano.

It's tough to smoke oregano. And it doesn't make you high.

We found time to attend most of our classes, but the house and the business were becoming increasingly more important, and certainly more fun.

One party lasted for more than four months, with only a few brief intermissions.

I had a plastic female torso from a Maidenform underwear display, which was perfect for the window in my front bedroom. I put a light bulb into an old railroad lantern and hung it in the window next to "Suzie." Before long, the building was a legend throughout the Lehigh Valley.

On Saturday nights, the local winos would perch on the curb opposite the building to try to catch a glimpse of the imagined debauchery and bacchanalia. Truck drivers from all over the country would stop by and offer to pay for admission with cash, grass or pills. I started changing the colors of the lantern bulbs at random, and the locals soon deciphered the non-existent code.

I once heard two Bethlehemers talking about the building. One told the other it was a hippie whorehouse for the students. He didn't realize that the hippies, the alleged whores and the students were the same people.

There were times that the party got too loud and the neighbors called the police. Once a somewhat-tipsy officer showed up on a noise complaint. He spied an equally-looped girl and said, "I like her; can I have her when I'm off-duty?"

Another night another cop came in because of a similar complaint. We were in Dave's living room and Dave had passed out on the floor with a can of Colt 45 malt liquor precariously balanced on his chest. The cop asked us whom the apartment belonged to. We all pointed to Dave. The cop asked what was wrong with Dave and we all said he was tired. The cop said it would be dangerous to wake him up, so he'd have to wait around to complete his report. He waited until after breakfast. One police officer advised us to control the noise: "I don't care if you rape my sister and abort her with the TV antenna up on the roof, as long as the neighbors don't complain about the screaming."

SEX, DRUGS, CURRY AND COPS

One of Bethlehem's police detectives was less complacent and more paranoid: he thought that the house was the center of an international drug syndicate, with prostitution on the side. We really weren't ingesting anything more powerful than low-grade grass and prescription amphetamines, and the sex was free. But Detective Don was certain he'd get us for something serious and maybe run for mayor based on his new-found fame.

Sometimes he'd come by on a noise complaint and carefully sift through our ashtrays, but he never found anything incriminating. One night he was *sure* he was going to advance his career by finding our drug factory. All he detected, however, were the combined scents of the Indians' curry powder and some photographic chemicals from the darkroom Dave and I had built behind the kitchen.

After that, our relations with the police were pretty good. I'd meet with Detective Don every six months or so to bargain over parking tickets. The procedure was like negotiating income tax in Italy. We'd sit on opposite sides of a conference table, and he'd spread out a pile of my unpaid tickets. I'd ask how much he wanted. He'd ask how much I had. We'd settle somewhere in the middle. I paid cash and don't know where the money went, but I got a good deal.

Relations with our neighbors were never good. They never spoke to us directly, but often complained to Dr. Steve about our noise. He defended us to them and chastised us very gently.

I had a TV antenna on the roof of the house, and its cable passed near a neighbor's window. She opened the window and cut the cable. I spliced the cable, taped an obscene message on the outside of her window, and nailed it shut from the outside. She never bothered us again.

Bethlehem, Pennsylvania was logically nicknamed *The Christmas City*, and any notion of separation of church and state was purely an innocent's illusion.

Our house was directly opposite a church that had an annoying custom of ringing loud bells on Sunday mornings. We could understand the need for church bells hundreds of years ago, but this was 20th century America, and people had alarms and clock radios to wake them for worship.

The church bells in the steeple even rang to announce class changes in Sunday school. There was no reason for school bells to be that loud and intrusive.

We bitched about the loud bells, but our complaints fell on deaf ears. We decided to fight noise with noise, and one Sunday morning we assembled several hundred watts of industrial-strength hi-fi equipment in the front windows facing the church. The church bells rang, and we countered with *Break on Through* by the Doors. The arresting officer said that complaints had come from over a mile away.

I had dismantled my speakers before the law arrived, but poor Jeff was caught, and busted for disturbing the peace. We pointed out that the Doors were no louder than the bells, but the Justice of the Peace was not impressed by our logic. I suppose he thought God was on *his* side. Jeff got the minimum fine, and we were advised that you just don't criticize a church in a city named Bethlehem.

The city was named on Christmas Eve in 1741 by Moravian Protestants who were fleeing religious prosecution in Eastern Europe; and along with Steel, Christmas dominated local activity and thought. The electric star on the top of South Mountain

119

DEATH AND SEX

burned brightly through the smog and soot and was visible for miles.

Volunteers assembled at the Post Office to answer letters addressed to Santa or Jesus, and extra clerks were hired to handle cards sent to Bethlehem for re-mailing with the seasonally significant cancellation.

When I lived there, Bethlehem's homes and stores got festooned with costly decorations that ranged from gorgeous to grotesque, and they all seemed to be displayed from Labor Day to Valentine's Day.

The city spent a fortune hanging colored lights on the utility poles. It was often difficult to distinguish between Christmas lights and the traffic lights on the same poles. I wrote a letter to the *Globe-Times* suggesting that driving would be safer if the Christmas lights could be raised or lowered a few feet.

The letter wasn't printed but I did get a late-night call from someone who said she worked at the newspaper. She called me "heathen scum," and told me to "mind my own business or get the hell out of town."

George Webster stopped working at Bethlehem Steel in 1969. He and Annie leased a mobile home in a retirement community near Orlando, and they deeded the family house in Bethlehem to their son Wayne. They loaded up their car and a big U-Haul trailer on Christmas Eve and they planned to start their drive south on Christmas morning.

Wayne Webster didn't want his parents to leave him, so he slit their throats while they slept, and then he had sex with the dog and went for a walk.

Chapter 32
My career as a beard, and a profit center

I got into the advertising business by accident.

In 1971 and 1972 I was audio-video editor at *Rolling Stone* magazine, and wrote reviews of lots of products. When I wrote good reviews, it was common for the manufacturers to ask permission to quote me in their ads. This was good for the manufacturers, good for *Rolling Stone*, and very good for my ego.

I almost always agreed, but I insisted on the right to review the ads before publication to make sure I was being quoted correctly and not made to seem like a complete asshole.

At one point I said something nice about a BSR turntable, and I got a call from someone at Kane Light Gladney, the turntable manufacturer's ad agency. He explained that they had done an ad with a quote from my review, and would buy me lunch if I'd come by and take a look at the ad. Their office was near mine, a free lunch was hard to turn down, so I agreed.

I met a couple of their guys at a restaurant, and then the three of us walked to their office, where a bunch of "rough" ad layouts were tacked to the walls in a conference room. I took a quick look, and saw that while the quotations were accurate, the ads absolutely sucked and I did not want my name to be associated with them.

With permission, I yanked a couple of layouts off the wall and sat down at the conference table, and within minutes I was an unpaid copywriter. It was easy, and I enjoyed it, and my hosts were impressed. They asked if I could come in on the following Saturday to do some writing for pay.

The Saturday freelancing went on for about a month, and then the agency boss Gerry Light asked me a powerful question: "How would you like us to triple you salary?"

He didn't realize it, but at the time I was only freelancing at *Rolling Stone* and making $75 for each column I wrote twice a month, so I didn't actually have a salary to triple.

The proposed advertising salary was MUCH more than I had been making, and I had a new wife, and I could keep doing the freelancing at *Rolling Stone*, so I quickly accepted their offer.

It was a strange change in environment, with a whole new set of policies and politics to get used to.

When I started work, there was a plaque on my new door that identified me as "Mr. Marcus." It was removed a few days later, and the next week a new plaque was attached to the door that said merely "Michael Marcus."

I found out later that the office manager got into a bit of trouble with one of the partners for labeling me a "Mr." before I had been on the job for a year. Office politics sucks.

My business card had an impressive title, "Associate Creative Director." After a few months I learned that the agency's one other copywriter had the same title. There was no Supreme Creative Director above the two of us. Perhaps our titles were intended to keep our egos in check, or to give us something to strive for.

I guess we were expected to associate with each other.

Although my work was creative and not administrative I also sometimes got to serve as the "account guy."

Mainly this meant that I got taken out to gaudy and expensive restaurants to hear sales pitches from extremely boring media salesmen that the agency partners or real account executives wanted to avoid dealing with.

I was often in an awkward position, creatively.

My straitlaced bosses were frequently too timid to show our clients what I felt was my best work. They were constantly telling me to "tone it down," but I had an edgy style, and was in my early 20s, writing for my contemporaries, as I had done when I was at *Rolling Stone*. We had several showdowns where I said, "You hired me because you like the way I write, so either show my work, or fire me." They almost always caved in.

Sometimes I'd come up with far-out ad concepts, and hold secret meetings with our clients and win them over. If the clients liked my stuff, my bosses had little choice but to go along.

There were other times I went to another kind of secret meetings.

In addition to our work turning out ads, press releases and sales promotion gimmicks, we also arranged dates for some of our clients, often with magazine models.

Jack, boss of one of our client companies, had a long-running affair with a *Penthouse* Pet, and sometimes when he was in town to be with her, I went along as the "beard." If any people saw the three of us, and they knew that Jack was married, they'd assume that *I* was with the Pet who had the cleavage deep enough to get lost in for several days.

I suppose I might have been flattered, but it was really a waste of my time and my only pay was food with an incredibly boring conversation. After dinner in a hotel dining room, the three of us would go upstairs in an elevator, but I'd make a quick U-turn and come back down to the lobby and go home.

I learned a lot about the ad agency business at Kane Light Gladney, but it was not always a pleasant educational experience. There was a lot of conflict, and they seemed to see me as a threat, as well as an asset, and their threat assessments had major lapses in logic.

I had a freelance client that made a unique headphone design called the HearMuff— "the first headphones you wouldn't kick out of bed." It was never very successful and I never made much money from my work. I did the work mostly for fun, and at the end I got paid in HearMuffs. I still have a few. The KLG partners tried to stop my HearMuff freelancing based on the absurd argument that two of the agency's hi-fi clients — AR and BSR — *might* decide to make stereo headphones in the future and my work *could* become a conflict of interest.

What these blind assholes somehow missed was that both AR and BSR *already* made record turntables, a *definite* conflict of interest that didn't seem to bother either company. And *I* wrote the ads for both companies.

Then the partners started referring to me as a "profit center" and urged me to work faster. In April, my boss told me that I had accomplished so much, that there was no need for any more ads to be done until September, and I was *out*.

There's absolutely no job security in advertising and an important rule that I was taught by several veterans was that "The day to start looking for a job is the day that you get a job."

Fortunately I had good contacts from my days at *High Fidelity Trade News* and *Rolling Stone* and I very quickly got a job as a copywriter at Muller Jordan Herrick. I then helped them to take the Columbia recording tape account away from Kane Light Gladney, who had taught me the ad business very well.

Revenge is sweet. Very sweet.

Muller Jordan Herrick wasn't a perfect place to work, but it was much bigger and better than KLG.

Our office was at 666 Fifth Avenue, in the Tishman Building, opposite St. Patrick's Cathedral. The floor below us was larger than our floor, and on nice days, we'd open our big windows and move out our chairs, phones, tables and typewriters and use the roof of the lower floor as an out-door office, dining room and tanning salon.

I won a big-deal award from the Advertising Club of New York while at Muller Jordan Herrick. We had mostly good clients with interesting products that I enjoyed writing about, and only one absolute idiot client.

That was United Jersey Banks, where marketing was controlled by castrated dullards in the legal department. (If anyone from that miserable bank is reading this, FUCK YOU! FUCK YOU! FUCK YOU! FUCK YOU! I still hate your guts.)

One time I had the brain-numbing assignment to write a boring ad about savings account interest rates.

The head guy on the bank's team, a government intimidated ball-less shyster, insisted that I write "*a minimum deposit of at least $500 or more.*" I tried explaining to this testosterone-depleted wuss that all this was repetitive and redundant and superfluous and unnecessary, and that we did not need to say all three!

The pathetic castrato would not give in and neither would I. I told him to write his own fucking ad and I left the room. My only regret was that I didn't shut the light off and slam the door and leave the asshole sitting in the dark, crying and caressing his empty nut sack.

It would have been worth getting fired for.

My office had a weird phone with two number-seven buttons on it, but no eight, and a very nice couch, inherited from the previous inhabitant.

I liked to close my door at noon time for a siesta, but my boss Andy Weiss hated closed doors and he had a nasty habit of opening the door and interrupting my naps.

For some unknown reason, Andy didn't mind if I took an hour to eat, but he didn't like the idea of me taking five minutes to eat and 55 minutes to sleep, even if it recharged my creative battery.

fter a while, my couch mysteriously disappeared and I had to sleep sitting up for 55 minutes.

FOOD, RELIGION AND SEX

Chapter 33
How a radio station lost business from the gay matzo maker

 One of Kane Light Gladney's clients was a major manufacturer of Jewish foods. While the company made a variety of products that were sold year-round, the bulk of their business, and the bulk of our advertising efforts for them, were focused on the eight-day Passover holiday in the spring. That's when Jewish people eat special foods, most notably matzo, a large thin, flat and crunchy bread substitute.

One February, representatives from the company met with several of us at the ad agency to discuss the upcoming advertising plans. We went over new products, the advertising budget, promotional themes, and media selection — both national and in the New York City metropolitan area.

One of the agency guys suggested advertising on the highly-rated, but controversial, Bob Grant radio show. One of the client execs quickly put up his hand like a cop indicating STOP, and told everyone in the conference room that Grant was an anti-Semite. The subject was quickly dropped, and the money was scheduled to be spent elsewhere.

I was the only other person in the room who had ever listened to the Bob Grant show. While I hated his right-wing politics, I knew he was no anti-Semite. In fact, although he was not Jewish, Grant was extremely pro-Jewish. However, Grant was very much anti-gay, and this matzo maker had just stepped out of the closet.

126

Chapter 34
What the blind man could see

Anton Bonn Inc. (the company deliberately left out the comma) was an advertising and public relations agency with two specialties: electronic equipment, and what many on the staff cynically called "wetbacks" — clients with limited command of the English language who were inadequately prepared for life or commerce in the United States.

Once or twice each year company execs would fly to Europe in search of potential clients. The wetter their backs, the more likely they could be convinced that Anton Bonn Inc. would be their savior, their source of riches in the new world.

Anton, the company founder, was an immigrant from Eastern Europe. His twinkling blue eyes, ample charm, and old-world courtliness appealed to many of the European manufacturers who yearned to make the trans-Atlantic leap and emulate Anton's apparent success. He looked a bit like Montgomery Burns on *The Simpsons.*

Unfortunately, Anton's twinkling blue eyes were failing.

He sometimes wandered into the art department and critiqued advertising layouts that were lying on a counter with their bottoms at the top.

Ad designs were often drawn on thin, nearly transparent paper, and one time a paper on a desk near an open window had flopped over, and Anton offered his opinion of an ad design while looking at the back of the page.

There were some things that Anton could see very well, however. When he looked out a window from his office many

DIRTY OLD MAN

floors above street level, he could easily determine which women crossing Fifth Avenue were bra-less.

Anton loved to look at — and to be seen with — beautiful young women.

He had a perpetual help-wanted ad running in the *New York Times*, with slight variations in job description from time to time, including "secretary to poet" and "secretary to playwright." Despite ads aimed at presumed intellectuals, Anton evaluated job candidates as eye candy.

Secretaries seldom stayed on the job more than a month. Some were so frustrated that they lasted only a day, or half a day. Their main duties were to read Anton's mail to him, read employees' mail to him, slice his fruit, and hold his hand and look beautiful as he wandered around trade shows.

Anton's second-in-command was hyperkinetic, abrasive, annoying, irritating, pretentious, egomaniacal, obnoxious, height-impaired and geeky Gerard P. LeDoux.

When the LeDoux family crossed the Atlantic, their last name was probably Ledewitz or Ledowsky. But just like my high school principal who morphed from Jewish Levine into fake French LeVine, the LeDoux clan seemingly preferred to mask its ethnic origins. But his wife shopped at a kosher meat market without hiding behind a mask.

Annie Leibovitz is one of the world's top photographers, and unlike the LeDoux folks, she didn't feel the need to Frenchify or shorten *her* name.

When little Gerard LeDoux made a phone call, he identified himself as "Mister LeDoux." At least he didn't say "Monsieur LeDoux."

Behind his back, however, other employees referred to Gerard as "The Vantz" — the Jewish word for a hyperkinetic, abrasive, annoying, irritating BEDBUG.

In the 1983 movie *WarGames*, the Matthew Broderick character consults a hyperkinetic geek named Malvin for advice on computer hacking. Malvin and Gerard are clones.

Bedbug Gerard was supposed to be the "rainmaker" for the agency, the guy who brings in the clients who spend the money to pay salaries and expenses and hopefully generate a profit. He would devise a list of potential wetback candidates, and then lead Anton in his periodic conquests of Europe. Sometimes it seemed that Gerard picked companies based on getting product samples he wanted to play with.

I don't know if Anton was ever a creative genius, but both his writing ability and his knowledge of business and technology had faded before he hired me. When he tried to get involved in the creative side of the agency, the results were disastrous, embarrassing and frequently funny.

He once failed to win the NEC computer account with a pun-based campaign that said, "If computers give you a pain in the neck, you need NEC." (The folks at NEC like their company name to be pronounced "enny see," and never "neck.")

Another time, the Bonn agency won the advertising business for a manufacturer of computer testing equipment, but Anton completely misunderstood the market.

He demanded that we produce ads that tried to sell the sophisticated test gear to computer *users*, rather than to computer manufacturers or service companies. It was like trying to sell wheel alignment apparatus and tire balancers to every person who drives a car.

Although some clients had stayed with the agency for many years, others left as quickly as Anton's secretaries. I remember seeing a telex come in from a new client, asking if we could recommend another ad agency.

Anton's son Martin supervised the creative side of the agency. He would never have gotten his job without the benefit of nepotism, but he was a passable writer, and a very convincing phony.

Along with his job, he had inherited blue eyes and some of his father's European ways, but his Continental aura was as temporary as a spray-on suntan. Martin Bonn normally identified himself as a vice president; but he morphed into a "managing director," to match the title of European executives he might have to deal with, and to make him seem more like them. He had a second set of Euro-style business cards with the foreign-sounding corporate title.

Even his voice changed if he perceived the potential benefit. When dealing with native-born Americans, Martin spoke perfect American English. But when he introduced himself to Europeans, he performed a retro-morph, to become Martin *Bunn*, the new immigrant from *Zee Continent* who had trouble *vid zee* American pronunciation.

The Bonns did not like to spend money. When they moved into new offices in the mid-70s, they reused an ancient cord switchboard, instead of getting a more modern phone system. When we wanted to make a call, we had to "flash" the operator, and nasty Gloria made it obvious that she resented interrupting her nail polishing to put in a plug.

We were always busy, but a lot of time and money were wasted redoing bad ads, and the place may not have been profitable. It was tough to get a raise. One time I was rewarded for coming in at 6 a.m. for nearly two months at a particularly busy time, with a lousy FIFTEEN BUCK weekly raise for my efforts above and beyond the call of duty.

Then we underpaid serfs found a way to use Anton's well-known paranoia and sneakiness to our own financial advantage.

If someone wanted more money, he or she would arrange to have a friend at another company send a letter on that company's stationery offering a new job, knowing that Anton would open the mail and learn about the bogus opportunity.

We'd wait a few days and then pop the question. Anton would assume he was in a bidding war, and would have to pay well to keep an important employee.

The agency had a public relations department, with some talented and hard-working recent graduates and old pros, and some who were not so talented or professional.

For a major trade show the agency distributed press releases with "challanges," "emphasizeng," and "discoteque;" they used commas to separate sentences, and spelled one client's name two different ways on the same page. Maybe Anton did the proof-reading.

I had worked at better ad agencies before Bonn, and this place was the equivalent of a "gut course" in college, where minimal work could earn an easy A.

It seemed to be an ad agency where I could stay for years, quickly cranking out stuff that impressed the bosses and clients, but was below my traditional standards and left plenty of time for naps and freelancing.

One day Anton approached me in the art department, and asked if I knew what a "sinecure" was. I said that I didn't.

Anton explained that it was a position in a church given to a respected elderly priest, where he could live out his life while doing very little work.

nton's eyes weren't very good, but the old coot sure saw through me.

Chapter 35
Spiderman meets Paul Newman

My 30-year dream came true in February, 2004. I bought a Spider, a Fiat 124 Spider. It's a little Italian sports car, a convertible, as red as an Italian tomato.

I wanted to buy one back in 1974, but needed a rear seat for packages, relatives and potential children, so I bought the slightly stodgier Sport Coupe version instead.

My 74-year-old Grandma Del, who was often in that back seat, thought I'd never be a success until I owned a Cadillac. However, she did feel the Fiat magic and acknowledged that the car seemed "geared to the road."

I removed most of the emissions controls from the '74, gave it an Ansa exhaust, Serra air cleaner, Bilstein shocks, Heathkit electronic ignition, racing steering wheel, super-powerful lighting, BWA alloy wheels with fat Michelin tires, and lots of TLC — including oil changes before and after driving in all-night rallies. I bought Armor-All shine-up fluid by the gallon, and washed the coupe several times each week.

The engine was clean enough to fry an egg on.

My Italian mechanic Ugo said "Anybody else come in, I fixa the engine, then I washa my hands. When you come in, I washa my hands *before* I fixa the engine."

At that time I was an advertising copywriter. My automotive clients included Castrol oil and Volvo cars, and I proudly wore my big Fiat belt buckle in meetings with the boring Volvo people.

Whenever it was parked, my beautiful "Fiata" drew crowds of curious and adoring people. It could go over 130 MPH, as steady as a train on a track, beat Detroit 400HP heavy-metal muscle cars on twisty roads, and could go through snow where FWDs had trouble.

On the other hand, the rear window leaked when it rained, the air conditioner couldn't be used on hot days, the oil pump failed during a rally ($1,500 repair), and I had to disconnect the battery to keep it from discharging when I parked at the train station.

That car was an absolutely gorgeous, fast-running, great-handling, piece of junk. I loved it, but it often seemed to hate me.

It's often said that the letters in FIAT stand for *Fix It Again, Tony* or *Fix It Alla Time*. It was also said that Fiats could have been wonderful cars if they were designed in Italy, and then someone carried the plans through Switzerland or Austria so the cars could be assembled in Germany.

Fiats are a *lot* of fun, but back then they were more like toys than transportation.

Older Fiats should never be the only vehicle in your garage and should *never* be depended on to get you to school or work in the morning. Turning the ignition key is like rolling the dice or playing Russian roulette — you never know what will happen.

Ultimately, the Feds made Fiat buy my sometimes wonderful 1974 coupe back from me because the engine was in danger of falling out— probably a first in American auto-motive history.

I had already bravely bought a Fiat Brava for my wife, and I then replaced the coupe with a Fiat Strada for myself. (They were both great-handling pieces of junk.)

Since then, I'd had a number of boring cars from Ford and Chrysler, but I always dreamed of getting a Fiat Spider. I even saved my stock of Fram PH7 oil filters, Marelli ignition pieces, and NGK spark plugs. I still had my tune-up test equipment, manuals and ancient parts catalogs. I even had a bright red Fiat driving suit, which I'll probably never fit into again.

In February of 2004, I spotted an absolutely gorgeous low-mi '78 Spider at a nearby dealer.

It had been a cold, gray winter here in Connecticut, but on 2/27/04 the weather was glorious — a perfect top-down Spider day. I went out to lunch with my brother Marshall while the car was prepped for my test drive.

The restaurant was nearly empty, but three guys were at the table across from ours. We overheard them and coincidentally they were talking about cars.

One of those guys, sitting a few feet away from me and talking about cars on this perfect top-down Spider day, was actor, philanthropist, food developer, car dealer and car racer Paul Newman. We spoke a little. He was very friendly.

It was a good omen. The car is great.

(Paul died while I was writing this book. I'm glad I got to meet him.)

Chapter 36
Marcia, Bob the giant penguin, and Harry's exploding belly

Our Latin 2 teacher in high school was Marcia Young. She was a few years older than the kids in our class — but she looked like she was younger — and could be best described as unsophisticated, sheltered and naïve. In short, she was no match for 30 wiseass suburban kids.

We definitely didn't dislike her, but Marcia was such an easy victim that she invited exploitation. I frequently "cooperated" on tests with the girl who sat in front of me. At first we passed notes back and forth. Later I built an intercom system for low-volume verbal consultations.

Here are two of the Class of 64's Greatest Hits:

◆Bob was a big kid. One of the other kids (probably me) had a pair of swim fins in his gym bag, and we persuaded Big Bob to put them on while he sat in the back of the class. When Marcia called on him to go up the blackboard to write something in Latin, Bob waddled to the front of the room like a giant penguin.

Bob kept a straight face.

Marcia was terrified.

The rest of us were hysterical.

YAY, BOB!

◆Our Latin class was interrupted by lunch period. One day I happened to have an inflatable life preserver vest in my gym bag. (I know it sounds weird, but I used the same bag for SCUBA diving classes after school.)

During lunch, Harry and I went to the boys' john and he put the deflated life vest on over his shirt but under his sweater, and we went back to class.

We did our normal Latin work for a while, but then Harry started moaning, and he waved his hand frantically. Marcia asked him what was wrong.

Harry stood up and slowly walked to the front of the room while hunched over and clutching his abdomen with both hands. He seemed to be shivering. Then he stood by Marcia's desk. Stammering, Harry said he thought he got food poisoning in the school cafeteria.

Harry's classmates and Marcia — who all ate the same food Harry ate — were horrified by Harry's condition and their own potential peril.

Harry told Marcia he had a terrible pain in his stomach. He said, "It keeps going up and down and up and down and..."

At that point, Harry sneakily put one of his hands inside his sweater and pulled on the ripcord which punctured the gas cartridge to inflate the life vest.

His torso seemed to double in size in two seconds.

Marcia screamed.

So did we.

YAY, HARRY!

Chapter 37
The right connections

Our high school guidance counselors pointed out that we could enhance our chances of college acceptance by participation in community organizations, particularly if we held important offices in those organizations.

Not wanting to miss a chance, classmates Howie, Barry and I formed a SCUBA diving club called the New Haven Finsters. We had been diving together for years, so why not formalize it? For the cost of a sheet of paper, an envelope and a stamp, we got listed in The International Roster of Diving Clubs, and our scam became reality.

To further enhance our credentials and impress college admissions officers, we decided that *each one of us* would be president of our important community organization.

I think we had different guidance counselors in school, so no one noticed the duplication. Internally we had different titles. Barry was the "lowest lump of whale blubber on the bottom of the Mariana Trench." I've forgotten what Barry called Howie and me but it was probably comparable. I remember a lot, but not everything.

Our esteemed organization was even listed in *Skin Diver* magazine and we started getting mail from all over the world, including offers on great bargains on lead weights. However, they were not such great bargains if the shipping charge from Louisiana to Connecticut was included.

In retrospect, I don't really know if the Finster presidency enhanced our college acceptability. Howie went to Yale, but I'm sure he would have gotten in even if he was not the leader of the Finsters.

On New Year's Day of 1964 we went ice diving.

It seems like a really stupid thing to non-divers, but divers think it's a great adventure. You find a lake, with suitably thick ice on top. You use a chain saw to cut a hole in the ice measuring about six by six feet and put a 10-foot ladder across the hole. A rope is tied to the ladder and the other end is tied to the divers.

On this particular day it was *ridiculously* cold out, something like six degrees Fahrenheit at Bolton Lake in north-central Connecticut, with a *wicked* 50MPH wind whipping across the ice.

The good news was that it was so fucking cold that there was little danger that the ice would melt and we would get dumped into the lake. The bad news was that it was so fucking cold that we were freezing our asses off.

Actually, we couldn't really freeze our asses off, because major parts of those asses were safely behind two layers of quarter-inch-thick neoprene rubber that raised the interior temperature about 30 degrees above the exterior temperature.

However the exposed parts of our *faces* were quickly covered with ice during the short walk from our car to the ice hole — and that's not healthy or pleasant. Also, the first stages of our regulators, the mechanical parts of our breathing apparatus mounted on the tops of our air tanks behind our heads, also froze up. We had to dip them below the surface of the lake to defrost them before making the dive.

People thought we were nuts to dive under the ice.

In reality, we felt comfortable and safe and it was really nice down there. It looked beautiful, with eerie light filtering through the ice and much better visibility than during the summer because there were no motor boats to stir up the mud and crud from the bottom.

The water temperature had to be above 32 degrees and the rubber "wetsuits" raised our temperatures another 30 degrees, so we were warm enough. It wasn't nuts to go *in* the water, but it was nuts to come *out* and get undressed in the six-degree temperature.

138

None of us wanted to strip down in the cold car so we decided to stay in our cozy rubber suits until we got home where it was warm and dry.

Unfortunately, when we reached New Haven, our car full of rubberized weirdoes collided with another vehicle crossing an intersection about a block from police headquarters, and the smash-up was, of course, witnessed by a cop.

He didn't want to write us up in the freezing weather, so he told everyone to follow him to the PD HQ.

It was a holiday, so we decided to have some fun.

Howie, Barry and I marched into the cop house wearing our swim fins and masks, carrying spear guns and with long knives strapped to our legs.

We could have been locked up "for observation" but we had guessed right and the cops were also in a holiday mood. They had a good laugh and they didn't even object to our awesome weaponry.

After a few minutes of discussion it turned out that both of the drivers had close relatives with important connections in City Hall. The official report of the incident stated that the traffic light was "simultaneously green in both directions."

None of the drivers got a ticket and we all got hot chocolate. One of the cops even tried my spear gun.

Chapter 38
Getting into Yale, early and unofficially

Like most of the Ivy League, Yale University was "boys only" for most of its existence. It finally became coeducational in 1969 after 268 years of complaining and masturbating.

Before the female students arrived, in an effort to provide a somewhat more normal social life for its cloistered male scholars, the university hosted "mixers" where freshmen could meet, dance with, and perhaps mate with female students from local colleges.

Since Yalies were considered to be good husband material, the girls who attended the mixers often revealed a bit more cleavage than on their regular campuses (especially in a Catholic school like nearby Albertus Magnus College).

They also wore shorter skirts, and were more likely to get into bed on a first date than on a date with a non-Yalie.

This attitude was well-known and resulted in packed dance floors. Theoretically the only males who were admitted were Yalies, but it wasn't hard for an enterprising New Haven high school senior to make a fake Yale student ID. The promise of abundant loose women stimulated convincing counterfeiting. (The fake cards were also good for admission to Yale's tennis courts and golf course.)

At one Saturday night mixer early in the school year I spotted a good looking girl who turned out to be an "Aggie Maggie" — a student at Albertus Magnus.

Beverly didn't ask to see my ID and never actually asked if I was a Yalie or asked a campus question I couldn't answer. She was majoring in secondary school education and came from Boston.

We danced, and talked, and eventually left the mixer with a few other girls and genuine Yalies I knew. We went to continue the partying in a freshman dorm suite.

We enjoyed Yago Sangria, grass, Dylan and the Beatles. We danced and made out and probably would have gone all the way but Beverly realized what time it was and had to get back to school before the 1 a.m. curfew.

I walked her back to her dorm, got her phone number, and we had a good goodnight kiss. I was looking forward to seeing Beverly again, but I was surprised at how soon I would see her and where we would be.

On the following Monday in my high school English class, our teacher introduced several student teachers who would be observing our instruction.

One of them was Beverly from Albertus Magnus.

I tried to hide behind my notebook, but eventually Beverly spotted me. I blushed. She smiled. Then we both laughed. The teacher and the rest of the class didn't get the joke.

I called her and we dated a few times. We lost our virginities together. She was my first "older woman," but not my last.

YAY, YALE!

Chapter 39
SHORT STUFF

This is a collection of really short, short stories that have little or nothing in common except their size. By putting them together, I may have saved half a tree.

What a putz!

In the Pennsylvania Dutch dialect, a "putz" is a three-dimensional nativity scene — a crèche.

In Jewish slang, however, the word is the equivalent of "schmuck," and means both "penis" and "fool."

Bethlehem, Pennsylvania's Christmas customs received the attention of a women's magazine in the late 1960s. It described the special meals and music, the decor, and the elaborate putzes assembled in many homes.

The small Jewish community in Bethlehem had a good laugh at the magazine's suggestion that tourists might "knock on any door in town and ask to see the family putz."

Oh Uncle Herman, there's someone here to see you!

Vinnie's water closet and circus

In what used to be the British Empire, "water closet," or "WC" is a euphemism for "toilet," or sometimes the smelly little room that contains the toilet.

In the early 1960s, in the Dr. Susan S. Sheridan Junior High School in New Haven, Connecticut, there was a real closet that often had water in it.

The old, original part of the school, like many schools built in the early 20th century, had a "cloak closet" across the rear of the

142

room, where kids would hang their jackets and coats. Heavy oak doors moved vertically in tracks, attached to sash cords with counterweights like old fashioned windows. When the doors were down, there were open spaces above and below them.

Vinnie Vetrone was one of my teachers at Sheridan. If he had reason to punish a student — and he often did, or often thought he did — the cloak closet made an excellent jail cell. The space above the door was just the right size for Vinnie to dump in a bucket of water onto the unfortunate prisoner's head.

It wasn't as bad as waterboarding at Abu Ghraib, but it sure wasn't pleasant.

A lot of innocent kids' coats got drenched, too; and on a cold day a soaking-wet coat did not provide much insulation on the walk home from school.

There was a very small student in a class a few years after me. Vinnie made him stand in a wastebasket like a circus sideshow freak while his classmates laughed at him.

I'm not sure if Vinnie is alive or dead, and I don't care and I'm not changing his name.

So, FUCK YOU Vinnie.

It took me nearly half a century, but I finally got a chance to dump on him.

Always a wiseass

In September, in the first swimming class at Hillhouse High School, instructor James J. Davin distributed 3×5-inch file cards to every boy.

He instructed us to "write down your name, home room, division, and YES or NO. If you can swim, circle YES. If you cannot swim, circle NO."

I yelled out, "If you can row a boat, circle OR."

What is the secret of life?

If I told you, it wouldn't be the secret of life anymore.

What does "In-A-Gadda-Da-Vida" mean?

In-A-Gadda-Da-Vida is a 17-minute, 10-second rock song by Iron Butterfly, released in 1968. It took up an entire side of an LP record.

If you hear a radio station play it during the daytime, there is a very good chance that the deejay is having a bowel movement or eating lunch.

If you hear it at night, the deejay is getting laid

Italian dog food

One time my mother drove to Luigi's, our favorite pizzeria, to pick up a pizza, lasagna, and a couple of hero sandwiches.

When she got home, she realized that one of the heroes was missing, so she left the food on the kitchen table and drove back to Luigi's to get the rest of our supper.

When Mom returned home for the second time, there was nothing on the table.

In the corner of the kitchen floor was the open and empty pizza box. Our dog Sniffer was sitting in the box, smiling and burping.

Buon appetito, il mio piccolo cane.

How *Rolling Stone* got screwed by *Screw*, and tried to screw me

Around 1970, porn tabloid *Screw* said some bad things about a personal vibrator made by Panasonic. A short time later, *Rolling Stone*, also a tabloid publication, was trying to get advertising business from Panasonic. The Japanese executive in charge of Panasonic's advertising confused the two publications, and refused to do business with *'Stone*.

In 1972, while I was audio-video editor at *Rolling Stone*, their book publishing division, Straight Arrow Books, wanted me to write a book about hi-fi.

I wasn't impressed with the advance and the royalty rates they offered me. My contact at Straight Arrow insisted that it was the best deal they had offered anyone, and would mail me a contract.

Someone at Straight Arrow goofed up, and put another author's contract in the envelope that was mailed to me. He was getting a much better deal, so I refused to do business.

Maybe I don't know as much as a caveman

The younger sister of a girl I dated in college was given a horse for her birthday. She named the horse "Vida," in honor of the Iron Butterfly song *In-A-Gadda-Da-Vida*.

The family didn't have much money, and couldn't afford to hire a professional trainer, so I volunteered to try.

I had generally been successful with animals. One of my tropical fish, a Kissing Gourami named Carl, grew huge and lived for six years. I liked dogs. Most dogs liked me and some dogs obeyed me. And a horse is just a tall dog. Right?

Besides, 15,000 years ago, the first Cro-Magnon who rode a horse didn't read any horse books or watch a horse DVD, and probably didn't know any more about horses than I did.

I decided to walk into the corral with an apple and a smile, and see what would happen.

I got kicked. I got pushed. I got knocked over. I got bitten.

Vida stomped on my foot and pushed it deep into the mud. Vida wouldn't even take the apple from me.

I have a new appreciation for Cro-Magnons.

Maybe grandsons are interchangeable

One time while I was in college, I took a weekend away from campus and drove to spend some time with my Aunt Fan and

Uncle Red on Long Island. While there, I phoned my Grandma Del in the Bronx, and we had the usual grandmother/grandson chat.

I said, "Hi Grandma," and asked how she was. She told me about a few aches and asked how I was. She asked about my folks, my brother and my sister. I asked about some relatives. She asked about school. I asked about her neighbors. She asked me about Uncle Steve and Aunt Judy.

I said, "Who?"

She repeated, "Uncle Steve and Aunt Judy."

I said, "I don't have an Uncle Steve and Aunt Judy. I must have called the wrong grandmother."

She said, "That's OK. I enjoyed talking to you. Please call me again. My own grandson never calls."

I was so bored, I learned how to bet, and I won

When I lived in Yonkers, New York, the man who lived next door loved to gamble. He and his wife would frequently go to Las Vegas or the Caribbean or Atlantic City for the casinos, or to the nearby Yonkers Raceway for horse races. They even bought a summer house in the Catskill Mountains near the Monticello race track.

He was friendly, and frequently invited my wife and me to go to the Yonkers track, but I had no interest. He persisted, and one time offered to buy us dinner in the track clubhouse to celebrate my birthday. It was easier to say yes than to keep saying no, so we agreed.

We ate an OK meal, and then began the torture of watching people scream at animals running in circles.

Bored, I began to read the racing program to see if I could figure out what the attraction was. After a while, I was able to decipher the recent racing histories of the horses that were running that night. I noticed two that had previously demonstrated their ability to win, but hadn't won lately.

It seemed like they were ready to win. And since I had no inside tips or reasons to bet on any other horses, and didn't want to be a party pooper who didn't bet at all, I went to a betting window and put a few bucks on the last two races of the night.

Both of "my" horses won. I even did better than the expert who took me to the track. He never invited me back.

Why real people sometimes need to speak like Beverly Hillbillies

On the popular 1960s TV sitcom "The Beverly Hillbillies," Jethro Bodine called the pool table, *the green eatin' table*, and the swimming pool, *the cee-ment pond*.

Some syllables were spoken with too much emphasis, and others didn't get enough

Sometimes there's a legitimate reason for non-hillbillies to mispronounce words.

In England, one of the major prep schools is Eton. It's pronounced like Jethro's *eatin* and was founded in 1440 by King Henry VI. The school has a very long list of distinguished alumni, including 18 former British Prime Ministers.

The Duke of Wellington said, "The battle of Waterloo was won on the playing fields of Eton." At Eton, team sports are considered essential to education

Starting in the 19th century, young boys were required to wear the "Eton suit" with huge, stiffly starched white collars. The Eton suit was copied by other English schools and even crossed the Atlantic and became a style of dress-up clothing for young American boys in the 20th century.

However, if a salesperson in an American clothing store suggested the garment and referred to it with a proper British pronunciation, a prospective customer might think the sales-person was a hillbilly and that the suit was suitable only for *eatin'* grits, chicken-fried steak and ham hocks.

I sold boys' clothes in a store where the personnel were instructed to mispronounce the name of the school and the garment as "<u>ee</u>-tahn."

Jethro would probably have been very confused.

Get it in writing

When I was audio/video editor at *Rolling Stone* magazine, one of our inexperienced and ultra-aggressive advertising salesmen sold an ad to a maker of car stereo accessories.

They made an adapter that allowed a car radio to be used indoors, and the ad salesman offered my services to write the ad. He neglected to check with me first, and he also neglected to get the client's signature on a contract.

The deal was done verbally, and sealed with a handshake. The ad was sold for something like "eighty-five-ninety-five."

The owner of the company nearly went into cardiac arrest when the bill arrived. He expected to pay $85.95. But *Rolling Stone* wanted to collect $8,595.

But Daddy, I'm not a gangster

When I was in junior high school, one of my teachers summoned my father to school for a special meeting.

Nate Franco told my old man that he was very concerned about my future because I had been skipping classes, playing hooky, smoking in the boys' room, and had joined a teenage gang that was using drugs and stealing cars.

My father knew that I might not do all my homework, but these other accusations were clearly out of character; and he asked Franco where he got his information.

Franco picked up and waved a manila file folder that was labeled MARCUCCI.

My father then explained that our name was MARCUS. Franco responded like Gilda Radner's Emily Latella character on *Saturday Night Live:* "Well, never mind."

But that's not *our* corpse

A few years ago my wife and I attended a funeral about 50 miles away from home, in a city we were not familiar with.

The proceedings started with a religious service in a synagogue, and then there was a long procession of about 20 vehicles that meandered though the city streets to the cemetery for the burial.

Our car was near the end of the line and when we reached the cemetery, we sensed that something was wrong.

Instead of familiar Jewish stars, most of the gravestones were engraved with crucifixes, and we saw lots of statues of Jesus and Mary. Most of the mourners were black, not white.

Apparently as some of the cars navigated through a complex intersection, we separated from the main group and had merged into a different dead person's procession.

We never found the right cemetery, but we had a very nice lunch at Legal Seafood.

The battle to dominate the Sears Tower

Some years ago my house was burglarized, and among the purloined property was a tool box filled with my nice Craftsman tools.

Our home was insured by Allstate. Allstate, like Crafts-man, was part of Sears.

After I submitted my claim for the loss, the Allstate adjuster applied a depreciation deduction formula for the stolen tools, based on their age and presumed decrepitude.

I responded that Craftsman tools are sold with a Lifetime Warranty, so there can't be any depreciation. I told him that I could take a bent, dull, rusted 30-year-old Craftsman tool into any Sears store and it would be gladly and immediately replaced with a bright and shiny new model.

The adjuster responded that "everything depreciates except land," and he gleefully pointed out that "a brand new Cadillac drops 20% in value when it leaves the dealer's lot."

I told Mr. Allstate that I would rather drive a Craftsman than a Cadillac and I was not giving up and he'd better check with corporate headquarters.

Apparently there soon was a battle for supremacy in the Sears Tower in Chicago and it was ultimately decided that the image of Craftsman was more important than the profitability of Allstate. I got every penny I wanted.

Er, ah, um, what about the tracks?

Once while I was on a commuter train going home from Grand Central Terminal, I heard a brief conversation between a man and a woman, apparently a married couple, as we approached the station where they planned to exit.

The man cautioned her to look closely and be careful getting off because there would be a large gap between the train and the platform.

The woman replied, "Well, why can't the driver just move the train closer?"

Phone sex

In our eighth-grade science class, teacher Anthony Accurso required us to do current events reports on new scientific discoveries or developments in technology. One day Susan was at the front of the class telling us that the Bell System was beginning to deploy roadside drive-up public telephones. This was long before cellphones.

According to Susan, a driver could stop his or her car next to one of these phones, roll down the window, insert the appropriate number of coins and "call across town, across the country, or even call abroad."

The young teenagers in our class thought calling "a broad" was hysterically funny and it took a long time for Accurso to stop our laughing.

Tie Score. Psycho-drivers: 1, Michael: 1

Around 1972 I was walking along a major avenue in the Bronx where children were playing on the roadway. The traffic light turned green and a hot-rod burned rubber and leaped from the intersection as if it was in a drag race. I was concerned about the kids, and yelled, "Slow down, asshole!" Despite his noisy exhaust, the driver heard me and got out of the car and ran towards me. I ran into a supermarket to hide. The speeder found me, punched me in my face, broke my glasses, and told me to mind my own fucking business.

A little while later while I was driving in a tough neighborhood in Queens, a driver cut me off and I gave him the finger. He slammed on his brakes and blocked my car from moving. He opened his window and started waving a baseball bat and swearing at me. I yelled at him to get out of his fucking car and fight like a man. He got out and started walking toward me. When he was a few feet away, I stomped on the gas pedal and sped down the block in reverse. By the time he got back in his car, I was far away and moving fast.

Drilling him a second asshole

When I was a teenager, my bedroom was a former guest room in our basement. The house was a split-level and the room was above ground and had a normal window. It was nice, definitely not a dungeon.

Late one night I was awakened by sounds outside my door. I got out of bed and opened my door slightly and I spotted a neighborhood "bad kid" going through my mother's pocketbook.

He had apparently gotten in through the unlocked back door and sneaked upstairs, grabbed the pocketbook, and took it downstairs to separate the cash from the other stuff.

A normal kid would have been scared shitless and kept silent until the burglar left. But I've never been accused of normalcy. I decided to defend my home from the invader.

151

I had no Colt or Winchester, but I was a SCUBA diver and I had a powerful spear gun powered by a monster-size surgical rubber tube. According to the salesman who sold it to me, the gun was strong enough to penetrate a car door!

In the past the spear gun had never been aimed at a creature any more treacherous than a flounder (and I didn't catch a lot of fish) but desperate times call for desperate measures.

I quietly and carefully pulled back the rubber loop and hooked it onto the notch on the stainless steel spear.

I stood by the door edge and took careful aim at the middle of the intruder's ass. I didn't particularly want to kill him, but I hoped to punish him, and keep him from running away until the cops arrived.

Unfortunately I missed his butt crack.

I was sleepy and shaky and not a great shot, even from eight feet away. My spear tip approached his ass at the wrong angle and bounced off the wallet in his back pocket.

He was startled, however. And when he saw me standing in my underpants and realized that he nearly gained a second asshole, he said, "Are you fuckin' nuts? You could've killed me." Then he dropped my mother's money on the floor and ran out of the house through the back door.

I don't know if he ever tried to rob us again, but we did keep the door locked from then on.

Chapter 40
Mein Doppelgänger

 In 1971, I was audio-video editor at *Rolling Stone* magazine. The 3M Company sponsored a press trip for some writers and editors to travel from New York to their factory in Minnesota to learn about a new high performance recording tape.

After the plane landed in Minneapolis, we boarded a bus to take us to our hotel, where we were scheduled to have lunch with 3M execs and scientists. I sat in the first seat, right behind the bus driver.

When we got near the hotel, I took out my comb, and looked into the driver's rearview mirror so I could neaten my hair and beard after the flight.

BUT, no matter how hard I moved my comb, my image wasn't combing its hair and beard. And its tie was different.

The mirror wasn't defective. I was seeing the reflection of the guy who was sitting next to me. He could have been my clone.

I turned to the left and we two guys stared at each other and trembled, and then we broke into insane giggles and shook hands.

Michael Edelson, an editor at *Popular Photography* magazine shared my beard, my nose, my cheeks, my hairline, my occupation, my religion, my physique, and even my first name. (He's on the left.)

Someone took a picture of us and captioned it "The Stereo Twins." It's still hanging in my house.

Chapter 41
My parents' other kids

Hardass brother

"Hardass" is slang for a tough guy. At least once in the history of the world it was literally true and not just slang.

One time my younger brother Marshall did something wrong. I don't remember what it was, but it got my mother so pissed off at him that she gave him a good kick in the ass.

Apparently Marshall had a *real* hard ass, because Mom broke a toe. His ass didn't break.

―――

Once when Marshall was an infant sitting in his high chair, I was trying to feed him some baby glop. I guess he didn't like it, because he stuck a finger in my nostril and gave me a nosebleed.

―――

When he was a little bit older, the family was eating a Passover meal. While the adults were concentrating on prayer and food, little Marshall picked up a bottle of wine and filled his glass. He really liked the sweet grape flavor and quickly emptied his glass, and in a few minutes there was a giggling four-year-old drunk at the table.

―――

When he was about two years old, my mother bought Marshall a pair of red shoes that he hated. He really wanted blue shoes, but they were unavailable in his size.

One day, instead of waiting for Mom in the front of our house as instructed, Marshall went for an unsupervised walk down the block and he threw the shoes and his socks into a sewer and then he walked home barefoot and defiant. I don't know what was wrong with the socks. Maybe he just liked being barefoot. Or defiant. Mom replaced the red shoes and Marshall was not allowed to wear them unsupervised.

Marshall was actually continuing a pattern that I had established earlier. When I was young I disposed of a dirty piece of paper by flushing it down the toilet.

Unfortunately the piece of paper, while dirty, was a perfectly functional $10 bill.

———

My baby brother grew up fast. In addition to getting drunk when he was a little kid, Marshall demonstrated sexual desire long before puberty.

Our family belonged to a beach club and a girl I was dating once carried Marshall where the water was too deep for him to stand with his head above water.

Marshall clung to her tightly. She probably thought he was afraid of falling into the water and drowning, but this well-built young lady was very wrong.

When we got back on the beach, Marshall told me he had been touching her breasts. I never got to do that, and Marshall bragged about his accomplishment for years.

Symbiotic sister

This isn't a funny section. At best this section is mildly amusing, but it would not be fair to talk about my brother and not about my sister Meryl. (Funny Meryl is on page 90.)

Symbiosis is a close cooperative relationship, often where a member of one species does something that the member of the other species can't do, and vice-versa.

155

Although my younger sister Meryl and I were both classified as Homo Sapiens as children (and presumably we still are), we had different talents and different shortcomings; but when we got together, we were able to accomplish what we had to do.

At one stage in our development she had trouble turning doorknobs. I was perfectly willing to open doors for Meryl, and she paid me back by tying my shoelaces — a task that I did not master until much later.

I now avoid laces completely. I wear only Crocs, slip-on boots, or sneakers with Velcro straps.

Our symbiosis even extended to the dining table.

With hard boiled eggs, I ate only the yolks and she ate only the whites. With salads, I ate tomato but not lettuce, and she ate lettuce but not tomato. We did a lot of productive trading. No one went hungry and no food was wasted.

Despite this apparent cooperation, Meryl and I really did not get along. Like most big brothers and little sisters, we fought like cats and dogs, until I was a senior in high school and she was a sophomore. Then we could try to fix up her friends with my friends. We were very symbiotic, even for two Homo Sapienses.

Chapter 42
Crawdads in Manhattan

A crawdad, or crawfish or crayfish, is a freshwater crustacean that looks like a tiny lobster and tastes like a mixture of rock, mud, dust and frog spit.

Crawdaddy, on the other hand, is the name of a rock club in England where the Rolling Stones played their first gig, in 1962. It's also the name of an American magazine, founded in 1966, that published serious writing about rock music even before *Rolling Stone* magazine. I have the singular honor to have served as the hi-fi editor of both *Rolling Stone* and *Crawdaddy*, and the distinctive displeasure of having eaten a few crawdads on one unforgettable night in Manhattan.

Crawdads are also known as mudbugs and there is no reason to eat one unless you are starving to death. I have never come close to starving to death. But having eaten some crawdads, I think that death might be the more pleasing option.

In the southern U.S., particularly in Louisiana, crawdads are often boiled with salt, cayenne pepper, lemon, garlic, bay leaves, potatoes, corn on the cob, onions, garlic and sausage. The elaborate seasonings may result in tasty potatoes, corn and sausage, but won't help the crappy crawdads.

My wife used to have an old aunt named Cristina. She was usually called Aunt Tina, or even "Teeny." There's no point in mentioning her last name here, but I will point out that at around age 80 she decided to add an extra "m" in the middle of her last name.

Tina was born and raised in the Bronx, but headed west with her new husband before World War II. They settled in Albuquerque, but she kept a sizeable and growing secret stash of money in a bank in the Bronx where it was safe from her distrusted husband. Tina was an excellent investor, and when she died, she had multiple millions that he never got to.

According to the family, her husband was both a philanderer and a fascist. He was born in Italy and during the War was imprisoned as a supporter of Mussolini and a potential threat to the United States.

Once each year Tina would travel east to visit her money. Although the bucks were in the Bronx, she usually stayed in a hotel in Manhattan. She used to tell us that she preferred to stay in the worst room in the best hotel, rather than the best room in the worst hotel.

One year she picked the wrong hotel. The elevators failed and she was marooned 30 flights up for two days. Room Service took food up to her, but she refused to walk down because she knew she couldn't walk back up.

A couple of times she stayed in our house. She'd get up early to perform an elaborate skin preservation ritual. Upon completion, her face was as white as Marcel Marceau. Underneath the white paint, as thick as the pink/yellow glop that Tammy Faye Bakker used, Tina may really have had the skin of a five-year old toddler. I don't know, because I never saw the real Tina. Only her embalmer knows for sure.

One year Tina decided to stay at the New York Hilton. It was an excellent hotel, so she presumably reserved their worst room. She invited Marilyn and me to join her for "a fine dinner in Manhattan." I would have been perfectly content to eat in any of the many wonderful restaurants inside the hotel, but Tina wanted to hit the streets.

She asked the concierge for his recommendations for nearby eateries and she made notes. I have to wonder if maybe he didn't want to recommend places that provided better food than the company that provided his paycheck.

We walked about a block to the first restaurant on the list. I no longer remember its name or cuisine. Tina scanned the menu on display by the door and quickly dismissed it with no comment. She clutched my wife's hand and escorted us around the corner to restaurant number two.

Here, she more carefully studied the convenient outdoor menu, and also dismissed it with no expressed reason for her dissatisfaction. I'm sure the reason was not the price.

She then marched us to the third of four restaurants on the list. This restaurant also had a conveniently displayed menu. Strangely, Tina completely ignored it and quickly opened the door and pushed us in ahead of her.

It was a fake-French bistro with lots of dusty bottles of wine and some large dead fish on display.

We were escorted to a table and Tina insisted on ordering a bottle of wine. After the bottle was uncorked and I gave it the obligatory sniff test, I attempted to pour some wine into Tina's glass. She then surprised me by putting two fingers across the top of the glass and said, "No, No, I never drink wine. It's all for you and Marilyn." Then Marilyn surprised Tina by explaining to her that she hates wine. I was not a big wine drinker, but I knew what I liked, and I did NOT like the wine Tina had ordered. There was no way I was going to drink the whole bottle. I barely drank one glass.

159

After a pretty bad start, things got *really* bad.

The elaborate bilingual menu had a great many choices— but not even one that appealed to me.

The eight pages revealed that the kitchen had a huge inventory of ingredients, but the perverted chef combined them in ways that would induce nausea, not salivation. "Would monsieur like some prime calves' liver marinated in cauliflower juice and goat urine and covered with mayonnaise, sauerkraut and chipotle? For a special treat, please consider a side order of raw garlic gloves dipped in melted chocolate and sprinkled with chives, sea salt crystals and wild boar dandruff."

Uh, no thank you.

If I had been allowed to combine the available ingredients the way I wanted to, I'm sure I could have easily whipped up a satisfying meal, even if it was just a burger.

Instead I carefully studied the menu and suppressed the urge to barf on the fine linens. The least objectionable choice was sautéed crawdads. Always helpful, Tina assured me that "they're just like lobster," so I placed my order and prepared for the worst.

I was inadequately prepared.

I got a plate of cockroaches wearing lobster costumes.

I could not find any way to extract either flavor or nourishment from the ugly red rocks. Tina and Marilyn were only slightly more successful with their choices.

I hope the waiters enjoyed the wine I left behind.

We then walked back to the Hilton. I wanted to quickly ditch the old lady in the lobby and go get some real food. When we got into the hotel, Tina announced that she was thirsty and suggested that we sit down in the lobby bar and talk for awhile before going upstairs to admire the view from her room.

Now it was my turn to treat and I was relieved that she ordered just a 7-Up and not a bottle of champagne. Unfortunately even a simple soda has an inflated price in a major Manhattan hotel. The price of Tina's 7-Up was seven bucks! She had two sips, pronounced it excellent, and abandoned about $6.80 worth of bubbling fluid on the table top.

As we walked from the bar to the elevators, Tina offered a weak apology for the dining disaster. If I was a nicer person, I would have murmured something like, "That's OK. It's the thought that counts."

Instead I kept silent.

What I *really* wanted to stay was, "You stupid bitch! You senile idiot! If you rejected two restaurants *after* reading the menus, why the fuck would you pick a restaurant *without* reading the menu?"

SEX AND VIOLENCE

Chapter 43
Oral sex can be unhealthy

As a professional journalist, I know that I should not publish any stories that I can't verify. However, this one is so good that I am willing to temporarily suspend the hallowed rules of reporting.

And besides, since I only promised you that this book is 80% true, I'll take a chance.

Here we go: ALLEGEDLY, one of my naïve female high school classmates was convinced by the owner of a local car dealership that he would provide her with a beautiful new car if she would provide him with beautiful oral sex.

Since her desire for the vehicle strongly outweighed her common sense, she was soon down on her knees on the carpet behind the desk in his private office.

Without getting up, she took a brief intermission to discuss the vehicle color, optional accessories and delivery date.

He then revealed that he had not been serious about the transaction.

She bit off a chunk of his scrotum.

Chapter 44
Who's listening to you?

It can be useful and fun to determine who pays attention to you, and who ignores what you say.

When people who don't know me, call to sell me printer cartridges or Wall Street stocks and ask, "How are you?," I'll say, "Medium." I don't ask how they are because I really don't care how they are.

Many of them imagine that I did ask, and they say, "Fine, thank you" anyway.

If they hallucinate, I won't buy their inks or their stocks.

When my Grandpa Walter was asked about his health by people who definitely didn't care, or even listen to his answer, he used to say, "Sick in bed, thank you." They never noticed.

Try it yourself. It's really funny.

Chapter 45

Objects seen in the rear-view mirror may not be what you think

From around 1975 to 1985, I frequently competed in sports car rallies. I drove, and my buddy Ralph was the navigator. Ralph and I met at an advertising agency where we worked. We were both automotive outcasts. I owned a Fiat and he owned a SAAB. We knew they were great cars even if the rest of the world didn't agree.

A rally is not a race, but a contest to follow a set of often cryptic clues to arrive at a final destination at the proper time. Penalties are assessed for each hundredth of a minute early or late. Really good rallyists can have amazing low scores like 6 or 13 even after hours of driving. Others can have scores in the hundreds or thousands. Some do not finish at all.

In those days cars were divided into classes by the sophistication of the primitive mechanical computing equipment they used. Some used none, and were considered to be running SOP (Seat Of the Pants). It was a cheap way to rally, and it was fun.

It was an honor to make it to the finish line, and there was usually abundant food and drink and plenty of trophies at the end, including one for DLBF — *Dead Last, But Finished*, a good way to encourage newbies to compete.

Along the route, cars were logged in at surprise checkpoints. Their arrival times were recorded, and then they were restarted on the next "leg" of the event.

The instructions gave clues such as "bear left at third yellow awning" and "increase speed to 37MPH at green cow." Under stress, it was easy to misread an instruction. One time Ralph thought "MR" meant "make right," but it was really "mile reference." It was tempting to drive faster than the prescribed speeds to allow time to compensate for when you're off-course. But if you're zipping along at 60 instead of 37 and turn a corner and suddenly you're 10 minutes early at a checkpoint, you get a 1000 point penalty.

Many rallies were simple three hour Sunday afternoon suburban jaunts. At the other extreme is the Paris to Dakar rally which includes a segment across the Sahara.

The big challenge for Ralph and me was an all-night rally, "The Connecticut Classic," operated by the Fairfield County Sports Car Club. It could take 14 hours and cover 300 of the crappiest roads in the Nutmeg State.

Because the rally route often ran through some really bad terrain, after the third year I learned to keep my own car safely in the garage. Instead, Ralph and I rented Mustangs from Hertz. The rental contract said we couldn't race, but it didn't mention rallies. Not worrying about scratches, scrapes or crashes definitely gave us a competitive edge.

We stuck on some racing stripes and big numbers and mounted a bar on its roof with about two zillion candlepower of Boeing 747 landing lights to shine our way through the New England forests. With those lights you could feel the heat 10 feet away, and could probably defrost a turkey. We hoped to avoid turkeys. And also trees, deer, bears and hunters.

While these events were called *sports car* rallies, and many of the vehicles were traditional MGs and Triumphs, there was nothing in the rules to keep out our Mustang, or anything else. We saw some basic Hondas and even a few pickup trucks at the parking lot where the rallies started. But one year a strange vehicle surprised us many hours after the start of the event.

Around three in the morning we were on a dirt road deep in some God-forsaken state forest, apparently hours behind schedule. We were bashing through the wilderness as fast as we could, aided by our airport illuminators and with total disregard for the posted 15MPH speed limit. It had been a long time since we had seen any other vehicle.

Suddenly two small lights appeared in my rear-view mirror and they quickly grew larger. In a moment, the moonlight revealed that there was a large white Jeep station wagon behind us, and I could even see that the wagon had a long antenna sticking out of it. It had to be some kind of a law enforcement officer on patrol.

I didn't want to slam on the brakes to reveal that I had been speeding before I saw the cop, but I pulled my foot off the gas pedal. We were going uphill and fortunately our speed quickly dropped from 40-something to the posted 15.

The wagon was now about one car length behind me, and stayed at that uncomfortable distance, just waiting for me to do something wrong. Every time I looked into my mirror, I expected to see a revolving red light.

I stayed at the legal speed limit for a miserable nerve-wracking half hour until we finally reached the end of the dirt road and left the state forest and drove into a checkpoint to get our miserable score recorded.

That's when Ralph and I discovered that the large white station wagon with the tall antenna was not driven by a forest ranger or a state cop. It was just another rally car, and the driver was pissed-off at *me* for driving so slowly and costing him penalty points into the checkpoint. I told the SOB that *he* made me drive slowly and that *he* should have driven a sports car or a Honda, not something that looked like a goddam cop car.

Chapter 46

I swear it's true, but if I saw it in a movie, I'd yell BULLSHIT

During lunch hour one day in 1971, my buddy Ken and I were wandering around the upper east side of Manhattan trying to find a BMW dealer. I don't remember which one of us was shopping for a car and which one was just looking, but the dealer wasn't where we thought it would be.

There were no cellphones in those days, and even a pay phone wouldn't help, because we didn't know the actual name of the place. We needed a Yellow Pages phone book, where we could go through the classified listing of car dealers until we recognized the right one.

You might think it would be easy to find a phone book in Manhattan, but on that day it wasn't. Every phone booth we found was barren of books. Bodegas, bars and newsstands had White Pages but no Yellow Pages. A restaurant owner said their phone books were for patrons only. A kindly dry cleaner offered his directory, but vital pages had been ripped out.

Disappointed and dejected, and with the end of our lunch hour approaching, we decided to give up and go back to our offices in midtown.

As we walked, a big delivery truck pulled up to the curb ahead of us. A driver and two helpers got out of the cab and opened the side door of the cargo area and set up a ramp to the sidewalk. They went up the ramp into the truck, and then they rolled out three hand trucks, loaded with five-foot-tall stacks of the Yellow Pages. We each got a book.

Chapter 47
A platinum card is as good as Medicaid

Years after I moved out of the Bronx, I was visiting someone who still lived in the Bronx.

I saw posters and heard amplified announcements proclaiming the availability of FREE CHEESE, being distributed by the Department of Agriculture. Apparently our taxes subsidized the dairy farmers and they overproduced, so this was a way of paying back something to the blood-sucked taxpayers.

I didn't need the cheese, and if I did, I could afford to buy my own, so I ignored the announcements.

After awhile, the audio announcements turned frantic. Apparently, any cheese that was not given away by 4 p.m. would be thrown away.

There was no provision for storing it locally, or returning it to government warehouses or to the dairies that made it. Our government agents were begging us to take it away.

I did not want to turn down my government in a time of need, and accepting free food was certainly less of a burden than joining the Army or paying a tax surcharge, so I went to the community center and joined the giveaway line.

When it was my turn, I was asked for my welfare card. I said I didn't have one.

Then I was asked for a Medicaid card. I didn't have one of those, either.

Then I was asked if I had a Medicare card, and I didn't have one of those.

The woman on the opposite side of the counter said, "Sir, we'd really like to give you the cheese, but Federal regulations require us to see some identification."

I smiled and asked, "Do you take American Express?" She said, "Sure." I showed my platinum card and I got a huge 10-pound block of cheese.

T hank you, Mr. President.

SEX

Chapter 48
Unplanned chick magnetism, how rich people eat, an overdue confession, and an amazing coincidence

Also known as If I saw it in a movie, I'd yell BULLSHIT (the sequel)

When I was in junior high school, like many Jewish kids who lived in Connecticut, I spent February school vacations at the Concord resort in New York's Catskill Mountains, which were also affectionately known as the "Borscht Belt."

The Catskills were where the movie *Dirty Dancing* took place, where such comedians as Milton Berle, Buddy Hackett and Jerry Lewis first got famous, and where my own father worked as a waiter during his college vacations.

(**Inside Secret Revealed**: Pop told me that if he was "waiting a table" with eight people who ordered steaks with a mix of rare, medium-rare, medium, medium-well and well-done, he'd tell the cooks to make them all medium. His subterfuge made all of the meals ready at the same time and made it much faster and easier to pass out the plates. Only a small percentage of guests would notice, fewer would complain to the overworked and underpaid waiter or busboy, and almost none of those would want to invest the time in waiting for a replacement meal. If anyone did complain, Pop would apologize, and blame a mythical recent immigrant cook who hardly understood English.)

"The mountains" were always a place where women hoped to find husbands and where men hoped to get laid.

It was where teenage boys of my generation learned to ice skate and ski. They dreamed of getting laid, but a little more realistically, boys hoped to reach *second base*, preferably touching a bra that contained a genuine breast, and not merely a wad of Kleenex tissue or a foam rubber falsie.

In February of 1962 I was 15 years old and in ninth grade. On my third day of skiing I was bored and feeling unjustifiably confident in my progress, and I decided to promote myself from the beginners' ski slope to the intermediate slope. It didn't look too much steeper or any more dangerous, but what I didn't notice was the ice where I expected soft snow to be.

I lost control, spun around, flipped and flopped, lost my skis, heard a CRACK and I hurt like hell.

I waved my ski poles and screamed for help and a few minutes later I was sliding down the hill in a sled-mounted basket aided by two ski patrolmen. I was a bit disappointed that I didn't get visited by a St. Bernard dog with a keg of brandy around its neck like in the cartoons.

An ambulance transported me to a local hospital for X-rays and I was informed that I had a broken ankle. My parents were summoned and they took me back to the Concord with a cast and crutches.

My skiing was obviously over for the week, but I saw no reason to skip the teen dance that was scheduled for that night. It was no more likely that I could dance than ski, but perhaps some sexy 16-year-year-old girl — or maybe even several of them — would notice my wound and offer to sign my cast or provide other comforts.

Although I had a brief career as a model around age four, I was a shy teenager who never attracted much attention from girls. But when I hobbled into the teen dance that night at the Concord, I was like Carly Simon's unnamed subject of *You're So Vain*. Like Mick Jagger or Warren Beatty or possibly someone else, I was the guy who walked into a party and all the girls dreamed that they'd be my partner.

The plaster cast and crutches were great chick magnets and I was immediately the center of attention. A returning war hero or a rock star in a Ferrari couldn't have attracted more admirers than I had that night.

Falling on my ass on an icy hill did not require any high degree of bravery or talent, but all of the babes wanted to hear how I got wounded and soon my white cast was covered with blue ink and red lipstick kisses.

I also collected some names, addresses and phone numbers on pieces of paper and one of those notes led to a romance that lasted a few years.

Alicia was very smart and very pretty and the only child in a family that lived about 20 miles from me. The relationship began by mail and after my ankle healed I started riding my 10-speed bicycle the 20 miles to visit her on Saturday afternoons. Unfortunately it was mostly uphill.

Although both of our families spent winter vacations at the same Catskill resort, our worlds were different. My own family was "comfortable" but Alicia's family was *loaded*. We had a Chrysler. They had a Cadillac.

All the girls I knew had plain names like Susan and Judy and Harriet. But even Alicia's Jewish friends had glamorous WASPy names like Muffy and Buffy and Sondra. They spoke WASPy, too. After a sarcastic remark from a friend of mine, Alicia replied, "You're uncouth." A New Haven teen's retort would have been, "You're an asshole."

Alicia's parents always took Alicia and me out to eat at expensive restaurants or to their country club, and it was when we ate — no, better make that *dined* — that I discovered that these people were in a class above my own family.

I had been brought up not to waste even a morsel of precious food. If I rebelled about finishing a meal that I hated, or even if I was genuinely full of food, my mother would say, **"You'll eat it and you'll like it and there are thousands of people starving in Europe!"** Under the same rebellious conditions my usually com-

172

passionate and coddling grandmother would coldly remind me of the "**starving Armenians**."

Even as a very young child I detected a large gap in the dining table logic of these two women.

Somehow I never quite understood how my eating every last disgusting lima bean or LeSeur green pea that was glaring at me from my plate would help fill the gaunt bellies of unfortunate refugees in Novi Pazar, Vagharshapat, Hrazdan or Yeghegnadzor.

Confession: Mom, I often hid the despised green things under a plate or a napkin or under the table, or even stuffed them in my pocket or handkerchief for later secret disposal.

I would gladly have mailed them across the Atlantic to any country where they would be appreciated and improve either the standard of living or the child mortality rate.

My mother bragged about the diverse foods she ate and she apparently thrived on weird stuff like kale, okra and Brussels sprouts, but she could not tolerate even the *smell* of kasha which my father and I loved. She hated to cook it and would leave the house when Pop and I ate it.

Mom had a perverse ritual to demonstrate that she was the supreme ruler of the land and I was a mere serf with minimal rights, but with better living conditions than provided at Auschwitz. Once each year she'd force me to eat food that I hated: those disgusting LeSeur peas and shepherd's pie. I doubt that Dr. Spock would approve, but I couldn't convince Mom to ask him.

Mom was an excellent "company cook" with special recipes that would impress our visitors. But family meals sometimes included salt soup, barely defrosted French fries and burnt chicken. Mom knew I liked only the white meat from a chicken but apparently she didn't know it was possible to buy only the white meat, or to buy additional white meat.

173

(My dog eats only white meat chicken, too. He'd happily eat the dark meat, but my wife won't let him. She's convinced that white meat is healthier, so that's what he gets.)

On the other hand, Mom was a talented baker and did a great job with lamb chops, London broil, pot roast, chocolate pudding and fried flounder, so **I hereby forgive her**.

My father never complained about Mom's cooking. Although he appreciated fine foods, he gladly ate things that few other humans ate (like lox "wings") and Mom called him "the human garbage disposal."

After our family thought it had eaten all the meat from a turkey, Pop would render the carcass into something resembling a pile of sawdust and toothpicks. The first time my wife met my parents, she assumed she was acceptable because my father took her plate and finished what she didn't eat.

Alicia was the archetype Jewish American Princess who never had to eat anything she did not like to eat. Being an only child, her position in the familial line of succession was perfectly safe and she was secure from sibling rivalry. Her face was the only face immortalized with a gilt-framed oil portrait over the marble fireplace.

Not only did Alicia never have to eat food she didn't like, she didn't have to finish any food at all.

In fact, she told me the exact opposite of what my mother had told me. Alicia's instruction was, **"You should always leave some food on your plate."**

According to the rich people's rules taught by Alicia's parents, finishing a meal implies that you are hungry and poor and *you actually need a meal*. I never before knew there were people who thought like that.

After a great meal — which I usually finished like a famished member of the destitute lower class who didn't know the rich rules — we'd go back to Alicia's house. Her parents would go to the den to spend the evening watching TV. Alicia and I would go to the living room to spend the evening making out.

174

SEX

She was probably 14 when we started dating, so real sex was out of the question. At least it was out of the question for "nice girls" of her age. Or maybe it was just not a good idea when parents were in the next room and the TV volume was too low to mask the sounds of heavy breathing and squealing.

We had marathon French-kiss sessions and after a few weeks of fumbling I eventually became an expert at one-handed bra unhooking. I could do it either lefty or righty, and in the dark. I was smooth and quick like a good professional shoplifter.

By one in the morning, it was time to go home.

After five highly stimulating but unfortunately unfulfilled hours, I usually had a severe case of *blue balls* ("temporary fluid congestion in the testicles and prostate region in the human male often accompanied by a cramp-like ache and tenderness of the testes caused by prolonged sexual arousal and lack of orgasm").

In that condition, I couldn't ride a bicycle 20 inches, let alone 20 miles.

Fortunately, Alicia's parents liked me. Her father would help me put my bike in the trunk of his Cadillac, and he drove me back to New Haven. He'd do absolutely anything for his Princess Alicia and almost anything for me.

Eventually I got my driver's license. This solved some problems, but presented another problem. You see, despite all of Alicia's wonderful qualities, she did have one quality that I perceived as much less than wonderful.

Alicia had a braided pony tail. NO! Wait a minute. It was not a mere *pony* tail. It was a goddam *horse's* tail, almost long enough for a giant Budweiser Clydesdale, which reached down to the middle of her ass.

She probably started growing it the moment she popped out of her mother's womb, if not sooner, and she never allowed even a micro-millimeter to be clipped. I wondered if she was trying to set a Guinness Book record.

175

Alicia seemed to like it more than anything else in the world, but I hated the fucking thing and I was embarrassed to be seen with her because of it.

During the time that our dating involved my biking up to her town, there was little chance of us being seen by anyone who knew me.

But once I had a driver's license and the use of a car, my new mobility meant that I could take her on dates almost anywhere. There was now a heightened risk that we might be seen by someone who knew me, and any friend or classmate would certainly give me shit about the strange growth that extended from the back of Alicia's head to the middle of her ass.

I had to come up with excuses why we couldn't go to the big city of New Haven for movies or concerts.

▶ **Long-Overdue Confession:** Alicia, I really liked you *a lot* and the reason I didn't ask you to go to my high school's junior prom was because I really hated that fucking hair thing and I didn't want to be seen with you.

▶ **Really Weird Coincidence:** One time I was in the back yard of Alicia's house with her father, talking about cars. His new Cadillac was nearby in the driveway.

I mentioned that I had read that despite all the many millions of cars that General Motors had made, they only had 1,000 different key patterns.

I said that I happened to have the key for the Chevy Corvair Greenbriar van that my father's store used for deliveries, and that it was possible that the Corvair key would open and start his Caddie.

He laughed, of course.

I tried it, of course.

It worked, of course.

I swear it really happened; but if I saw the scene in a movie, I'd yell BULLSHIT.

Chapter 49
Not Strictly Kosher

✡ + ✝ = ?

When I was in fifth grade, our synagogue distributed a survey with questions about parental attitudes on interfaith dating. (If you haven't figured it out yet, I am Jewish.)

At the age of 11, there was little chance that I would be a traitor to the Chosen People and date a pretty blonde Gentile girl (a "shiksa"); and my politically liberal mother — probably without much thought about the future consequences — indicated on the survey form that she and my father would allow me to date a girl who was not Jewish.

Fast-forward from age 11 to age 17.

In my senior year in high school I was working part-time in my father's clothing store. So was Maria. She was not a blonde, but a beautiful dark-haired Italian-American who was a senior at Mary Immaculate Academy — unknown territory to someone who had studied religion at B'nai Jacob.

It was easy to be attracted to Maria. She was gorgeous, smart, played the guitar, and seemed to like me.

We engaged in some mild flirting. I made frequent visits to her cash register to get change for big bills. One time I asked her to give me "three threes for a nine." She laughed. It was a good sign. The flirting was a little awkward at first, partly because I was the boss's son. If this happened today, I could be accused of sexual harassment.

IRRESISTABLE LUST

Red Skelton, a popular TV comedian at the time, had done an episode about an alien landing on Earth and needing change for the parking meter near his flying saucer. Red played the saucer pilot who asked a friendly Earthling something like, "May I have three hizzins for a hern." I printed up a piece of hern currency in the store's sign shop and I asked Maria for change. She laughed at that, too.

My attraction to her was pretty obvious, and some employees encouraged me.

Mickey, who was the buyer for teenage girls' clothing, even revealed Maria's impressive bra size (34C) and urged me to ask her out. Eddie, an Italian-American who worked with me in the men's department, cautioned me to stay away. He said, "Don't shit where you eat." I wondered if he was trying to give me useful advice, or just wanted to protect a member of *his* ethnic tribe from an alien marauder.

Eventually, the hormone pressure was impossible to resist. After years of dating girls with last names like Cohen, Kaplan and Berkowitz, it was time to try a name that ended with a vowel.

In 2009 the notion seems quaint; but in 1963 I either told or asked my parents. I don't remember the dialog other than that there was a negative reaction. But when I reminded Mom about the form she filled out years earlier, she gave me the keys to her Plymouth.

We dated on and off, even after I went away to college. It was a time of transition for both of us. I let my hair grow longer, grew a beard and discovered sex (but not with Maria). She dated some older Yalies. We hung out at the *Exit* coffee house, and drove to Greenwich Village.

Our families tolerated the relationship. Her mother was a great cook, and I loved Italian food. I was terribly disappointed to learn that Italian mothers never cooked lasagna in the summer because it made the kitchens too hot.

Maria also crossed over the ethnic food line and liked to eat Jewish kosher deli foods. She even introduced me to Peking duck and Chinese rice chips.

Late one night, when we were a year or two under 21, we were in a car in a country club parking lot, drinking beer and eating corned beef sandwiches.

Suddenly, we saw the revolving light of a police car approach. When the cop got out of his car and aimed his flashlight into our car, Maria was frantically stashing our Heinekens under the front seat.

He caught her with her hands under the seat, but he couldn't see the beer bottles. He asked what she was doing, and she quickly said, "Oh, I'm just looking for some salt for the corned beef." Fortunately the officer of the law didn't know enough about kosher cold cuts to realize that no one puts salt on corned beef; and Maria and I were not arrested for underage drinking. I assume that after 40-plus years this confession can't get us in trouble.

Although I liked her a lot (and maybe I loved her— whatever love is for a teenager) and thought about marrying her, I only called Maria, "Maria" one time. It just sounded *too Catholic* to me. Every other time, I used her nickname, "Marty." I also was not prepared to have a crucifix or a Jesus picture on the wall of my home. Religion ruins a lot of good things.

So does bad communication In 2009 I learned that Maria considered me to be her boyfriend back in 1963 and '64. It made me feel good, even though she was now a grandmother. Back then we both dated others and I didn't realize I was that significant to her.

Revisionist History: in 2009 I also learned that Maria had become disenchanted with Catholicism back in high school. Had I known in 1964 what I learned 45 years later, I might *not* have thought our relationship was doomed and I could have tried harder to keep her as my girlfriend, and maybe even make her my wife (but not at age 18).

179

Despite her physical beauty and a relationship that lasted over a year, we never got beyond holding hands, hugging and kissing. One time we were at a beach and she asked me to rub suntan lotion on her. I was tempted to do some additional rubbing, but I restrained myself. I don't know now if I was shy, stupid, scared, over-indoctrinated to be a "gentleman," or afraid of getting slapped and losing her, or a victim of the Madonna/ Prostitute Syndrome.

Maybe it was all of the above.

Sigmund Freud apparently invented the term "Madonna/Prostitute Syndrome," where males divide females into two types. There are the nice girls ("Madonnas" like the Virgin Mary) and the overtly erotic, uninhibited and available "prostitutes." A man would choose one woman for love and another for sex, but none for both.

Some males, at least at some time in their lives, assume that females must fall into one of the categories, but never both; i.e. nice girls can't be sexy and sexy girls can't be nice girls. I now know differently.

Just as Groucho Marx said that "I don't want to belong to

any club that will accept me as a member," many young men wanted to have sex with the "prostitutes," but preferred to marry the "Madonnas." The beautiful girl with the Catholic name from Mary Immaculate Academy was appropriately — but unfortunately — a Madonna to me.

In later years I wondered if Maria was insulted or disappointed that I didn't "try something" at the beach or another place, or if I just didn't turn her on, or if she just wasn't ready. Was the request to apply lotion a hint to do more? Maybe it's better if I don't know the answer. As time goes on, I care less about the answer.

How would I have reacted if she was sexually aggressive? I'm not sure. In later years I was with sexually aggressive women who said, "I need to get laid" — just as a man might. I like it just fine. But back in 1964, aggressiveness might have moved the needle on the Madonna/Prostitute scale away from Madonna and I might not have liked it.

Allegedly "men think with their dicks," but sometimes there can be a battle for control between the penis and the brain. If the brain wins, the result can be erectile dysfunction or the avoidance of sexually stimulating encounters. Animals with small brains don't have this problem.

Toward the end of my relationship with Maria I began dating "X," who might not want to be named here. I respect her privacy and there are good stories about her that I've left out. If X writes her own book, I'll be glad to buy it.

X was Jewish and my soul mate. We were two halves of one whole. In the 1965 movie *A Thousand Clowns*, we both identified with eccentric Uncle Murray. She was the first woman I definitely wanted to marry. We seemed to like and dislike all of the same things, but we were so much alike that it might not have been a good marriage. It's probably better to have debate and second opinions.

X referred to Maria as "Lubavitcher." I'm not sure if it was because she couldn't remember the Italian name, or a sarcastic disapproval of my dating a gentile. It could have been both. The Lubavitcher Rebbe was the leader of a group of Hasidic ultra-Orthodox Jews based in the Crown Heights neighborhood of Brooklyn.

I was a year ahead of X in high school. I no longer remember if we knew each other then, or even when and how we met. The peak of our relationship was 1966-'67.

That was supposed to be my junior year at Lehigh, but I had screwed up and was back in New Haven. I had enrolled in the University of New Haven, but seldom went to class. I worked part time, but don't remember much about the rest of the time, except for my time with X.

Although she went to college out of town, we spent a lot of time together. I sometimes visited her at college, and sometimes she came "home" to see me. We wrote a lot, and were together many days in the summer.

One time I joined her family at another relative's beach cottage. X didn't feel well and did not want to go in the water so her 15-year-old sister and I swam out to an island. When we got there, the sister lied down on her back to collect some sunbeams. She had an adult's body and a small bikini. I positioned myself to look into her cleavage and watched her breasts move as she breathed. I was soon having "should I" and "what if" thoughts.

Eventually common sense prevailed and I went into the dark cool water to hide the evidence of my excitement. I had to wait about two years before I had sex with a 15-year-old girl.

The guest room in the basement of my family's house became my bedroom when I was 12. By age 19 it morphed into a "bachelor pad" with a bar and a condom collection. I had my own door from the street, and young ladies could enter and leave without encountering my parents.

X was very affectionate. Sometimes too affectionate. When we were out on the street, her PDAs (Public Displays of Affection) embarrassed me and I sometimes asked her to cool it, at least until we got back to my place. We never went "all the way" but we were "on the way." Several times I had worn Levi jeans when we went to a movie, but I changed into thinner and looser chinos for "improved tactile sensation" in make-out sessions in my room later on. She stripped down to her underwear. I feel a tingle in my dick just writing about it.

After one particularly stimulating session we talked about getting married. I gave her a college pin from Lehigh, and she decided to call herself my "pindel." I remember going to work the next day in a haze and telling some of the other employees that "I think I'm engaged, but I'm not sure."

One time when I visited X at her college, we decided to check into a motel, presumably to consummate our relationship. X and I had a debate in the car about whether I should register as just "Michael Marcus" or "Mr. & Mrs. Michael Marcus." In retrospect, I doubt that Mr. Patel would have cared if I signed in as "John Smith," "John F. Kennedy," or "Pope John."

There was no consummation that night. X spent most of the time crying. This was the beginning of years of unhappiness and depression for her.

At one point X's doctor decided that I was the cause of her problems and we were forbidden to see each other. We had a last goodbye in the summer of 1967. It was the last time I saw the woman I once thought I'd spend the rest of my life with. I cried. X did not cry. She could not cry. Therapy had robbed her of emotion. She was like a zombie, and nothing like the funny and affectionate girl I had fallen in love with.

Over 40 years later I was relieved to learn that X's troubles were caused by her mother, and I was officially non-toxic.

L ater I married Marilyn Cafarelli. Marilyn's father Joe was a non-church-going Catholic Italian. Her mother Sally was Jewish. That makes a good combination, even if it's not strictly kosher.

Sally's culinary repertoire was multi-ethnic. She served luscious lasagna, perfect pasta "fazool" and spaghetti sauce with sausage and pork chops in it; as well as magnificent chopped liver, chicken soup, potato pancakes ("latkes") and stuffed cabbage— but not all at the same meal.

Sally's kitchen was a wonderful place for a gourmand like me and her cooking probably helped Marilyn induce me to pop the question.

FETISHES

In August, 1971 we were introduced by Judy, who worked with her in New York and who used to live across the street from me in New Haven. Marilyn was tired from unpacking after moving from the Bronx to Manhattan and fell asleep the first time we met — not a strong testimony to my conversational abilities — but I was strongly attracted even before I had tasted Sally's cooking.

Marilyn resembled both Maria and X. My fetishes seldom varied. My standard package: five feet tall, dark hair, large breasts. Hmm. That describes my mother, too. The Oedipus complex doesn't end at age five, Dr. Freud.

Marilyn and I were both dating a few others at the time. My social calendar was full and I waited about a month before calling her, but I passed the word via Judy that I was interested and I eventually called her. She thought her falling asleep had turned me off, but I'm a napper, too, and it didn't bother me. We started dating regularly and by October or November we planned a quick marriage in December. It seems ridiculous now. It probably was ridiculous then.

If we knew each other longer, we probably would not have gotten married. We argued *a lot* (and we still do). At one time we considered canceling the wedding, but one of us said (and I don't remember who said it), "What the hell, the invitations have already gone out, so let's do it."

I no longer remember why it was planned so soon, but I'll state here for the record that she *wasn't* pregnant.

I do know we got a good deal from a caterer who had a cancellation on the date we picked, so maybe that was an influence. We probably also saved on taxes by marrying by the end of the year. Maybe we were just extremely in love and wanted to get married ASAP. That's a good reason.

Marilyn's cousin Manny was a printer, and he offered us free invitations as a present. Unfortunately, they arrived with my father's name wrong. When Manny reprinted them, he got Pop's name right, but he printed the wrong *year*.

(but maybe not until they're adults)

We didn't want to ask Manny for a third freebie or insult him by taking our business elsewhere. (He kept a gun strapped to his ankle and I used to refer to him as *Mafia Manny* although I had no real knowledge that he was in the mob.) The wedding date was rapidly approaching so my future mother-in-law used a pen to correct the year on each invitation. It wasn't very elegant — in fact, it looked like shit — but it was definitely a rare collector's item.

Unfortunately the printing was just the first in a series of nuptial fuckups.

Depending on whom you ask, the wedding was either very nice, OK or terrible. The photographer was a tyrant and made Marilyn cry while posing for pictures. And while he had us posing for pictures, we missed what were said to be the best latkes (potato pancakes) in the world — even better than Sally's homemade latkes.

Marilyn's Aunt Hilda (Mafia Manny's mother-in law) complained because there were no cigarettes on the dining tables, fomenting loud disagreement over whether it was the responsibility of the bride's family or the groom's family to finance the wedding guests' lung cancer.

Marilyn had designed her own wedding gown, and on the day of the wedding, she realized that it was not the right decision to have a vertical seam down the center. But it was too late to change.

When we went to cut the cake, the two of us applied all of  our power to the ceremonial knife. We tried slicing, sawing, stabbing, pressing and poking, but we just could not penetrate the icing on the beautiful triple-decker. We wondered if the cake was frozen or if we were victims of a joke.

After what seemed like two

hours of snickering from the guests, the catering manager came out of the kitchen and whispered a little secret to us.

Apparently someone had neglected to tell us that this gorgeous cake was a wood and plaster *fake* and we were supposed to just *make believe* to cut it when everyone sings "The bride cuts the cake, the groom cuts the cake..." The servers had a sheet cake in the kitchen already cut and ready to roll out and serve to the guests.

About a month after the ceremony, the photo studio delivered the wedding album with Marilyn's name spelled wrong on the cover. They eventually provided a corrected replacement, but in 38 years we have not been motivated to switch the covers. I'm not sure if we're too busy, too lazy or just sentimental. More likely, we just don't care anymore.

We got some really nice wedding gifts, but the one I liked best was a bunch of McDonald's gift certificates that Ken Irsay gave us. It's easy to spend money. It's harder to make me smile. Judy, the woman who introduced us, stiffed us. Maybe she felt that introducing us was a sufficient gift. Maybe so, but a toaster would have been useful, too.

Marilyn did not approve of my eating habits, and promised to make me home-made soup every day of our married life if I'd give up eating canned Campbell's soup.

We got married on December 12, 1971, and she's already made enough home-made soup to take us through January 8, 1972. That's lunchtime, not supper.

Marilyn is an excellent cook who hates to cook. I would be a lot less frustrated if she was a lousy cook.

She does a great job microwaving the contents of doggy bags and ordering meals to be delivered, but there's no one in the world who can make a better roast chicken or turkey. Not only do they taste delicious, but they look good enough to be on the cover of *Good Housekeeping*.

Marilyn can't resist a bargain at the supermarket and our freezers periodically fill up with large plastic-wrapped carcasses bigger than bowling balls. Unfortunately she seems to give away more frozen poultry than she defrosts, cooks and feeds to me.

Despite abundant and consistent negative reviews, Marilyn insisted on buying a particular $7,000 *professional style* stove because of the way it looked. On a good day, we're lucky if two of its six burners work. I would have been happier if she hung up a pretty picture of the $7,000 failure and bought a bunch of $1.59 cans of Sterno that can be reliably ignited with a match.

Marilyn has trouble deciding anything and is constantly re-playing decisions made years and even decades ago. Her most common phrase is, "Maybe I shoulda got." Marilyn is always looking back, but I never look back, except through the rearview mirror when I'm driving.

Our first house could have been carpeted with the little carpet samples she collected. Our second house has wooden floors because Marilyn couldn't pick carpet for it.

Big decisions, like picking a house or a car or a husband, come much easier than the little ones, like picking carpet color or deciding on coleslaw versus string beans.

If Marilyn asks for help making a decision, I give her a very quick answer, knowing it doesn't matter what I say because she'll soon change her mind anyway.

Our "regular" waiters have learned to wait a few minutes before telling the chef what to prepare for her because there's a good chance that Marilyn will soon run into the restaurant kitchen to change her order. Maybe even twice.

We disagree on almost everything, and Marilyn and I have been happily at war since 1971.

Her difficulty in deciding and her extreme cautiousness and paranoia can be very frustrating and terribly time-wasting. I grew up in a family where if you weren't ten minutes early, you were late. I often refer to Marilyn as "my late wife" and I'm sure she'll be late for her own funeral.

I know that she really means the best for us and I love her for it — and in spite of it — and she's kept me out of trouble many times. Marilyn is my second-guesser, my censor and my conscience.

Marilyn sometimes says she wishes she could be fearless like me, but it's probably better that she's not like me.

Opposites attract. But two of me would be in jail, or maybe dead.

Our friends who seemed to get along perfectly well, got divorced long, long ago. Apparently they just didn't care enough to fight.

⌘　⌘　⌘

☺ADVICE FOR A LESS-UNHAPPY MARRIAGE

Michael's Alternate Victory Plan

Forget about compromise decisions. If one of you wants black walls in a room and one of you wants white walls, and you get gray walls, neither of you will have what you want. You'll both be pissed off when you enter the room.

Try alternate victories. Let your mate make some unilateral decisions, and try to ignore the paint, carpet, car, vacation destination and furniture that you hate. Then *you* make some unilateral decisions, and you'll get to enjoy your personal victories.

Overall, life together will be a compromise, and that's nice.

Warning: My alternate victory plan doesn't apply to everything. It's probably best that you agree on the city and the house you live in, and on kids' names. My father let my mother pick my middle name. I hated the name for many years and I wish he didn't give in. See Chapter 82.

Chapter 50
Yakkity Yak, Don't Talk Back

For several years, my wife had an extremely talkative and extremely annoying friend. Louise would talk to anyone about anything at any time; and it made absolutely no difference if the other person had no time to listen, or no interest in the subject.

She'd often call at 11 p.m. with a report of the day's activities, complete with every real or imagined insult from co-workers, relatives, storekeepers and strangers, and full details of every one of her biological functions.

Louise would call again at seven in the morning with a rehash of the previous day's activities, plus her nocturnal emissions, remissions, secretions, defecations and expulsions of pus, phlegm, mucus, blood clots, earwax, and other bodily fluids, solids and gases.

Louise was obsessed with the functions of the human body — especially her own body — and upon first meeting her and hearing her initial medical report, one might think she was a doctor, or at least a medical student.

She actually had planned to become a doctor, but half way through medical school she discovered that blood made her vomit. So rather than treat bleeding patients, she left medical school and her life's work became talking about her own blood and vomit.

Louise assumed that everyone she met was deeply interested in her innermost functions.

It was not unusual for her to tell men — even on a first date — about the gory details of her most recent menstruation. They seldom asked her out again.

I didn't *hate* Louise, but I certainly found her annoying and often disgusting, and I resented all the time she was taking from my wife for absolutely no useful purpose.

I found one cool way to get back at her.

She was one of just two people who called us with blocked Caller ID.

If the phone rang at 11 p.m. or 7 a.m. and the screen on the phone said "restricted," I'd pick up the handset and say "Hello Louise." She knew I was in the phone business and so she assumed I had some special equipment that was able to override her privacy feature, and she got really pissed off (but probably not as pissed off as I was about her twice-daily calls about nothing).

One New Years Eve we went out to dinner with Louise and Harry, her boyfriend. (Originally Louise told us that Harry was her husband, but that's another story.)

We went to a Japanese restaurant, and had to wait about a half hour for our table. Three of us went to the bar, but Louise stayed at the coat check room. She treated the unfortunate coat checker with her life story, complete with the details on every pimple, rash, abrasion, contusion, splinter, hangnail, allergic reaction, cramp, belch, fart, manicure, pedicure, prescription, diagnosis, misdiagnosis, urination, bowel movement, psycho-analysis, chiropractic adjustment and surgical procedure.

When we were notified that our table was ready, we went to get Louise and we learned that the coat checker did not understand English.

H e didn't know how lucky he was.

Chapter 51
What I learned in college

Good advice: In the first Phys Ed class of my freshman year at Lehigh University, the athletic department head, who was described as a wise and kindly "grandfather" to each incoming class of young men, gave us some good advice.

He told us how to determine when our gym suits needed cleaning: "Gentlemen, when your shorts, socks, T-shirts and jockstraps are able to stand up by themselves, it's time to put them in the washing machine."

And he told us how to avoid venereal diseases and un-planned offspring: "If you're gonna take it out, and you're gonna get it wet, put a raincoat on it!"

Bad joke: Lehigh wisely recognized that freshmen were hope-less slobs, and our room and board fees included maid service. We put charts on our doors indicating our first class of each day in a futile effort to keep the cleaning ladies from barging in at six if we didn't have to wake up until nine.

In addition to dusting, vacuuming and making our beds, these substitute moms would help us start the day with a few words of encouragement, and efforts to fix us up with a daughter or neighbor, and a stupid riddle or lame joke.

One day Katherine asked me, "What did the bathtub say to the hopper?" ("Hopper" was a Bethlehem term for "toilet." Coal was a big influence on local lingo.)

I told her I didn't realize that tubs could talk.

According to Katherine, the bathtub told the toilet, "Ha-ha! I get twice as much ass as you do but I don't have to take any shit."

Chapter 52
Where are all the fat mommies?

In 1952, at the age of six, our family moved from the Bronx, New York, to New Haven, Connecticut, while I was in the first grade.

We crossed just one state border, moved just 60 miles, and stayed in the same time zone; but to say it was massive culture shock is a massive understatement.

The transition was a mix of *Beverly Hillbillies* and *Moscow on the Hudson,* with a bit of *Planet of the Apes.*

I had lived the first years of my life in an apartment house, in a city where people traveled by bus and subway and sent their dirty clothes to the laundry, and kids played at playgrounds and cooled off at public pools or under the spray of a fire hydrant.

In New Haven, people had individual houses, that were separated by grass — not concrete alleys — and had cars and washing machines, and swings and pools in their own backyards, or went to the beach. Parents drove cars and kids rode bikes. There were no subways. Only poor people rode the bus.

In New York, people too-awked like I did.

In New Haven, the people sounded funny to me, and I sounded funny to them. My first-grade teacher sent me to the principal's office so she could listen to my strange accent. I was exhibited like a freak in a circus sideshow.

In New York, many kids have elevators in their houses, and lots of stores have elevators and escalators.

In New Haven, it was a big deal for my country classmates to go downtown to ride the escalators and elevators in the Malley's department store. What stupid hicks, I thought.

In New Haven, there were Jewish women named "Mary." That's not permitted in New York.

My best friend in New Haven had a top sheet on his bed. I never saw one in the Bronx.

A New York frankfurter was eaten with mustard, but a New Haven hotdog might have ketchup or even (OH-MY-GOD!) mayonnaise on it.

A long fat sandwich was a hero in Manhattan or a wedge in parts of the Bronx, but a grinder in New Haven.

In New York, pizza was perfectly round, always had eight slices, and had mozzarella cheese and sauce on it.

In New Haven, the pizza could be any vaguely oval shape, with a random number of slices, and no two slices were the same size. Pizza could be topped with strange things like meatball chunks, eggplant or clams, was spelled "apizza," and pronounced "ah-beetz." The mozzarella cheese, pronounced "mootz," was optional.

There were many changes in pronunciation and sometimes even in spelling on different sides of the border.

"Kaufman" was pronounced "cowfman" in New York but "cawfman" in New Haven.

A New York "ant" is a New Haven "ahnt." Except for Ant Jemima. The pancake lady is an Ant everywhere.

Someone attending the second year of high school in New York (and probably in most other states) is a "sophomore," from the Greek words for "wise" (sophos) and "foolish" (moros). In New Haven, I heard it pronounced "southmore."

When a department store advertised a set of bedroom furniture pieces, it was described as a "bedroom <u>suite</u>." In New Haven, people who were enticed by the ad and went to the store would ask to see a "bedroom <u>suit</u>." Some of them were probably shown pajamas.

CROTCH, AND VIOLENCE

Some local stores — either out of ignorance or in an effort to correct the pronunciation of their ignorant customers — advertised "bedroom <u>sweets</u>," thereby setting the English language back to the pre-Chaucer era.

As a teenager I sold clothing and shoes in my father's store, and my ears were offended several times a day.

Many people tried to buy "posturepedic" shoes. Posturepedic is a brand of mattresses made by Sealy. Orthopedic shoes are designed to correct foot problems.

Not everyone in New Haven was educated at Yale.

Men who were buying pants (and the women accompanying them) would discuss having the "crouch alternated" instead of the "crotch altered." I was often tempted to say, "Yes, madam, we have an extensive line of alternative crouches."

Working for a clothing store, I got first crack at new fashions. I was one of the first to wear ski gloves to my high school. When I approached the school entrance, a classmate spotted them and exclaimed, "Man, them mother-fuckin' gloves is co-legent!"

I hope he learned how to pronounce "collegiate" by the end of his southmore year.

A common beverage with New Haven ah-beetz was birch beer, which was unknown in the Bronx. On the other hand, it was tough to find cream soda in New Haven, and my father had to teach New Haven restaurateurs how to make an egg cream, which was available on every corner in New York. It contains neither eggs nor cream, by the way.

In New York, baseball fans were devoted to our home teams, the Yankees, Dodgers, or Giants. Our one city had three major league baseball teams. The entire state of Connecticut didn't even have one, so most folks were focused north on the Boston Red Sox, still within New England.

In my first days in New Haven I actually got beaten up twice because it was assumed that any kid from the Bronx had to be a Yankees fan. The Red Sox fans thought they could beat me into

194

submission, to change my assumed allegiance to match my new New England address.

In reality, I had no interest in baseball and didn't give a shit who won a game, or the World Series, or if neither team ever played another game. But not caring about baseball was un-American and un-masculine and I might have gotten a worse beating if my new neighbors knew I didn't love baseball, than if I merely didn't love the Boston Red Sox.

We moved to New Haven in May, towards the end of first grade. But first grade in New Haven was so far ahead of first grade in the Bronx, that it was decided that I should repeat first grade to learn what I had missed.

Apparently it wasn't a big deal because I don't remember much about it. I don't feel stigmatized or traumatized, because it was the fault of New York City, not me.

And besides, when I was in New York I was deemed to be such a genius that I had skipped kindergarten and was pushed ahead to first grade. (I'm kidding. I was actually pushed ahead because there was no room in kindergarten.)

So when New Haven made me repeat first grade, I ended up with my proper age group, and I'm still close to some of the kids I met many years ago in my second chance at first.

To this six-year-old, the biggest difference between my old city and my new city was not food, transportation, education or vocabulary, but the size and shape of the mommies.

The standard Bronx mommy was five feet tall and weighed at least 200 pounds.

They were zaftig. Well rounded. Full figured. Rubenesque. Pleasingly plump. Prosperous. Well fed. Nicely developed. Had something to hold onto. They were built like Gertrude Berg, Eleanor Roosevelt or Big Mama Cass.

But New Haven mommies — and even grandmas — were at least six inches taller and 80 pounds lighter.

They were tall. Slim. Like a model. Thin. Skinny. Bony. Emaciated. Unhealthy. Undernourished. Wasting away. Needs a good meal. Like from Auschwitz. If not like Twiggy, maybe like Cher, or Michelle Phillips.

Beauty is in the eye of the beholder. And standards may change even when you change your area code.

Life has strange cycles, and strange recycles.

NY➔CT➔NY➔CT

I moved from New York to Connecticut a second time, when I was 55 years old — 49 years after the first time I made that particular transition.

By then I had learned to understand, if not actually become a fan of, the national pastime.

But despite my move, my baseball team allegiance — if I have to have any — stays with the Bronx, the borough of my birth. So...GO YANKEES. (And...fuck Boston!)

Chapter 53
Wow, I'm an assistant editor. Oh shit, the editor is a back-stabbing thief.

Since I went to college to become an electrical engineer and then switched to journalism, and had summer and part-time jobs in retailing, I was the ideal candidate for my first after-college job. I became assistant editor of *High Fidelity Trade News*, a magazine that went to hi-fi stores.

I knew about hi-fi. I knew about stores. I could write and edit. It seemed like the dream job.

Although my starting salary was only $115 per week, I was working for a *real magazine* and my business cards and the magazine's masthead showed my title as "ASSISTANT EDITOR." I was working in MANHATTAN, while other recent journalism grads were in places like Allentown and Fresno.

I enjoyed most of my work, but I soon became aware of some unpleasant office politics. They didn't teach us about this in our journalism classes.

One of my first assignments was to write an introduction to our company's annual *Hi-Fi Trade-In Guide*, a "blue book" that helped dealers decide how much to allow on traded-in audio equipment.

I wrote something about how trading in old models for new has been an American tradition since someone turned in an aging model A Ford for a new model T, and submitted my manuscript to my boss, Jay the editor.

Jay didn't say anything about it to me, but the publisher showed me a note Jay had attached to it and given to the publisher. Jay implied that I was an ignoramus for writing that the

Model A came out *after* the Model T. Jay insisted that I should have written about trading a T for an A, not an A for a T.

I was not ignorant, but Jay sure was. I knew T and A better than he did. (You're supposed to chuckle, or at least smile, after reading that line.)

What I knew, and Jay didn't know, was that there were *two* Model A Ford cars.

One was first built in 1903, *before* the Model T, which was produced from 1908 through 1927. Another Model A was first built in 1927, *after* the Model T was discontinued.

▶ MEMO TO BACK STABBERS: check your facts before you unsheathe your knife.

Jay got in trouble two more times for messing with me.

I used to go to a lot of press conferences where new hi-fi products were announced. I'd take pictures, and write about what I saw. A roll of film had space for at least 36 pictures, but a press conference seldom required that many. Usually five or six shots told the story just fine.

Very often on the way back to my midtown office, I'd use some of the film to take pictures of anything that seemed interesting. It didn't cost any extra to develop the film, and if I wanted any personal prints made, I'd pay the photo lab myself.

One day I saw a film crew on Fifth Avenue with an elaborate van and a huge amount of movie gear filming a commercial. The hardware seemed interesting, so I took a few pictures. Strangely, the "contact sheets" with my pictures never came back from the lab, and Jay said he didn't know what happened to them.

(but maybe not until they're adults)

A few months later, I picked up an obscure magazine called *Making Films in New York*, and in it I found a full page displaying three of my photographs, and crediting Jay for taking them.

When I challenged him, Jay concocted a fanciful story, claiming that the editor of that magazine had been visiting, and must have stolen the negatives.

Jay, if he stole them from you, why would he have published it in his magazine and identified you as the photographer?

Another time, also on Fifth Avenue, I saw a man picketing with a large sign proclaiming that short skirts would be the downfall of America.

Naturally, I took pictures. Again, the "contact sheets" with my pictures never came back from the lab, and Jay said he didn't know what happened to them.

A few weeks later, I was looking through a copy of *Women's Wear Daily* (I read lots of stuff), and saw the picture I took, with a photo credit for Jay.

In the years since, my websites have been plagiarized by competitors more than a hundred times, that I know of.

▶ MEMO TO THIEVES: if you're going to steal something unique, don't display it where the victim will see it.

Chapter 54
First job, last drunk

The first big assignment on my first "real" job, as assistant editor of *High Fidelity Trade News* was to cover the 1970 Consumer Electronics Show at the Hilton Hotel in New York City. I was expected to wander around the show and ask what's new, take some pictures, shake some hands, and kiss the behinds of the advertisers who made my glamorous $115-per-week job possible.

As a "trade magazine" that offered free subscriptions to hi-fi dealers, our only source of revenue was advertising from the companies that made hi-fi equipment, so it was vital that every actual and potential advertiser was given the impression that they were VERY IMPORTANT to us.

The real boss of the magazine was not the editor or publisher, but Ken the ad manager; and he directed a steady stream of reporters, editors and photographers to the booths, press conferences and "hospitality suites" of each company.

We had an intense rivalry with another trade publication, *Audio Times*; and it was important to provide more editorial coverage of important advertisers than they did — or at least create the appearance of doing so.

Our editorial staff actually consisted of Jay the editor and me, and a couple of freelancers who would write for anyone for a nickel or a dime per word.

For important events, we were augmented by shills. At one press conference we had two real editorial people, plus the production manager making believe he was a reporter, and an ad guy making believe he was a photographer. He flashed his strobe light at dramatic moments, but there was no film in his camera.

There was a lot going on in electronics in 1970.

Cassettes were challenging both 8-track and open-reel tapes. Open-reel monochrome video tape recorders were being marketed for home use, and several companies had battery-powered portables. Pre-recorded video was starting. Direct-drive and linear-tracking turntables were attracting attention. Different varieties of Quadraphonic Sound were competing for market share. Speakers were shaped like end tables, conga drums, human ears and sculpture stands.

The faceplates of audio components were shifting from silver to black. The Feds were trying to stop companies from exaggerating the number of watts coming out of amplifiers. "Console" stereos were being replaced by "compacts." Detroit's car radios could now be augmented or replaced with higher technology and more power. Answering machines were starting to be sold, instead of just rented by the phone companies. "Solid State" was the hot label that appeared on TVs and even lipstick.

There was a social shift along with the changes in technology. This was the era when electronics makers first noticed the "youth market." Hippies who once were thrown out of stores were now invited to spend big bucks on audio gear. Stereo equipment ads talked about rock instead of Bach.

I had invited my college buddy Dave to see CES with me. He wore a press pass, carried a camera, and acted like he belonged there. We spent about eight hours cruising the show floor, over and over and over again, with little rest and no food.

When the show closed at 5 p.m., the action shifted upstairs in the Hilton or across the street to the Hotel Americana, where the manufacturers welcomed retailers, journalists and even competitors to their hospitality suites.

In most cases, a hospitality suite was an ordinary hotel room, with the bed put in the bathtub so products could be displayed in the center of the bedroom, and a well-stocked bar.

ALCOHOL

Dave and I worked our way from one end of the Hilton to the other, and one end of the Americana to the other, stopping in dozens of suites and drinking in each one. By 10 p.m. Dave and I had probably walked 10 miles, drunk three gallons of liquor, and eaten two shrimp, a pretzel and a celery stalk.

We could barely stand up, but we were commanded to go to a party where some industry biggee was celebrating the launch of a hi-fi store franchise chain, in another hotel near the Hilton.

This event called for still more hand-shaking and strobe-flashing, a lot more drinking, and maybe a little more celery, pretzels and shrimp. I don't remember what happened during the next few hours, but the editor said I spent some time sitting in the lobby of the hotel, embarrassing our company by reciting fake Japanese poetry, and one guy reported that I tried to crawl up Fifth Avenue, towing my camera case behind me.

I do remember waking up in a strange bedroom, with no knowledge of where I was or how I got there. The phone next to the bed had familiar letters and numbers on it, so I figured there was a pretty good chance I was in a friendly country.

After a while, my spinning head slowed down enough so I could stand up, and I noticed a door at the end of my bedroom. I walked out, and discovered I was in a hospitality suite belonging to Pickering, the phonograph cartridge company. I found another door. It led to another bedroom, and Dave was in there, starting to wake up.

Dave told me that Tom, the Pickering sales manager, had rescued us from somewhere, taken us out to eat at BrewBurger, and then got us upstairs in the Hilton and put us to bed.

It was now about 6:30 a.m. Going home was out of the question, and I had to be at my desk at 8:30. I threw some water in my face, left the hotel, and started walking, taking a very long route from 56th Street to 45th Street, and getting a little bit more sober with each step I took.

I got to work on time, and managed to type a few pages. I later ran into Tom from Pickering, and Dave called me on the phone, and we reviewed the night's activities.

Tom said I was too drunk to walk to BrewBurger, so he and Dave had gone to eat without me. But Dave insisted that I was at the restaurant with him, when I was really in bed.

H e must have been drunker than I was.

Chapter 55
OK, so maybe baseball isn't child abuse

When I lived in the Bronx, I lived just a few miles from Yankee Stadium, and only a few more miles from the Polo Grounds in upper Manhattan where the New York Giants played before they moved to San Francisco in 1958.

Despite all this nearby major league activity, I was no sports fan. I didn't give a damn about baseball, and couldn't understand why others did. When other kids asked who my favorite player was, I'd quickly answer, "Mickey Mantle." It was an easy answer, because Mick and I shared initials, and no kid in the school yard would challenge my choice. I was lucky that none of them asked me for his batting statistics.

My mother's parents, who lived near us in the Bronx, were big baseball fans and wanted to convert me. They surprised me with tickets to a double-header. It was a double-dose of torture.

It was the longest day of my young life.

It seemed like the 10 longest days of my life. I spent hour after interminable hour staring at white spots on a green field, listening to old men belch from their beers, while I kept asking my grandparents, "Can we go home yet?"

I loved Gramma Del and Grampy Jay, but this was child abuse.

In later years, I didn't get to like ballgames much more. In mandatory games during gym class, my favorite position was to be "left-out."

In college, I went through a strange metamorphosis.

There was an intramural softball program, and a bunch of hippies and assorted misfits thought it might be fun to form a team to play stoned, with absolutely no intention of winning. We'd get to smoke some weed, enjoy the great outdoors, work on our tans, and get free T-shirts. It sounded like a good plan.

What I didn't plan on, was that I turned out to be a "power hitter," a "homerun king" just like Mickey Mantle.

I found no joy in running around the bases, or catching balls hit by the opposing teams, but I loved to whack those balls as far as I could.

My teammates thought I was a traitor to the cause. The team fell apart, and it was many years before I picked up a bat or saw another ball game.

Around 1995, my nephew and nieces nagged me to take them to a Yankees game at Yankee Stadium, the site of my long-ago — but *never* forgotten — abuse.

I really didn't want to go, but I like the kids, so I agreed. I packed a radio with a headset and plenty of reading material and glumly resolved to pass the hours as pleasantly as possible.

When we arrived at the stadium, the butch-bitch rent-a-cop at the gate searched my bag and seized my plastic bottle of Diet Pepsi so her co-conspirators upstairs could sell me $8 drinks. She would not let me drink it before entering the stadium, or take it outside to drink, or reclaim it after the game. She slowly and sadistically removed the cap and poured out the soda into a trash barrel while I watched helplessly as my money and refreshment dribbled away. It was not a good omen for what was to come, I thought.

When we got to our seats I tuned my radio to WCBS, allegedly an all-news station, and was both disappointed and shocked to hear a play-by-boring-play description of the ball game in front of me. For some unknown reason, I didn't immediately select another station, and soon, for the first time in my life, I understood what baseball was all about.

In baseball, it always seemed to me that the hitters were the heroes. People like Babe Ruth, Ted Williams and Mantle (and even me) hit the homeruns that drove up the scores that won the games and the pennants. But what I learned from listening to the radio that afternoon was that it was the CATCHERS and PITCHERS, not the hitters, who were really in control.

Balls — not bats — made the big difference.

Throwing was more important than hitting; and it was the sneaky, stealthy, silent catchers, squatting in the dirt behind home plate, who signaled secret instructions to the pitchers who caused hero hitters to strike out.

Because of those good pitchers, even really good hitters seldom got a good hit. And when they did, the balls were usually caught by really good fielders, and the hitters did not score homeruns.

I actually *enjoyed* baseball that day.

If someone had properly explained baseball to me in 1950, my life might have been very different. I might have liked baseball enough to become a homerun king for the New York Yankees.

As Marlon Brando said in *On the Waterfront* in 1954, shortly after I left the Bronx, "I coulda been a contender. I coulda been somebody."

Chapter 56
Fired, hired, fired, hired, fired

In 1971, while I was assistant editor at *High Fidelity Trade News*, I got friendly with some folks at *Rolling Stone* magazine. A while later, I wrote a major cover story for *Trade News* about the exploding "youth market," and it inadvertently helped *Rolling Stone* get hi-fi advertising. Although the main audience for *Trade News* was hi-fi dealers, it also reached the important executives at the manufacturers. *Rolling Stone* decided to run ads in *Trade News* to get even more hi-fi advertising, and they paid me to write and design the ad.

Rolling Stone then decided to make a major long-term effort to develop hi-fi advertising, and wanted a regular column of education and product reviews, and I was the logical one to write it.

I wasn't sure if my company would allow me to freelance for another publication, so rather than ask and risk being turned down, I decided to go ahead with the plan, but use the pen name, *Mitchell Newman*. I wasn't deep under cover, however. Mitchell is an obvious variant of Michael, and my middle name is Neuman.

Rolling Stone agreed to pay me $75 per column, which would appear in each issue, every two weeks.

Unfortunately, I was soon in a terrible writer's slump at *Trade News*. For weeks, I found it very difficult to put words on paper, and I was fired from my then $125-per-week job.

I quickly persuaded *Rolling Stone* to hire me full-time at a bit over $20K per year to both guide the ad staff and write my column, now under my real name.

Rolling Stone's New York office at 78 East 56th Street was in constant turmoil. We were a remote satellite of the San Francisco headquarters, separated by 3,000 miles and three time zones, and seldom visited by boss Jann Wenner who apparently preferred the west coast.

In the two years I worked there, we went from trying to sublet half of our floor, to renting a second floor, to getting rid of the second floor. For several months we operated a specific New York City edition, and then closed it down. Years later, the San Francisco operation was closed down and New York became corporate headquarters.

We had an endless stream of publishers in New York, with a new one about every six months. The new guy would typically fire about 80% of the employees hired by his predecessor, and then rehire about half of them, and then he'd get fired, and the cycle would repeat with the next publisher.

Each day, the writers would go to work expecting to be fired, and eventually most of us would be.

I went through a particularly weird outplacement procedure. New publisher Larry, an evil prick who was hated by most of the staff, called me into his office to tell me that I was going off salary, and I'd be writing a column in each issue, which was the way I had started working for *Stone*.

This was not unexpected, or frightening, and there were lots of other publications I planned to write for, but I did ask for severance pay. Larry said I was not entitled to severance because I wasn't being fired. I was just changing my status.

A few months later, Larry told me he no longer wanted me to write my column. I again asked for severance pay. With a sadistic gleam in his eyes, Larry explained that in Rolling Stone's version of *Catch 22*, freelancers are not entitled to severance pay when their work is no longer wanted.

A bit later Larry was gone. Since he wasn't a freelancer, the prick probably got severance pay.

Chapter 57
Three in a bed (sort of)
The "why I married your aunt" chapter

 At the time my income at *Rolling Stone* was reduced from a salary of $400 per week, to a freelancer's fee of $75 every two weeks, I was seriously dating three young ladies.

Actually, it was more than dating. I was *auditioning potential wives*: Marilyn, Virginia, and I forgot the third one's name. I do remember that she lived in Brooklyn and she had a southern accent.

Number Three got pregnant by someone else and had a painful abortion. She recuperated in my apartment. I was a very good friend.

Anyway, for a normal bachelor in Manhattan, a drop of over 80% in income would make a serious impact on dating. But things are different for a journalist with abundant freeloading options.

There were plenty of ways to have free dates.

Writers and editors and their companions could go to free movies and concerts just by requesting "review tickets." There was even plenty of free food at lavish press conferences, and sometimes invitations to check out new restaurants and bars.

Even without an invitation, it was easy to crash an event with a free meal at the New York Coliseum or a hotel by wearing a badge from some previous event or showing a press ID or a business card.

The gatekeepers would never risk offending a member of the press, even someone with dubious credentials who was not on the invitation list. The cost of food and booze was minimal compared to the potential benefit of positive press coverage, or the risk of negative coverage after turning someone away.

And for gifts, there were always trinkets from trade shows and press conferences, free samples, and plenty of free records and tapes sent to us to review.

When my wife audition process had narrowed to the three leading contenders, I needed a tie-breaker, and my Marilyn was the only one of final trio who was willing to sleep with me and with Long John Nebel.

No, I'm not talking about a *Ménage à trois* with three living people in the bed. Long John Nebel did a late-night talk radio show, and I like to sleep with the radio on.

Fortunately, Marilyn accepted me and didn't object to John, and she didn't ask how much money I was making.

Even in 1971, $37.50 per week didn't go very far.

1971 was a time of granny gowns, granny glasses, going bra-less, and anti-materialism, and it never occurred to Marilyn to ask about my salary. And besides, *she* had a real job with a decent salary. I knew how much *she* made.

Marilyn swears that if she ever remarries, she'll demand to see the next guy's paycheck and previous year's tax return before she says, "I do."

Anti-material Marilyn didn't want an engagement ring but she later changed her mind and I gave her a diamond ring on our fourth anniversary. Her mother complained that the stone, selected with assistance from my brother — an alleged jewelry expert — was cloudy.

Marilyn and I are still together after 38 years, and the radio is still on all night. There *is* a third real live body in our bed now, but he's a Golden Retriever.

Chapter 58
Three in a bed (for real)

For a while in college and shortly after I finished, I had the hots for a kinky, lusty and loose young lady named Nina. We dated, but she was never my girlfriend. We even dated while she was another guy's girlfriend. Her boyfriend was 400 miles away in medical school. She sometimes said they were engaged but she wore no ring, and didn't act betrothed.

I read that Marilyn Monroe regarded her spectacular sexuality as a *gift* to be given to JFK and others, and it often seemed that Nina felt the same way.

Sometimes Nina had the hots for me, sometimes for either of two friends of mine and sometimes she was hot for Danny, our art professor.

I don't know that Nina qualified as a nymphomaniac, and I wouldn't call her a slut. (But others did.) She just *loved* sex. She was into traditional as well as somewhat more exotic erotics such as simultaneous salad tossing (see *Urban Dictionary* if you need an explanation), streaking, outdoor, mild bondage, flashing truck drivers, and performing in personal porn; but she drew the line at girl-girl sex. Nina was not wife material, but she was definitely fun to be with— with a trustworthy prophylactic.

One night Nina and I were at Professor Danny's apartment to look at 35mm Kodachrome slides he had taken at European museums during several summer vacations. He could not afford to have prints made from the thousands of slides, and had hocked his slide projector to pay his rent.

SEX, DRUGS AND ROCK & ROLL

We sat around his dining room table and held up the tiny slides in front of the chandelier bulbs to see them. It was not much of an art exhibition.

After a while, Danny brought out some wine, and then some joints and put Procol Harum on the stereo; and pretty soon we three had a serious buzz on.

Before the end of *A Whiter Shade of Pale*, Danny moved his chair so he could sit behind Nina.

He started massaging her shoulders and back and occasionally reached around to rub her bra-less breasts through her thin satin blouse. He kissed her neck and her exposed shoulders. Then he took her right hand, kissed it, held it, and stood up and invited her into his bedroom.

Nina stood up, too.

She smiled at him, and then she turned her head and she smiled even more brightly at me.

She playfully grabbed my right hand with her left hand, touched it to her right breast and invited me to come along.

This was the 60s, so I went along.

Pretty soon one professor and two students were naked and squished together on a double bed. Since it was Danny's home and he was our professor and he had issued the first invitation, I felt he deserved to be first with Nina, and I was relegated to "sloppy seconds." I hate even typing that phrase, let alone partaking in it, but horniness, wine and marijuana can overcome a lot of reservation and revulsion.

Unfortunately for Professor Danny, he couldn't get hard, and he resorted to packing poor Nina with Vaseline in an effort to ease his entry. It didn't help.

Frustrated, Danny told me to take over.

My position in the sexual sequence had improved suddenly and greatly. I had moved up from Sloppy

Second to Top Dog, Leader of the Pack, Ichi-Ban, Numero Uno... and the nutty professor started rubbing my penis to get me in the mood.

I could tolerate three in a bed, or maybe four, but not another man's hands on my private parts. And I certainly had no intention of returning the favor.

Danny's effort to get me in the mood, got me out of the mood. I quickly rolled off the bed, grabbed my clothes, and got out of that apartment as fast as I could.

Danny gave both Nina and me A's in the course.

Nina was an excellent artist, a good student, and deserved the top mark even without extra credit for sex.

I probably deserved a B-plus, but the embarrassed and cautious professor apparently gave me some "Please-keep-your-big-mouth-shut" bonus points to boost my average into the A range.

He later married another one of his students and Nina married one of my friends. I don't know if Danny ever had prints made from his Kodachrome slides.

Chapter 59

On second thought, maybe we will hire you, if you'll cut off your penis

Sometime in the 1980s, I was looking for work as a copywriter. Conveniently, at the same time, the New York Telephone Company was looking to hire a copywriter. I went for an interview high up in their new headquarters on Sixth Avenue in Manhattan — the same wide roadway that tourists call Avenue of the Americas.

I was informed that I was the top candidate. No one else who had applied for the job could match my experience and writing ability, my broad knowledge of business and technology and my specific knowledge of telecommunications.

Unfortunately, this was during an affirmative action drive, and they were trying hard to hire non-whites and non-males and people with disabilities and unconventional sexual orientations and sundry minority classifications.

The ideal candidate apparently would have been a 90-year-old left-handed one-legged cross-eyed red-haired albino Samoan Wiccan lesbian with bad breath who had served in the Korean War and was deserted by her husband.

My interviewer apologized for the situation. He admitted that the company, its customers and its stockholders would suffer by not hiring me, but they had to hire a woman to counteract past gender discrimination.

On the bottom of my employment application, was a list of government agencies I could notify if I thought New York Telephone Company was discriminating against *me*.

Chapter 60
What's more important, your brain or your teeth?

The best advertising agency I ever worked at was Scali, McCabe & Sloves, under the creative supervision of legendary art director Sam Scali and writer Ed McCabe. Marvin Sloves was the business man of the founding trio. Bob Schmetterer joined them as an account executive and eventually became president, although his name wasn't on the door.

I worked on prestigious accounts like Perdue chicken, Volvo cars, Pioneer stereo, TDK recording tape, Barney's, Castrol, and others. However, I was not working in the prestigious part of the agency.

I was a copywriter on the lowest floor we had in the building, in the sales promotion department. We did some national ads, but our specialty was local advertising, radio scripts, packaging, contests, and even T-shirts.

I did a lot of T-shirts. Sometimes I still see people walking around wearing shirts that I designed over 30 years ago. It's a good feeling. A couple of times I spoke to people wearing "my" shirts. One wanted me to autograph it. One thought I was nuts and ran away.

One out of two ain't bad. Actually, it's pretty good.

While at Scali, I was paired with two very talented art directors at different times, Barbara Schubeck and Larry Lee. They both had famous family connections. Barbara was the sister of TV newsman John Schubeck. Larry was the nephew of architect I. M. Pei.

215

The basic creative team that does the work in an ad agency consists of an art person and a word person. They respond to directions from the client, relayed through the account executive. Either the art director or the copywriter may come up with the concept for an ad or a sales promotion project, and then the two people work on it together.

While they have to work together, there is often a subconscious jealousy or rivalry because there's a big difference in titles and perks.

The person who draws is called a DIRECTOR, but the person who writes is just called a writer.

The art director gets to hire photographers and models and photo retouchers and choose typesetters (back then), filming and photo locations, and various suppliers. Art directors get to travel to exotic locations; they influence the spending of tons of money each year, and are rewarded with lavish gifts at Christmas time. Bottles of liquor or even cases of Champagne were not unusual. The lowly copywriters — who were usually the source of the creative concept that made the Champagne possible — were lucky to get a $5 box of chocolates. Getting nothing at all was more common.

Most art/word teams fought constant battles, with the art directors wanting to chop words to make the ads look better, while the copywriters insisted every word was vital.

I was much more flexible than most of the other writers. Although I took great pride in every word I wrote, I had gone to art school as a child, and had great respect for the visual images that accompanied my words.

I also knew that perhaps 90% of the people who saw an ad, would see the picture and headline, and they'd never read another word, no matter how hard I had worked to choose the word and pick its position.

At Scali, the upstairs art-and-copy teams made the big bucks and had more prestige than our lowly sales promo department. But we frequently functioned as a top-secret "skunk works" which management knew they could call upon to produce a last-minute miracle when the high-paid upstairs teams came up dry.

Several times Victor, an account exec, came to us in the late morning, ashen faced, and explained that his clients were coming for a campaign presentation ("dog and pony show") at the end of the day, and the highly-paid "national team" that had been working for six months, had turned out worthless crap and the agency was in deep shit.

This was our time to show off — and eat well.

In order to get in the proper creative mood, we'd insist on being seduced with a culinary bribe.

At Victor's expense (or maybe the client's expense), we'd order in a banquet of Japanese food from Mr. Yakitori for everyone in our department, plus a few favored secretaries from other departments and even the mailroom guys and assorted hungry hangers-on.

After a leisurely meal, and postprandial cigars, we'd finally get to work around 2 p.m., and by 5 p.m. we'd have fantastic stuff that wowed the clients, and pissed-off the jealous overpaid big-ego upstairs team that didn't get free cigars or the food from Mr. Yakitori.

Although Scali, McCabe & Sloves was a great place to create advertising, like all ad agencies, politics took its toll. The problem was not the agency's internal office politics, but client politics.

Often, particularly with Japanese clients, it was just not possible to get a simple "yes" or "no" when we needed approval for one ad or an entire campaign.

Sometimes there would be six people from the client company in a conference room for a presentation. They'd all sit with blank faces, waiting for a smile or a frown from Big Boss-san; and if the chief inscrutable Oriental didn't show emotion, no one else did.

After meetings like that, I'd go back to my office and show *my* emotion.

217

I'd kick a hole in the wall and label the hole with the name of the client and the date of the meeting. Every few months, I'd replace the Sheetrock and start kicking again.

While I worked at Scali, my wife hit the Big Four-Oh, and was very depressed. Her last words at night and first words each morning, were, "I'm so depressed."

I'd leave for work, have a little vacation during my half-hour subway commute, and then I'd face Adele, our department secretary, who'd greet me with an all-too familiar refrain, "I'm so depressed."

It was very depressing.

When the agency chose a new health insurance company, the personnel department distributed a survey form to determine what optional coverage the staff wanted.

Psychiatry won over dental care, six-to-one.

At one time, the employees of Scali, McCabe & Sloves were summoned to gather together on an unoccupied floor of our office building, for drinks, snacks, and an important announcement.

One of the partners, probably Ed — but maybe it was Marvin or Sam — told us that the agency was being bought by international advertising giant Ogilvy & Mather.

He reassured us, saying that although the partners were going to make a lot of money, the operation of the agency would stay pretty much the same.

"We're not selling out; we're just cashing in," he said. I thought it was an award-winning headline.

Chapter 61
Even Connecticut has hillbillies

While I was in high school, I worked Saturdays and summers at a clothing store in a shopping center.

For a few days each summer, employees would haul out slow-selling stuff and specially purchased bargain merchandise, and display it in front of the stores for a sidewalk sale.

These sales were fun. We had a carnival environment with balloons, music, clowns, costumes, cotton candy and silly announcements. It was very different from our usual way of doing business. Even the customers were different.

Instead of our usual solid middle class patrons, the sidewalk sale drew in the dregs of society. But they were nice dregs and we never had any trouble.

The super-low prices attracted trailer park trash and hillbillies who would be more appropriate on the stage of the *Jerry Springer Show* than in our classy store. These were the people who never went to a dentist, and attended family reunions to evaluate potential spouses.

They didn't mind buying slightly soiled underwear, shirts with missing buttons, a red sock paired with an orange sock, or pants that had faded from being displayed in the window. They didn't mind the smell of mildew.

Some of these customers loved to bargain, and some of our salespeople were such skilled hagglers that we sold merchandise for higher prices than on normal days. Sometimes we got out-haggled, but it was all fun.

Walter McAfee was a regular sidewalk sale customer who showed up every year. He always carried a rolled-up sheet of soiled brown wrapping paper with the outlines of the feet of his six children. He'd expect me to recommend shoes to fit each absentee kid, and apparently I did OK, because Walter came back, year after year.

One year I just didn't have anything that would fit his oldest daughter without exceeding his budget. He did like one pair a lot, but it was obviously a bit too small.

Ever the optimist, Walter said, "That's OK, I'll just tell Abilene to curl her toes up just a tad."

Chapter 62
And so does Pennsylvania, but why is this town named after the capital of Libya?

Pennsylvania is smaller than Texas, but it's still a BIG state. It has more than 12 million people, about 50,000 square miles, and measures about 280 miles from west to east. Pennsylvania's southern border is the famous Mason-Dixon Line. States north of the line were "free states" during the Civil War. South of the border were the "slave states."

The western end of Pennsylvania is Midwestern, with steel mills, coal mines, oil wells, forests and deer hunters. It touches Great Lake Erie.

The east end comes close to the Atlantic Ocean. It has Philadelphia, with its Philadelphia lawyers, universities, hoagies, pretzels, cheese steaks, Rocky Balboa and the Liberty Bell. It's part of the Washington-to-Boston East Coast metroplex.

Within the Keystone State's borders are the usual mountains and rivers and turnpikes and tunnels, and even something known as the "Grand Canyon of Pennsylvania." PA's diverse populace includes Philly's cheesesteak makers, Slippery Rock students, Pottsville brewers, Pittsburgh Steelers, Pocono honeymooners, Three Mile Islanders, Hershey chocolatiers and Intercourse Amish.

The most exotic Pennsylvanians I ever encountered were gathered one Sunday in the late 1960s at Ontelaunee Park in New Tripoli. They wouldn't have seemed exotic or out of place in rural

Georgia, and some of these creepy country folks could have acted, quite naturally, in *Deliverance*. Ba-da-bing-bing-bing.

New Tripoli is in Lynn Township, in Lehigh County, between Allentown and Scranton, and it seemed like it had been transplanted from well below the Mason-Dixon Line.

Strangely, for a reason that's long forgotten, it is named after the capital of Libya, immortalized in the *Marines Hymn* ("From the halls of Montezuma, to the shores of Tripoli"). But it's pronounced differently: nu-tri-PO-lee.

The area was settled mostly by Pennsylvania Dutch (who were really German, not Dutch), who had farms and small businesses that supported the farms.

New Tripoli is known for farming, country music and crappie fishing. Apparently the crappie fishing was good, not crappy. On the other hand, I think most country music *is* crappy; and had I known about the country music connection, I probably would never have gone to New Tripoli.

From 1929 to 1988, New Tripoli was the site of Ontelaunee Park, a woodsy recreation area with a carousel, miniature train, swimming pool, picnic tables, and a stage that featured country music performers.

Over the years, the park showcased the talents of countless country performers whom I never heard of, like Shelby Nestler, Al Shade and Shorty Long; as well as Conway Twitty and Loretta Lynn. I did know of them.

Although I own CDs by Willie Nelson, Johnny Cash, K. D. Lang and the Dixie Chicks, I *hate* most country music.

When I was in college, I was a partner in a booking and management company that supplied bands for bars, discos, and fraternity parties. Our bands performed Motown, classic rock, blues, psychedelic, oldies, hard rock and heavy metal, but *no* country.

We heard that there was going to be a "battle of the bands" at Ontelaunee Park. It would be an opportunity to showcase one of our groups, and perhaps even win some prize money. Unfortunately, we had no idea that Ontelaunee Park was hillbilly territory, and might not be the best place to exhibit Oredad.

Oredad (from "metal" and "father") was a high-wattage heavy-metal group, with lots of banging and clanging, and long drum solos and minimal lyrics.

The Ontelaunee audience, on the other hand and unbeknownst to us, was into acoustic a-pickin' and a-pluckin' and a-twangin' and a-strummin' and very sad lyrics about adulterers and gamblers.

After a long and dusty ride (that sounds like a country lyric), we unloaded the U-Hauls near the stage, and waited our turn for what we were told would be the "rock segment."

After endless hours listening to pedal steel guitar and banjo plucking and songs about wayward wives and worn-out mules (or maybe it was worn-out wives and wayward mules), we learned that Oredad *was* the rock segment. Apparently other rock bands had the good sense to do some research, and they all stayed away.

At least we seemed to have a good chance of winning first prize in the rock category. Maybe all three prizes.

The musicians in Oredad were high school kids, and did not have the freedom to shave their heads, pierce their chins, grow fluorescent pink Mohawks or have tattoos like adult heavy-metal bands.

Their clothing was tamer, too, with no Kiss-like leather and spikes. They wore ratty jeans, scuffed work boots and faded T-shirts like regular high school kids, which contrasted with the polished cowboy boots, fringed leathers, bandanas and 10-gallon hats worn by the other Ontelaunee performers. Oredad's appearance marked them as alien invaders the minute they took the stage, even before a string was stroked.

The emcee announced who they were and the groupies and sisters and parents who had made the trip applauded.

The rest of the audience was cynically silent, and we heard unpleasant murmurs and rustling as people noticed the band members had no fiddle or pedal steel or banjo or dulcimer.

NEAR-DEATH EXPERIENCE

Oredad's performance began with the lead guitarist, rhythm player and bass player silently facing the rear of the stage. The keyboard guy stared into space, above the audience, his fingers motionless. The drummer started whaling away with sticks and feet, and began his trademark 15-minute drum solo.

Within seconds, the audience was in wide-eyed shocked silence.

It was like the scene in *Back to the Future* when Marty McFly leads the band in a noisy version of *Johnny B. Goode* and startled the kids and Principal Strickland, who put fingers in his ears.

The silence at Ontelaunee quickly turned into loud boos and catcalls. And then the hillbillies started throwing food at Oredad. And then beer cans. And then came the sticks and the stones.

Oredad was definitely the best rock band to perform that day at Ontelaunee Park in New Tripoli, Pennsylvania. But they took no trophy home. Actually, they were lucky to leave alive.

Chapter 63
Lemme outa here!

 I was attracted to electronics quite early. In first grade my father and I built a telegraph set; and later, with no parental assistance, I built a radio out of cardboard. (Well, at least it looked like a radio, and my first grade teacher was very impressed).

I later went on to make fake walkie-talkies, fake telephones, fake robots, a fake car videophone, fake computers, and eventually some real ones.

In ninth grade I won a prize for a computer I built that used a rotary telephone dial to input numbers to be added and subtracted. It was based on the *Eccles-Jordan Bistable Multivibrator*. You can look it up.

I wrote a lot of letters to electronics manufacturers. They were impressed by the tech questions that my teachers could not answer and I frequently was able to mooch freebie parts for projects. Sometimes I even got invited to visit the factories. Unfortunately some of the most interesting factories were 3,000 miles away, and airfare was not included with the invitations.

Although I understood the science behind it, the telephone was always magical to me. I loved the notion of a voice going in one place and coming out somewhere else.

Whenever a telephone repairman was in the neighborhood I'd beg him for spare parts, old instruction manuals, surplus tools and bits of wire. I was a cute kid and usually got what I wanted.

CONFESSIONS: ❶ Twice when I desperately needed parts for an important project I deliberately broke a telephone in our house so a repairman would come and I could mooch some supplies. ❷ Once when I was in fourth grade I raided a repairman's truck when he was busy in our house. I took a bunch of wire from his scrap bag and an old dial. I doubt that it impacted the phone company's finances.

Starting around age 12, I supplemented my pathetic allowance by installing intercoms and public address systems, and I was in the phone business long before it was legal to compete with Ma Bell. Years later the U.S. Supreme Court decreed that it was OK to do it.

A misguided high school guidance counselor strangely ignored the facts that my math College Board scores kept going down and my "verbal" scores kept going up. She decided that I should become an electrical engineer. She knew I liked electronics. But the electronics that I liked was based on soldering irons and screwdrivers and she apparently didn't really know what engineers really did.

I went to Lehigh University and was quickly disappointed to learn that engineering was mostly math, and slide rules were not nearly as much fun as soldering irons. I wanted to build things myself, not to design things for other people to build.

As one of the few literate people in my engineer-filled freshman dormitory, I quickly built a lucrative business editing term papers.

It seemed to me that most of the engineering students were familiar with only the six of the 26 letters of the English alphabet (A, B, C, X, Y and Z) that were necessary for plugging into mathematical formulas, plus the few Greek letters that went into formulas or were needed for identifying fraternities. These guys were good customers for my coaching.

In those days Lehigh had peculiar anti-technology rules for a college known for training future engineers. Personal computers were not prohibited because they did not exist yet, but students could not have televisions in their dorm rooms. The rule seemed illogical because it did not stop kids from watching TV. There was a TV in the lounge of our freshman dorm and there were others around the campus. The prohibition did not seem based on power consumption either, because we could have stereo systems in our dorm rooms with no limitation on wattage; and music could certainly be as distracting as television.

We were also not allowed to have telephones in our rooms and there was just one public pay phone near the front door that the kids were constantly trying to hack into for free phone calls.

One kid's girlfriend lived less than 20 miles away, but it was considered a long-distance call. He was constantly "modifying" the phone to make free calls and the phone company threatened to take it out if he didn't stop.

This guy also forced other freshmen to swallow chewing tobacco. When he needed extra money, he had an elaborate sucker bet to extract money from his classmates. He would carefully open a pack of cigarettes and remove one cigarette. Then he'd meticulously close the pack so it looked absolutely virgin. Next he would choose a victim and engage in some small talk about the accuracy of modern packaging machinery was, and how no cigarette pack ever leaves the factory with just 19 cigarettes.

It didn't take much effort to get the sucker — confident in technology — to bet $20 that there were indeed 20 cigarettes in the apparently randomly selected package. The victim looked over the pack, opened it up, counted the contents, and paid up!

I got into deep shit for installing an intercom system between my room and a friend's room two floors below. There was no specific prohibition against intercoms, but perhaps I antagonized some higher power because "our" red phones were labeled BELL SYSTEM PROPERTY. I also had trouble explaining the presence of a pay telephone in my suitcase in the storage room.

There was one Lehigh administrator, Clarence "Clarabell" Campbell, who had a really dumb title, Dean of Residence (Dean of all people who live anywhere?).

Apparently Joe, my super-straight dorm counselor, found out about the hotline phones installed between my room and Jim

VanderKloot's room on the first floor. He didn't have to be much of a detective. It wasn't hard to miss the wire hanging out my window and heading down to Jim.

Super-Straight Joe ratted me out to Clarabell who searched my room and luggage and founded the illicit payphone. I had "liberated" it from a Connecticut beach club during the off-season. Then Clarabell called his contacts in the Pennsylvania Bell Telephone Company Gestapo, who alerted their contacts in the Southern New England Telephone Company Gestapo, who called my old man.

The phone company was mostly concerned that I had ripped off a big bunch of their dimes. I couldn't care less about the money, and the coin box was empty when I pried the phone off the wall. I just thought it was cool to have a pay phone. I now have 14 pay phones and two phone booths — all bought legally.

My father, a pillar of the community, rolled over. He turned over my illicit phone collection and even got rid of some of my favorite traffic signs.

A while later at about 4 a.m. while studying for a calculus exam, a mighty voice from an invisible source said to me, "Michael, are you sure you want to do this for the rest of your life?"

I said, "No."

Then the powerful voice said, "Michael, do you want to do this for four years?"

I said, "No," again.

And then I heard from the mystery inquisitor one last time: "Do you want to do this for the rest of the semester?"

I shouted, "HELL, NO!"

The next morning I went to the counseling department and switched from engineering to journalism.

I've been writing ever since, but I still play around with phones.

Chapter 64
Boys are dumb

The Great Jockstrap Debate: At our first gym class in

seventh grade in junior high school, we were given a list of supplies we would need: sneakers, thick white socks, white T-shirt, white gym shorts, combination lock for our clothing basket, and something few of us were familiar with: an athletic supporter (more commonly known as a jockstrap) to protect our precious and fragile genitalia.

A week later, we reported to class with bags of our new or hand-me-down supplies; and as we waited on the benches for our teacher to appear, the jockstrap became the subject of heated debate.

The 12-year-olds were evenly divided as to whether the strange garments were to be worn under our underpants or over our underpants.

We were completely unprepared for the shocking truth that was revealed when the teacher finally showed up and gave us instructions for "suiting up."

Jockstraps are worn *instead* of underpants. Ooh.

Where do babies come from? When I was at the

Quinnipiac Day Camp in the summer between fourth and fifth grades, Alfie told me that babies came out of an opening in a woman's upper leg called the *magenta*.

Sal, a year older, insisted that they came out of the belly button.

Chapter 65
A tale of two sisters

For Teresa and Loretta, the best of times together ended before the beginning of World War I. For the rest of their lives, which ended in the early 21st century, if they were with each other, speaking to each other, or even just thinking of each other, it was the worst of times.

Loretta, born second in 1910, quickly and involuntarily made the transition from cute baby sister to oppressed victim of four-years-older terrorizing Teresa.

They were born in the Bronx, and as adults stayed far apart. Teresa married Luigi in 1928 and moved far west and settled in Albuquerque. Loretta married Albert in 1935 and moved just a little bit west, and lived in Rockland County, New York. She had a son the next year who was shunned for most of his adult life. She divorced Albert in 1955, and soon married her hair dresser, Donald, who was five years younger than she was.

Loretta and Donald were both Catholics, but not permitted to marry in a Catholic church because of her divorce. They tried to have the divorce labeled an annulment so they could have a Catholic wedding, and made appeals all the way from parish priest to Diocesan Tribunal to the Pope. They were turned down by all, despite promised huge donations. They settled for an Episcopal wedding, which Loretta deemed "almost as good as Catholic."

From around 1975 through 1990, my wife Marilyn and I saw Loretta and Donald once a year, on Christmas. Their house was a strange mix of futuristic and pathetic, ancient technology. On the roof was an elaborate solar water-heating system. In the kitchen were a 1940's phone, and a *gas-powered* refrigerator.

Neither Loretta nor Donald spoke of Albert Junior, Loretta's son from her first marriage. He was out west, teaching at a small college. He never spoke to his mother on the phone. Cards, not presents, were occasionally exchanged at Christmas.

There was no picture of him displayed in the house but his old toys were still in the attic. He died of an unnamed disease in 1993 — quite possibly AIDS. A relative said that he was gay and that's why Loretta disowned him and he then rejected her. Near the end of his life, Loretta wrote to him and her letters were returned, marked "Address unknown. Return to sender." The marking was in Albert's handwriting, not a Postmaster's.

Loretta was politically conservative as well as theoretically Catholic. She insisted that Richard Nixon was "our greatest president," thought Democrats were communists, and detested gays. We knew never to discuss politics on Christmas.

Giuseppe, father of Loretta and Teresa, was born in Italy in 1877 and sailed to the United States in 1895. He soon met and married Maria, 11 years younger. She would become the mother of Teresa and Loretta, Giuseppe Junior, and Arturo. Giuseppe was a musician, an instrument maker and a dreamer.

Over a century ago, in 1903, Giuseppe invested 50 cents a week in his American dream — to purchase a plot of land in Mizpah, New Jersey. It's in the "Pine Barrens," about 25 miles inland from Atlantic City.

The Pine Barrens (less-derogatorily known as the "Pinelands") is a forest covering more than a million acres of flat low-lying land in southern New Jersey. The name reflects the sandy, chemically hostile, nutrient-depleted soil which could not support the farm crops planted by early European settlers. The soil, however, does support the species that depend on fire to reproduce, and fortunately for them and not for humans, fire is very common in the Pine Barrens.

Optional Biblical Backgrounder

A great many centuries ago, in Old Testament times, Mizpah was a village in ancient Canaan.

The name means a "watch tower" or a "lookout." The Bible tells a tale of intra-familial deceit and intrigue that ends at Mizpah. It's an eerie precursor of what happened between Teresa and Loretta that began at the American Mizpah, thousands of years later and thousands of miles away.

Genesis relates the rivalry between Jacob and Esau, the twin sons of Isaac and Rebecca. Esau decided to kill Jacob. When Rebekah found out, she sent Jacob to live with her brother Laban.

Jacob stayed with Uncle Laban for 20 years and worked as a shepherd. Jacob wanted to marry Laban's younger daughter Rachel. Laban pulled a wedding night switcheroo, substituting older Leah for Rachel. When Jacob protested, they negotiated a package deal for him to marry both Leah and Rachel.

Through some slick wheeling and dealing, Jacob ended up with most of Laban's animals and other valuables. Apparently fearing a revenge attack by his cousins and uncle, Jacob headed back to Canaan with his family, animals and household goods while Laban was away shearing sheep.

Laban caught up to him at Mizpah where he planned to attack Jacob and take back his daughters, grandchildren and sheep. Laban changed his mind after a dream in which God warned him not to hurt Jacob.

The final parting of Laban and Jacob was peaceful, and they erected a stone monument to serve as a physical reminder of Laban's final blessing for his daughters: "God will watch over us when we are apart."

Other Mizpah-like monuments were erected elsewhere to symbolize an emotional bond between people separated by distance or even by death. The word "Mizpah" and the blessing from Genesis appear on gravestones and lucky charms.

Teresa and Loretta inherited a piece of Mizpah, New Jersey. Unlike its namesake in the Holy Land, it came with no blessing and no emotional bond.

In spite of the unfriendly conditions, the Pine Barrens have supported human endeavors since prehistoric times. The Lenape tribe of Native Americans passed through in annual migrations from inland to the Atlantic Ocean, and they hunted as they traveled. Colonists from Europe built farms and factories including ironworks, and sawmills to harvest the abundant trees.

After less-expensive sources of iron were developed farther west in Pennsylvania, new industries such as papermaking and glass making started up. Cranberry and blueberry growing have been important for many years.

Despite its closeness to Philadelphia and New York City, and major highways that run through it, the Pine Barrens are still mostly rural, and quite barren. There are few people, then and now called "Pineys." Villages were formed near local industries, and when the factories failed or moved, the homes were often abandoned and the land was reclaimed by the forest.

Development in the area is under control by a state/federal commission. Some areas are off-limits to construction, and a large part of the Barrens are State Forests and Wildlife Management Areas that attract hunters and hikers — not home builders.

A major real estate company has a web page devoted to Mizpah. It has about a dozen categories of homes for sale, and *not even one* home listed in any of the categories. Clicks on links for community information or school information reveal nothing. It's like a ghost town with a name but nothing else.

If you were to parachute into a random part of Mizpah, you are much more likely to scare a bird, a dear or a skunk, than to be greeted by another human being. When you walk around, what you see will be pretty much what has been seen for thousands of years — or never seen before.

Despite this depressing environment, the abundant land attracted the attention of a real estate developer at the beginning of the 20th century.

This huckster divided hundreds of cheaply-bought acres into small house-size lots, on streets with fanciful names like Broadway, Main Street and Paradise Avenue.

Some roads are named for distant and more glamorous municipalities. Mizpah has a New Orleans Avenue and Los Angeles Avenue and Riviera Street, and strangely even a Brooklyn Avenue. Both Boston Avenue and Venice Avenue dead-end in the trees. Mizpah has a Zip Code and a part-time Post Office not much bigger than an outhouse, but no school or movie theater.

The real estate mogul peddled his vision of a rural utopia to recent immigrants sweating in the squalor of the South Bronx. The easy payment plan and attractive promotional brochures attracted the attention and nickels of many, including Giuseppe.

Giuseppe never moved there nor built a home there. He never even saw his rural real estate in the 10 years he owned it. He died in 1913, at the age of 36. He left behind a widow, four young children, and a deed to a small part of America.

There was little life insurance, and young widow Maria had no way of supporting her children. She recognized that education would be the family's savior, put the children into foster care, and studied to become a nurse. When she graduated and got a job, she sought to reclaim her family. Teresa, Loretta, and Giuseppe returned home. Arturo, the youngest, had died, apparently of neglect, while in an institution that was supposed to care for children.

Maria was still young and pretty and had a source of income, She soon attracted a new husband named Rafaelo, who became the father of Thomas. Unfortunately, Maria was soon a widow again, and again had four young children to support.

Maria quickly attracted husband number-three, Stefano. Unlike the first two marriages, this union produced no offspring, but it was like those marriages in another unfortunate way. Maria outlived Stefano. Maria outlived three husbands and a child, and even a grandchild.

For over 70 years, through most of the 20th century, Maria paid the annual real estate tax bills, which gradually escalated from $12 to $29 per year. It was not much money to keep her first love's dream alive.

When she died in 1984 at the age of 96, the deed was passed to the two surviving children of Giuseppe — the warring, seldom-communicating Teresa and Loretta. Both sisters realized that with their mother gone, there was probably little point in continuing to pay the real estate tax to keep the property, but it made little real impact on their bank account balances.

Neither one was willing to surrender her half to the other, but since they were in their 80s, they had the uncommon common sense to realize that if they did not reach a settlement, after they both died there could be a dozen or more heirs of Giuseppe and Maria who would have to agree on a solution.

Loretta, a well-off and clever investor, decided that the best solution was to sell her share to her even wealthier sister Teresa. The heirs of their deceased brother Giuseppe just wanted the land to go away as simply as possible.

Naturally Loretta wanted to extract as much money as possible from her sibling, partly to get back at her for years of teasing and criticizing, and Teresa wanted to pay as little as possible, preferably zero dollars and zero cents.

Somehow, I was recruited to perform the role of impartial investigator and real estate appraiser, to help the two old crones make a deal.

Armed with the ancient deed and real estate developer's map and a crappy rented Ford Pinto paid for by Loretta, Marilyn and I ventured south on a nice day in 1991.

Our first stop was at the Mays Landing Town Hall. We hoped we'd have an easy way out, and find some "comparative values" for recent sales of similar property. Alas, there were no recent sales, and almost no ancient sales.

Our next stop was at a local real estate agent. He reinforced the impression we got from the government. He also advised that in the foreseeable *centuries* there was little chance that there would be a market for the land we hoped not to inherit. He said that unless we knew we would use it, our best option was to stop paying taxes and surrender the land to the town.

That sounded like a good option, but curious and duty-bound, we resolved to see and set foot on Giuseppe's ancient dream. We might be his only relatives to ever do so and maybe the only human beings to be there since the Lenape Indians last hunted there.

There was no Global Positioning System in those days, but I've always been good with maps and I have an accurate internal compass. With some basic directions from the real estate agent, we headed toward the wilderness.

The main road into and through Mizpah is Route 40, the dreary "Harding Highway." We saw some homes and businesses on the road, and there were clusters of development both to the north and south. We had been directed to turn right and travel north. In a few minutes we were beyond any indication of recent economic activity, and clearly in the Pine Barrens.

The overwhelming impression was failure, and our over-whelming emotion was sadness.

We saw exactly two businesses: a garage and a dilapidated grocery store, and very few moving cars or people. Mizpah seemed to have been trapped in suspended animation. We saw dozens of house foundations that never had homes built upon them, and the remains of homes that were completed, perhaps inhabited, but burned down and never replaced. The scenario was like a post-apocalyptic sci-fi movie about a pleasant suburb after a nuclear war when vegetation was replacing humanity.

(but maybe not until they're adults)

There were some street signs in the forest, some recent, most ancient, and many wounded by shotgun pellets. With intensive navigation I was able to surmise where Giuseppe and Maria's Promised Land should be. I hiked beyond the road and paced-off what seemed to be an appropriate distance, walking on a soft carpet of fallen pine needles decorated with pine cones and broken branches. I saw one skunk, two deer, and too many squirrels to count.

When I reached the center of what could have been a good spot for a house, I carved a shallow "X" on a tree along with the year to indicate to anyone who might follow me, that at least one person had been there before.

After hiking back to the road, we drove some more. We saw more unfinished and burnt-down homes, lots of dumped mattresses and office furniture, and tires and abandoned cars. We finally saw a man in a driveway at a nice house on "our street" at a point just before it dead-ended at a wall of pine trees.

He told us that he had moved there about 20 years earlier, and his house was the newest in the neighborhood.

When we got back to civilization, I called Loretta and gave her an accurate report. She wanted me to type up a phony report to present to Teresa.

I was asked to inflate the value far upwards of zero, glamorize the neighborhood, and suggest that the Atlantic City building boom would soon make the land even more valuable. In reality, the boom reached just one block west of the boardwalk casinos, not 25 miles into the forest primeval that was Mizpah. And if for some weird reason someone did want to live in Mizpah, there were hundreds of other building lots available, much closer to civilization.

Because I would not lie for her, Loretta eventually told the truth to Teresa. They finally agreed to abandon the property that their father had bought for them 89 years earlier.

Loretta's husband Donald was both unpleasant and strange. He was a skilled hairdresser who wore one of the world's worst hairpieces.

Despite marrying Loretta, who was a customer, he despised most of his customers and co-workers. He originally owned a salon, and later worked for another salon owner. He hated his boss.

In one of his few concessions to modern technology, he was willing to accept a cordless phone as a gift from us.

Donald fought in the South Pacific in the Second World War, and hated anything or anyone Japanese. He was wounded in the war, and botched battlefield surgery caused him recurring pain throughout his life. Unaware of his prejudice, we gave him a top-of-the-line Panasonic phone. When he opened the package and saw the brand, he choked up and said, "I can't use this. Please take it back."

We replaced it with an AT&T phone. Like the Panasonic, it was made in Japan, but he couldn't read the fine print and he was much happier owning a phone with an American brand name.

Over the years that we visited them on Christmas, Donald's physical and mental health diminished.

In the early years, he'd offer us home-made wine, show off his woodworking projects, and tell us war stories. Later he hid from us, staying in bed allegedly because he had bad migraine headaches. In reality, he probably hated us.

Eventually Loretta and then Donald moved into a nursing home. We visited them even more often than before, to try to cheer them up and do some shopping for them. It was a difficult duty because they were cold to us, and confused. Their dementia was getting worse daily.

Loretta, bewildered, paranoid and weakened by a stroke, asked us to get her an attorney. She was afraid that less-disabled Donald had gotten her to sign a paper to turn over all of her money to him, and to give him the right to decide when she should die. Loretta did not trust the attorney, whom she thought was conniving with Donald and Marilyn. She even accused Marilyn of having sex with Donald.

Towards the end of his life, Loretta's son Albert Junior was too ill to work. With no income, he was in danger of losing his house. With no communications with his mother, he appealed to his wealthy Aunt Teresa to buy the house and let him live in it until he died. She turned him down and he died in 1993 at the age of 57.

Teresa could have easily afforded to buy the house, and probably could have sold it at a profit. She was loaded, with many millions that she hid from her unfaithful husband.

If there is any justice in the world — and in this story — it might sadly be this: Teresa tormented her sister Loretta for 85 years and refused to help Loretta's son to spend his last few months in his own home instead of in a hospice. But Teresa's own son soon died of cancer at age 51. Teresa lived to mourn her child for 13 years until her own death at age 97.

Chapter 66
Sex in the sixties: my first dry hump

Maybe because of Betty Friedan and Anthony Quinn, 1965 was much sexier than 1964.

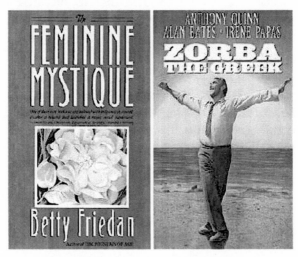

The attitude about sex for most baby-boomer boys who became teenagers in the late 1950s and early 60s was not much different from the attitude in previous decades and centuries, dictated and reinforced by religion and parents.

Boys wanted to do "it," but nice girls didn't do it.

Therefore, the girls who did it were not nice.

A man would choose one woman for love and another for sex, but none for both.

Before the feminist revolution, the girls who did "it" were frequently perceived to be whores or sluts or pigs; or were fat or flat or ugly or pimply and provided sexual favors to attract and keep a boyfriend, unlike the more desirable girls who could remain virgins until their wedding night.

Before the feminist revolution, sex was assumed to be pleasurable for most men but not for most women.

Women were advised to look at the ceiling during sex and think about something else. On a wedding night, and through decades of marriage, women often endured sex because it was considered a marital duty, and necessary to keep the husband from straying, and to perpetuate the species. I heard women, born in the first decades of the 20th century, speak of being "bothered for sex" by their husbands.

The human female is among the few creatures that engage in sex during non-fertile periods, and this facet of evolution may have developed to keep the man around to protect and provide for the family. This leads some feminists to insist that marriage is legal long-term prostitution.

There's a lot of sex in the bible, and most sex was done by men to women. Jacob asked Laban for his daughter Rachel so he could "go in unto her." Moses ordered the men of Israel to "come not at your wives" before he went up Mount Sinai.

Although they are in the minority, there are several sexually assertive women are in the Bible. Ruth sought the advice from her mother-in-law Naomi for seducing husband Boaz. Naomi told her to wait until he was drunk and sleepy and "go in and uncover his feet [meaning genitals], and lay thee down."

For many wives, sexual pleasure was accidental, unthinkable, infrequent or impossible.

Betty Friedan's *The Feminine Mystique* and other books that followed helped establish women's right to not just equal pay for equal work, but also to equal pleasure from sex.

For a teenage boy in the early 60s, there were big internal questions about "what to try" and "what I can get away with." Some boys were slapped for kissing a cheek or touching a breast. Others — so I heard — received look-but-don't-touch stripteases or hand jobs while still in junior high school.

It seems quaint in the 21st century when 10-year-olds have oral sex and junior high school girls email nude photos, and there

FUCKING MATT DAMON

is endless talk about hooking up, friends with benefits, fuck buddies and booty calls; but back then it took guts to kiss a girl goodnight on a first date.

Thoughts of progressing from "first base" to a "home run" were more likely to result in wet dreams than in two-people sex.

The assumption was that since sex wasn't fun for females, they didn't want to have sex, and must be seduced, coerced, forced, persuaded, bribed, paid or drugged.

The vocabulary reflected this. Males "got something off her" or screwed, hammered, drilled, boffed, banged, bonked, boinked, porked, poked, schtupped, shagged, slammed of knocked-up.

Until recently, "fucking" was mostly done by males to females, but both genders can "get laid." Men are more likely than women to "get lucky." Women like to "make love."

"Fuck" is a transitive verb for a male, as in "Steve fucked Janet." But for a woman, at one time it was mostly intransitive, and a description of a loose woman, as in "Yeah, Janet fucks."

It was different in 2009 when Sarah Silverman proudly sang, "I'm fucking Matt Damon" to Jimmy Kimmel.

Females lack an appropriate and equally assertive or aggressive term to match "screw" or "bang." It may be that the physical essence of the genital apparatus leads to the imbalance. A hard penis just looks more aggressive than a soft vagina, and penetration is more assertive than being penetrated

In *Moving Beyond Words*, feminist author Gloria Steinem considered this language deficiency, and the most forceful verb she could think of for the female function was "envelop." That doesn't seem very assertive.

I dated a pretty girl in 1962-63, my junior year in high school. I had the normal desires for her— and the normal inhibitions to keep me from acting on them. We held hands and eventually got to goodnight kisses, but nothing more.

Physically she seemed much colder than previous girls I had dated, and had made-out with. The gossip at school was that she was "frigid." I asked my mother about it. She said, "There's no such thing as a frigid woman, only clumsy men." My mother did not suggest the possibility that this young lady might be a latent lesbian, and thus not receptive to any male.

In my senior year I dated several other girls. I liked one of them enough to think about marrying her. On the Freud scale, I considered her to be much more of a Madonna than a prostitute. We never went beyond kissing, and my balls frequently ached.

In the fall of '64 I went away to college and became aware of changes in sexuality. Male attitudes had shifted from "getting something" to "giving pleasure." Female attitudes had shifted from "letting him do it" to "wanting him to do it."

In *Zorba the Greek*, Anthony Quinn's character advised his younger companion, "God has a very big heart but there is one sin he will not forgive: if a woman calls a man to her bed and he will not go."

This movie scene was my first "official" notice that females might actually like sex. Alas, I no longer remember which girl I saw the movie with, or what we did after it.

I saw the movie during Christmas break at the end of 1964. In early '65 there was a dance in our freshman dorm, and my blind date from Cedar Crest College turned me on during a slow, close dance.

I made no effort to hide my erection. Rather than being outraged or offended, she seemed to accept it as a compliment. She did not slap me or move away. We danced closer and she grinded against me. It was my first dry hump, and wet ones soon followed.

So thanks, Zorba, for explaining the facts of life and changing my life. I just wish you did it a year earlier.

Chapter 67
Farts and breasts
(to help women understand men)

THE FART SECTION

**Q: Why do farts stink?
A: So deaf people can enjoy them.**

**One big difference between living together
and being married, is that married men don't
try to hold farts in, or leave the room to fart.**

Fart appreciation is a gender issue. Men are proud of their farts. Women are embarrassed. When men are without women, even if they are in their 60s, they still act like they are six years old and they love to out-stink each other — even if they are in the corporate boardroom and wearing $5,000 custom suits.

Kids know that farts are funny. When we're young, we all like to blow ass bubbles in the bathtub or the pool. Fart sounds are so cool that we make fake fart sounds, and we buy gadgets that make fake fart sounds and fake fart smells. There are even recommendations online for "fart foods."

But by a certain age we are taught to hold back our farts, and not even to laugh at farts. That's sad.

244

I think we should have one day each year when nobody is embarrassed to fart. A national "Freedom to Fart Day" is no more ridiculous than "Talk like a Pirate Day." Aaargh!

Farting is a very natural activity. Even presidents and popes and police chiefs fart. Presumably Michelle Obama farts in the White House. If we never farted, we'd be in big trouble. We'd explode from the build-up of ass gas pressure.

College freshmen with nothing better to do, hang around the dorm and light farts through their jeans or even through tubes stuck in their asses. Or they eat lots of baked beans and cabbage and drive around in an enclosed car for a while and then open the window to gross-out an unsuspecting cop.

I don't think the ladies of America engage in these activities. They might not even think they're funny. (Read chapter 7 to learn how I got in trouble for farting in school.)

My dog is the ultimate SBD (silent-but-deadly) farter. His farts smell as bad as his shit, but in eight years I've never heard him fart even once. His butt hole is a stealth weapon, striking with no warning.

THE BREAST SECTION

Most heterosexual men are attracted to female breasts. At an early age, even gay men and heterosexual females are attracted to female breasts. It's a fact of life, because the breast is the source of life.

Now many babies get their initial nourishment from bottles, but for millennia, vital milk actually came from mothers. If babies were not attracted to breasts, there might never have been a second generation of human beings — or even a second generation of dogs or monkeys or any kind of mammal.

Mammals are a class of animals whose name is derived from their distinctive feature, mammary glands — the breasts that feed young mammals.

The word "mammal" comes from "mamma," the Latin word for breast. "Mamma" is often the first word said by an English-speaking baby. Variations include "mommy,""mummy," "mom," "mammy," "ma," "eema" (Hebrew and Estonian), "meme" (Albanian), "mere" (French), "maji" (Hindi), "mama" (Dutch, Spanish, Chinese, German, Russian and Italian), etc.

The widespread use of similar words in diverse and distant cultures implies that babies learn to extend a basic sound of happiness while suckling and nuzzling ("m") into a real word. The sound is obvious in "mother" and "maternity." The breast may be the source of not just life-sustaining milk, but of speech.

Breast allure for most male human beings extends *long* after the need for breast feeding. The female breast can be a life-long source of attraction and sexual excitement. It's possible that men who were breast-fed as babies are more breast-focused than babies who were bottle-fed. I can appreciate a fine behind, but I was breast-fed and am definitely a "tit man," not an "ass man."

Young teenage boys are driven to see, touch, nuzzle and more— but they may not be initially aware that females can receive pleasure from being seen, and even from being touched.

Some women resent being "ogled," or complain that men look at their chests, not at their eyes, during a conversation.

Other women are willing and eager partners in the relationship that perpetuates the species. They display cleavage, wear push-up bras, wear falsies, get breast implants and dance naked to attract mates— and human life goes on.

When I was in advertising, one of the sexiest women I knew was 25 years old and as flat as an 11-year-old girl. Even though she did not have much to display, she often dressed with multiple open blouse buttons and she never wore a bra. The men she worked with tried to position themselves to see her nipples.

Women may not like this, but it's a basic part of being a mammal. It's God's plan. It's human nature. It's vital for the continuation of life on Earth. Get used to it.

If you've got it — even a little bit of it — flaunt it.

Chapter 68
They don't need a telephone man; they need a psychiatrist

After years of writing magazine articles and advertising during the day, and installing phones for friends and family at night, I reversed my schedule around 1980 and became a full-time phone guy. I installed phones and phone systems for businesses and homes. I worked for ordinary people and famous people, very rich and not-so-rich, normal and nutso.

After years of dealing with the public I learned that certain stereotypes apply. About 85% of the time.

• Doctors were the cheapest.
• Lawyers were the crookedest.
• Interior decorators were the nuttiest.
• People with old money tended to be looser with their money than people who had just recently struck it rich.

Superstars and billionaires defied stereotyping. They could be the nicest people in the world, or bitches and bastards and raving lunatics. Some rich people felt they had plenty and had no objection to others making money. Others felt that any dollar that someone else had, was one less dollar available for them to have.

It's hard for me to think of my worst customer. There's probably a three-way tie. Actually, if I keep thinking, maybe it's a ten-way tie.

I said that the decorators were the nuttiest and the lawyers were the crookedest. Mrs. Statler was a decorator, married to lawyer, and together they drove me nuts. I had installed a phone system in their house, but this esteemed "officer of the court" wanted the bill made out to his business so he could claim it as a tax deduction, and he offered to pay me in cash so he could avoid paying sales tax.

Mrs. Statler insisted that I remove all of the light bulbs from their phones because they were "too-businesslike." But then she and he complained because they were constantly interrupting each other's calls and dumping calls off hold.

One time Mrs. Statler summoned me to her house and complained that the phone in her bedroom sounded like crap, and asked why it couldn't sound as good as the phone in her husband's den.

I checked the bedroom phone, and of course it was fine. I then went into the den and encountered Mr. Statler. He said, "I'm glad you're here. This phone is a piece of shit. Get rid of it and get me a good one, like the phone in the bedroom."

Arnie was also a lawyer, married to a Sharon, a well-known soap opera actress. They moved into a beautiful and huge new custom-built house on Long Island that I wired for phones, audio, video and computers.

Arnie's personality ranged from a kindly Dr. Jekyll to a vicious Mr. Hyde. Apparently his mood swings were triggered by Sharon, but I never saw what she did to cause him to make the shifts.

She was always cold to me. On the day after they moved in, I was chatting with them in the kitchen and I asked how the unpacking was going. Her highness replied, "Do I look like someone who unpacks?"

When Arnie was in his nice guy mode, he'd chat pleasantly about music or politics, give me presents, serve me meals and trust me to watch his young daughter.

But twice when there were problems with equipment I had installed, this esteemed officer of the court threatened to cut open my chest and "rip out my liver and eat it."

No other customer ever said that to me. Arnie sure had a flair for the dramatic.

Later on he and Sharon divorced.

Arnie's mood swings stopped and he was Mr. Niceguy every time we spoke after their split.

Divorces are unpleasant and I don't know the details of this one, but I think he was lucky to escape with his mind intact. I blame her for his viciousness, not him. Although Arnie is on this worst customer list, it's only for the pre-divorce Arnie.

One valuable lesson in business that business people seldom learn early enough is that sometimes it's better to turn down business.

Once when I was young, foolish and hungry, I ignored a warning from a friendly competitor and I agreed to work for a customer who was an absolute lunatic who should have been strapped up and put away.

I was in Mandy's house for three very long days installing a state-of-the-art phone system, and during that time the tip of her nose was seldom more than an inch away from the tip of my screwdriver.

I don't know if she didn't trust me, was in love with me or was trying to learn the business. She was a real pain in my ass, but that initial pain was just the beginning of the torture.

The real agony began after I thought my work was finished. For two days, this maniac escorted me from room to room so I could fine-tune her telephones. She had me open up each telephone handset, and adjust the volume of the transmitter and receiver by inserting varying thicknesses of different kinds of cloth.

She had me experiment with diapers, napkins, felt, nylon stockings, perforated rubber — an endless parade of both natural and synthetic textiles. And when we reached the point when Mandy was finally satisfied, she asked her husband and their daughter for their opinions, and we started the agony all over again.

Somehow, I lived through the ordeal and I got paid and the check cleared. The phone system seemed stable — a lot more stable than Mandy — and I prayed I'd never hear from her again.

But I was not to be that lucky.

She called from a neighbor's house to complain that none of her phones were working. Reluctantly, I honored my obligation and I went right over. I found that the main "brain" of the phone system was blackened and smelled like smoke. I asked what happened. Mandy said her daughter's teenage boyfriend was using the phone system for a school science experiment.

I told her the warranty was voided and I quickly walked to the front door. As I gleefully skipped to my car I invoked the spirit of Dr. Martin Luther King, Jr. and loudly proclaimed to Mandy and her neighbors: "Free at last! Free at last! Thank God almighty, I am free at last!"

There is not enough money on Planet Earth to pay me to go back there again.

Chapter 69
For the birds

In the 1980s lots of people replaced the phones that they had been renting from their local telephone companies, with purchased phones. Buying was a good deal. People typically earned back the rental cost in less than a year.

While many of the purchased phones looked just like the rental phones they replaced, there were often technical improvements inside. Some had memory for automatic dialing of important numbers, or electronic ringers that could sound like warbles or chimes or chirps instead of the standard raspy mechanical bells.

Mrs. Weinstock was a nice elderly widow who had spent a small fortune renting three phones from New York Telephone Company, and she was eager to keep a bit more of her monthly pension check by buying three new phones from me. The work went smoothly. She seemed happy. I got paid, and I left.

A week later I got a frantic call from Mrs. Weinstock. Her daughter had just shown up unexpectedly, after driving all the way from Chicago to Scarsdale because she was not able to reach her mother on the phone and she was afraid something terrible had happened.

Mrs. Weinstock told me that the new phones I installed for her were fine for making calls but they never rang.

And strangely, ever since the time I installed the new phones, her two pet birds in the cage next to the kitchen phone were chirping much more than they did before.

251

Chapter 70
The lawyer was a liar

One time I had a customer with a very expensive apartment in Manhattan. Sheila was a mistress, a kept woman, being kept by Harold, a lawyer with a wife and kids on Long Island. Harold seemed to treat her well, at least in terms of spending money — except for one time.

Sheila ordered an expensive, ornate (and I thought ugly) Italian phone made with onyx and gold-colored metal. It cost about $400, which was a lot of money in the mid-1980s. It's a lot of money now, too. Especially for a really ugly phone.

When I delivered it and plugged it in, she seemed to like it, and she gave me a check. No problem, I thought.

A few days later she called me and said she wanted to return it because it was not what she ordered.

This didn't make any sense. She had no complaint when she first saw it. She had ordered from a color catalog page; and that page, and my order form, and the phone's package and the label on the bottom of the phone all showed the same model number.

I figured that Harold blew up when he saw her check book. $400 was a lot of money for a really ugly phone.

I refused to take the ugly phone back. I had done nothing wrong. I could not return it to my supplier. It was extremely unlikely that I could sell that onyx monstrosity to anyone else.

Harold was not happy, and he stopped payment on the check. I sued him in small claims court. The court was inconveniently located near the bottom of Manhattan, and Harold and Sheila missed the scheduled court session. They, the defendants, got an automatic postponement to a new court date, which really pissed me off.

The law was very unfair. If I, the plaintiff, didn't show up, the case would have been dismissed and the defendants would have gone home victorious. They could have kept the phone for free. It's not so ugly if you don't pay for it.

Harold and Sheila did show up the second time. Harold was used to trying cases in fancy venues like the Supreme Court of the State of New York. Snooty Harold had a Harvard law degree and clearly thought my small claims case and the appointed referee were several rungs beneath his exalted stature (there was a six-month wait for a "real" judge). Harold expected an easy victory and to keep his four hundred bucks.

As "Defendant's Exhibit A," Harold showed the referee the catalog page that Sheila had ordered the phone from. With excruciating detail, worthy of a forensics expert tracing blood spatter, he pointed out what he insisted were significant differences in the grain pattern of the onyx in the photograph, and of the actual onyx in "Exhibit B," the telephone which he showed to the referee.

The referee, a graduate of Brooklyn Law School, was as streetwise as King Solomon and as knowledgeable as a Nobel scientist, and was not impressed with highfalutin Harold from Harvard.

He pointed out that onyx was not molded plastic, and it was not realistic to assume that two pieces of stone that came out of the earth would look the same.

I easily won Round One.

Harold then shifted strategies to portray evil me as unresponsive to his complaints. He told the referee that he left a message with my answering service when he first saw the phone, and that I did not return his call.

It seemed like I should have already won the trial after the referee's lecture about the earthly origins of onyx, and that this move by Harold was — as Perry Mason said — "incompetent, irrelevant and immaterial."

But rather than objecting to the testimony, I decided to take advantage of it... and maybe have some fun.

Harold was more accustomed to being the attorney who questioned witnesses, and not being a witness himself, and he got careless. I was now the sharp-toothed legal shark and I smelled blood in the water and it was my turn to examine the witness.

I had what seemed like a simple and innocent question — almost a time waster — but I was really hoping to set him up to commit perjury and lose the case.

I asked Harold if he spoke to a man or to a woman when he called my answering service.

Without hesitation, this esteemed officer of the court and professional bullshit artist told the referee that he spoke to a woman.

I then shifted from being an attorney to being a witness. I said to the referee, "Your honor, I don't use an answering service. I use an answering *machine*, and it answers in my own obviously male voice."

I got paid for the phone, and I recovered the court costs. I wasted a lot of time, but I *love* playing lawyer.

My only regret was that Harold was not disbarred for perjury in a courtroom. But he did eventually get paid back many times over for fucking with me.

You see, Harold's wife Lorraine found the apartment lease and discovered that he had been shacking up with Sheila, and she beat him up in a very costly divorce.

And by then Sheila didn't want him either.

She got pissed off at him because he didn't want to pay for the onyx phone that she liked so much. She moved out of their love nest and started dating others, and eventually she married the referee from Small Claims Court, and she went back to college and became a divorce attorney.

Justice usually does prevail. Sometimes it just takes a while. Sometimes verdicts are reversed after years of imprisonment. Sometimes defendants are pardoned *after* they're executed.

It took me over 50 years to tell you about my sixth-grade teacher.

Chapter 71
I lost the trial but won the case

In the mid 1970s I lived in a brand-new luxury high-rise apartment building in Queens, New York. My wife and I planned to live there for three years, and then buy a house. The building was filled with lots of other young couples who had similar plans and dreams.

Unfortunately, we all soon realized that each month that we stayed in the building meant that the prices of houses we might want to buy would go up, and we'd be paying about $600 to the landlord, instead of using the money to build equity in our own real estate.

Some of the other couples broke their leases early but had to pay huge penalties, often agreeing to keep paying rent until a new tenant moved in. The building still had virgin apartments, so there was no incentive to the rental agents to steer prospective tenants to previously occupied apartments.

I, however, had an advantage over my peers.

I was a *big* pain in the landlord's ass.

The landlord hated me, and wanted me out.

I was active in the building's tenants' organization, and became reporter, editor and publisher of the *Tenants Times*. My neighbors loved it. Our landlord hated it.

Every time that the landlord announced a new rule or he claimed that some activity was a violation of the lease, I'd do some research and publish a special issue to point out that the landlord was full of crap.

I knew the lease better than he did. A lot better. This was a talent I inherited from my father — a retailer who was a master lease negotiator who knew the contents of his landlords' leases better than the landlords or their attorneys.

One time my landlord tried to ban cookouts on our balconies, claiming that they violated the lease and were a terrible fire hazard.

I was pleased to point out that the lease *didn't even mention* outdoor cooking. I also interviewed the local fire chief, who said that in the last 40 years in the entire Borough of Queens there was no record of any fire being caused by cooking on a balcony. I published this information, along with some advice to try to minimize annoying smoke, and to keep a bucket of water or a fire extinguisher handy.

After this, the landlord did change the lease for new tenants to specifically outlaw balcony barbecues, and he determined to find a way to get rid of me.

The prick discovered that I had erected a huge Citizens Band radio antenna on the roof, and had snaked a cable down seven floors through a ventilation shaft to my apartment.

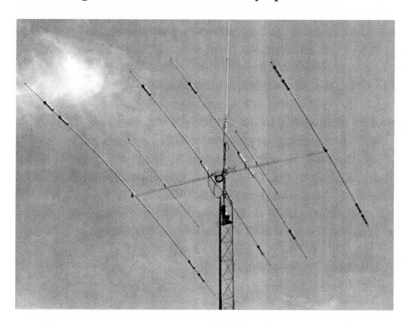

This, he was certain, was a violation of the apartment lease, and grounds for my eviction. Eviction sounded pretty good to me, because I could move out without penalty, and then pay my money on a mortgage for my dream house, instead of as apartment rent.

When we went to court, the landlord's attorney showed the judge several pictures of my huge antenna on the roof of the building, and a yellow-highlighted page from my signed lease, noting the prohibition of the installation of exterior antennas without permission.

Now it was time for me to use my secret weapon and win the war.

I opened my briefcase, removed a manila envelope, and took out a neatly typed letter on the landlord's expensive engraved stationery.

It was dated on the same day my lease was signed.

It was signed by the landlord's rental agent — who was also his *son*.

The letter, which was written as an enticement to get me to sign the lease to rent my apartment, gave me explicit permission to erect the CB antenna on the roof!

The landlord's attorney turned white and gulped.

The judge and stenographer tried hard not to laugh.

The lawyer made no effort to dispute the letter. He just wanted to find a way to get me out of the building ASAP.

He was engaging in pest control.

I negotiated the right to end my lease with no penalty or payment, and to move out at any time within the next 12 months. The landlord paid the court costs.

It was only years later, when I was examining some old papers, that I realized that I was officially evicted.

I still think I won the case.

Chapter 72
I skipped the trial but won the case

 I once got a ticket for an illegal left turn at a particularly confusing intersection in Scarsdale, New York. I thought the conditions might be ambiguous enough for me to avoid a fine if I got to speak to the right judge.

However, the maximum fine was only $45, and it would not jeopardize my license or raise my insurance; so it was quicker and simpler to just visit the court clerk and deliver a $45 check.

When I got to the court, I was horrified to learn that fines had to be paid in cash!

This court was in fancy-shmancy SCARSDALE, and they wouldn't trust a $45 check.

When I lost a traffic court case in crappy Jamaica, New York, they were quite willing to accept my check.

I told the snotty Scarsdalian bureaucrat that as long as I had to waste my time by coming back a second time; I wanted to change my plea to Not Guilty and have a trial. She modified the record, and put my name on the court calendar for trial a few months later.

On the scheduled day, I went to court. I had $45 in cash in my pocket because I assumed I would lose, and I dressed a little better than I normally did.

When my case was called, I said something like "Defendant ready, Your Honor," just like on *Perry Mason.*

However, there was no one there to represent the Village of Scarsdale. The Plaintiff was apparently too busy giving tickets to other drivers to come to court.

The case was dismissed and I got to keep my cash.

On the way out of town hall, I couldn't resist stopping by the court clerk's office for some immature gloating.

I held up the $45 and said, "If you accepted checks, this money would be yours!"

I was tempted to call her a stupid bitch, but, with great effort, I controlled my glee.

Chapter 73
But when is the trial?

One time my company was sued by an annoying customer.

He invented a lot of phony complaints, even alleging fraud because there was one name on my initial proposal and a different name on the final invoice.

There was no fraud. My company had changed names to get a better position in the Yellow Pages and we went from being a company to being a corporation.

The real reason for the suit was all-too-common "buyer's remorse." The customer had agreed to spend too much money, and was now looking for a legally-sanctioned way to avoid paying his bill.

The summons listed about a dozen complaints that I could easily challenge. When we got to court, our case was called, and the judge invited both parties into his private "chambers" for a pre-trial conference.

The plaintiff went through his bogus complaints and I made a very half-hearted effort to refute them, saving my stronger arguments and abundant evidence for the later courtroom appearance.

After a few minutes, the judge said, "Thank you very much; you'll be notified of my decision by mail."

I was shocked, and replied, "But Your Honor, when is the trial?"

His Honor said, "You just had it."

Chapter 74
Verdict for the amateur professional, or maybe the professional amateur

In the 1990s I lived in a townhouse condominium in Westchester County, New York. I was one of the original residents, and had moved there in 1978.

When the place was built, the builder, like other builders, needed to establish rules and regulations. He apparently went to an office supply store and paid a few bucks for an all-purpose document written by a lawyer who never lived in our condominium, never knew the people who would live there, and certainly had no idea how society would evolve over the following decades.

One important way that society did evolve was the emergence and popularity of the "home office."

Once home offices were limited to doctors, but by the mid-1990s, inexpensive computers and the Internet enabled a wide range of occupations to be carried out in underwear or pajamas, at any hour of the day or night.

Our condominium's bylaws specifically outlawed carrying out any occupation other than "professional" activities on condominium property.

The attorney who wrote the rule in 1970 knew what he had in mind, just as the folks who wrote and approved that "...the right of the people to keep and bear arms, shall not be infringed" in 1792 knew what they had in mind.

But in both cases, there has been lots of disagreement and interpretation over the years, selective prosecution, perhaps some persecution, and ample income opportunities for attorneys.

In my condominium, lots of occupational activities were carried out in apparent violation of the rules. School teachers corrected exams and read term papers. Salespeople wrote proposals. Bartenders mixed drinks. The ice cream man sold pops. Landscapers planted, mowed and trimmed. Lifeguards guarded lives. Carpenters remodeled kitchens. Doctors prescribed medication. Plumbers replaced water heaters. Cops and insurance agents investigated burglaries. Our managing agent managed. Our maintenance men maintained.

Lots of people — residents, visitors and even employees of the condominium — worked there every day in flagrant violation of the holy writ, and life went on just fine.

But one day, and I don't know why, the Board of Managers decided to sue me for violating the rules against operating a "non-professional" business on the premises.

My main business at the time was installing business phone systems. I installed them at the premises of my customers. Many of them were in Manhattan, or in New Jersey, or Long Island, or Connecticut — but certainly not in my own living room.

I made most of my money outside the house, but I did have a few business visitors each month. Some were salespeople showing me new products, and some were prospective customers, and a couple were customers picking up phones.

I certainly had no store. There was no showroom, no sign in the window, no bright lights, no factory with loud noises or noxious odors that would have violated the bylaws or zoning regulations. I had no employees. My business certainly drew less traffic than a perfectly legal doctor or a 17-year-old girl.

The traditional examples of permitted "professional" occupations, as envisioned by the ancient unknown lawyer who wrote our rules, were doctors, dentists, architects, and — of course — other lawyers. I had to prove to the judge that this group was much too narrow, and an unrealistic interpretation for the late 20th century.

OLDEST PROFESSION

I told the judge that many occupations were widely recognized as professions, and deserved to be included, starting most obviously and in chronological order, with "the world's oldest profession"— prostitution. Wasn't a hooker as worthy as a dentist?

I then told the court about professional wrestlers, professional golfers, professional tennis players, professional musicians, professional divers, professional gamblers and professional assassins. GMC makes professional trucks.

I showed the judge a copy of *Professional Boatbuilder* magazine and *Professional Hair Salon* magazine, and told him about magazines called *Professional Woman* and *Quilting Professional* and *Christian Professional.*

I also told him about the Professional Drivers Association and the Association of Professional Body Piercers and I showed packages labeled "professional screwdriver," "professional duct tape," and "professional toilet plunger."

The judge ruled that the term "professional" was now synonymous with "business," and merely meant the opposite of an amateur or non-business activity; and unless the condominium rules were rewritten to include or exclude specific occupations, neither the oldest profession, nor mine, were against the rules.

Chapter 75
How can a free dog cost $100,000?

 In 2002, neighbors announced that they were divorcing and moving away. The wife was getting custody of the kids and we could have the dog.

My own wife had never lived with a dog, but had gotten to like theirs, and was willing to go along with the deal, provided I agreed to clean up the crap.

Hunter is a Golden Retriever, with proper AKC papers. The neighbors had paid $1,000, but he'd be ours for just the price of food and a few toys and the annual shots.

HAH.

It didn't take long before we realized that Hunter wasn't happy going for morning and evening walks and spending most of the day in the house, so we spent $100 for a gate on our rear deck, and then $3,000 for a custom awning over the deck to keep him cool when it was sunny.

As he grew bigger, Hunter needed more room to roam than the rear deck provided, and he wasn't happy being tied up in the back yard, so we decided to have a fence put around the yard. A three-foot-high fence would have been tall enough to keep him in, and would cost about $5,000.

The very helpful salesman pointed out that if we spent just $2,000 more, we could have a fence that was five feet tall — tall enough to protect a pool, "just in case."

"Just in case" came the next year, and cost us about $75,000. We didn't buy the pool just for Hunter, but we probably would not have gotten it if we didn't already have the dog fence, and Hunter uses the pool much more than people do.

Hunter eats dog food, but only for snacks. Breakfast is a can of Costco chicken breast meat, costing over $2. Supper is roasted chicken breast from ShopRite, costing about $6. When he's thirsty, he drinks Poland Spring water. When we travel, Hunter has the co-pilot's position in the right-front seat and Marilyn gladly sits in the second row.

We take him on vacations to dog-friendly hotels, and he's never been left in a kennel. Hunter and I bathe together in our Jacuzzi and I brush his teeth. Our kitchen table has a stainless steel top. It's one of his favorite places to nap and lounge with Copper, his Chihuahua-Beagle girlfriend.

There's an animated movie called *All Dogs Go to Heaven*. I've warned Hunter not to die, because Heaven won't be nearly as good as what he has here and now.

Chapter 76
The beep line

 Long before AOL, MySpace, FaceBook, YouTube, and even long before the Internet, college kids were connecting with chat rooms accidentally provided by their local phone companies.

I don't know who discovered it, but when several people reached a busy phone number, they were connected together in a conference call, on a "beep line." People could speak to each other between the beeps, for free.

When I was a student at Lehigh University in Bethlehem, Pennsylvania in the late 1960s, young men at Lehigh used the beep line to try to get dates with young ladies from Cedar Crest College in neighboring Allentown, or even with "townies" who worked at Bethlehem Steel.

Around 8 p.m. on Saturday, a desperate dateless Lehigh guy would call his own busy phone number to reach the beep line, hoping a similarly dateless girl would have done the same thing.

The conversation might go like this:

"Hi BEEP I'm BEEP Steve BEEP a BEEP football BEEP player BEEP at BEEP Lehigh. BEEP. Does BEEP anyone BEEP want BEEP to BEEP go BEEP to BEEP a BEEP party? BEEP."

"Hi BEEP Steve BEEP I'm BEEP Cindy BEEP a BEEP hot BEEP freshman BEEP cheer BEEP leader BEEP at BEEP Cedar BEEP Crest. BEEP. I BEEP can BEEP be BEEP ready BEEP at BEEP nine BEEP. Call BEEP me BEEP at BEEP 86 BEEP 75 BEEP 55 BEEP 5 BEEP."

"OK BEEP Cindy BEEP hang BEEP up BEEP and BEEP I'll BEEP call BEEP you. BEEP Do BEEP you BEEP have BEEP a

BEEP car? BEEP. What BEEP kind BEEP of BEEP beer BEEP do BEEP you BEEP like? BEEP. Are BEEP you BEEP on BEEP the BEEP pill? BEEP."

I can't tell you how many of the dates actually happened, or how many of them resulted in romance. As in today's chat rooms, there was lots of lying.

Many of the alleged football heroes weren't; and the allegedly beautiful-and-willing blonde 18-year-old college girl might turn out to be a 14-year-old junior-high-school student, and might not even be a girl.

Eventually, Bell's central office equipment was "improved," and the beep line disappeared.

Chapter 77
But how does a quadriplegic dial the operator?

When I was a student at Lehigh University in the mid 1960s, geeks from the student radio station found a way to hack free long distance phone calls.

There was a basic black rotary dial telephone in the faculty dining room, with a lock that kept the dial from being rotated to make calls when the telephone was unattended. The phone was sometimes needed to answer calls at odd hours, so there was no lock to prevent picking up the handset;

Many of the radio station guys were ham radio operators, whose Morse Code experience enabled them to make ten quick taps with one of the hookswitch buttons on the top of the phone. Ten taps generated ten electrical pulses, and had the same effect as dialing "O" to reach the operator.

When she answered, the dial tone thief would say, "I'm a quadriplegic. Please call ...."

Sympathetic operators would always complete the call, and they never asked how the alleged handicapped person managed to dial the zero to reach the operator.

269

Chapter 78
Parental issues

What's worse, mom and dad, or moo-goo-gai-pan?

When I went home from college to visit my parents, I frequently got really bad migraine headaches.

When I went home from college to visit my parents, we frequently ate Chinese food. It wasn't available in Bethlehem, Pennsylvania, where I went to school.

Around this time, a theory started circulating that migraines were triggered by the monosodium glutamate that was used as a flavor enhancer in many Chinese dishes.

As an experiment, I decided to avoid Chinese food the next time I went home.

I still got a migraine.

The unavoidable conclusion was that it was my parents, not the MSG, which made me sick.

I hope my mother doesn't read this

In eighth grade, my friend Larry was at my house one day after school. We were in the kitchen working on a school project, and my mother was nearby in the dining room talking to Larry's mother.

I no longer remember the details, but I do remember that she was talking about me and said, "I knew he was right, but I couldn't tell him."

I didn't trust her after that. Not for a long time.

NO SEX

What came first, the chick or the driver's license?

I became 16 in 1962, during my sophomore year in high school.

The state of Connecticut let people drive when they were 16 years old, but my parents had different rules.

Mom said, "You don't need a driver's license because you don't go out with girls."

Hey Mom, did you ever think that maybe the reason I wasn't going out with girls was because I didn't *have* a driver's license?

So Dad, whose fault is it?

When I was a teenager, I fought a lot with my parents. I don't remember the specific issues, other than some crappy marks in school, and Mom and Dad not letting me get my driver's license when I was 16.

I once planned to run away from home, but when I started writing the farewell note and got to the part where I was saying goodbye to the dog, I got weepy and threw away the paper and decided to stay a while longer.

I guess I thought they were insensitive and intolerant and didn't understand me, just like most parents. Sometimes I'd stay in my room, and endlessly blast Bob Dylan's *Don't Think Twice, it's All Right*, but I don't think they got the message.

It was probably normal for teens to fight with their parents. My parents, however, didn't think it was normal, and sent me to an adolescent psychologist.

I didn't mind the chat sessions, but they didn't seem productive; and after a while, the shrink said that he wanted my folks to come in for some sessions so he could hear their side of the story.

When I told that to my parents, my father refused to go, saying "I'm not going to pay $25 an hour to be told it's MY fault that you're messed up."

And for balance, some nice things about my parents

My mother, Rita Marcus, is responsible for my lifelong love of reading and my drive to be productive before the chickens wake up. (I typed that at 3:44 a.m.) Both came together when I was in junior high school and we watched *Sunrise Semester* together on TV. It started at 6 a.m. Mom watched it to get her master's degree. I watched it because I liked classic Greek literature. *Lysistrata* is an extremely funny and sexy anti-war play, written over 2400 years ago by Aristophanes. I highly recommend it.

My late father, Bud Marcus, also encouraged reading by example, and he is the source of my interests in business, building things, technology, travel, history, maps, food, collecting, pranks, photography, law, language, cigars, tropical fish, and probably everything else I care about. He was one of the world's funniest storytellers and is a major influence on my writing (we both include lots of details and tend to be pedantic). During college vacations he worked as a waiter in a Borscht Belt hotel, but he could have been on the stage. Pop was my best resource and I felt both deprived and deserted when he retired to Florida.

Both of my super-smart parents went to high schools for "the gifted." Their intellectual gifts to me more than make up for any mistakes they made because I was the first-born child. And besides, if they didn't make those mistakes, this book would have been shorter and less funny.

Chapter 79
My 200-minute battle with Bill Gates (This may piss-off Microsoft.)

 I've installed lots of versions of Microsoft DOS, and lots of versions of Microsoft Windows. I did 3.0, 3.1, 3.11, 95, 98, 2000, ME and XP; probably every recent Operating System except Microsoft Bob.

In ancient times, I'd have to sequentially stuff a dozen or more floppies into my PC, and I knew that when I reached about 44 minutes into the 45 minute sequence, the installation would stall, and I'd have to start all over again.

In February 2007, I assumed the installation of Vista, with five years and 86 gazillion Microsoft dollars behind it, would also take about 45 minutes (at least until the first fatal error). Cynical Cousin Dave and I agreed to start the job when the little hand on the office clock tapped ten.

There were two minor setbacks.

I couldn't figure out how to open the super-cool new package. I got frustrated and threw it to Cynical Cousin Dave to open. (Despite his left-handedness, he's more dexterous than I am.) I aimed wrong and the package hit Dave's shoulder, and it conveniently opened right up and two DVDs spilled out.

The next problem was caused by the unexpected presence of the two discs: one labeled for 64-bit PCs and one for lowly 32-bitters. I assumed that my super-duper PC with a dual-core Athlon "64" CPU would use the 64-bit Vista — but it wouldn't load.

After I shoved in the 32-bit DVD, the installation got started. There was no stall, no unexpected crash, and much to Cynical Cousin Dave's surprise, no smoke spewed out of my hard drive.

I let Vista check online to see if there were any updates (UPDATES? Sheesh, the software had just been released the day before, and Mr. William Henry Gates The Third wants me to check for updates? I doan need no steenkin updates.)

Next, I had the opportunity to accept the licensing agreement, which I did, without reading it, just as with 3.0, 3.1, 3.11, 95, 98, 2000, ME and XP. I probably wouldn't have read the Bob agreement, either.

And then, Microsoft wanted to check my compatibility. I hoped it wouldn't be like an online dating service where people lie about height, weight and affection for things that they assume potential mates would like. Fortunately Micro-soft found me to be compatible. (For $259.99 plus tax, I damn well better be considered compatible).

At 10:18, I was informed that "potential issues were detected with installed applications." Even Microsoft's own Windows Messenger 5.1 — which I never use and didn't know I had — had a potential issue.) None of the apps were important enough for me to abort Vista, so I told my machine to move on.

At 10:19, Vista started copying files, and I reached the important 50% milestone at 10:20, and hit 100% at 10:22. Cynical Cousin Dave asked, "Is it done yet?"

At 10:23, I was feeling really good. My screen told me that Vista was "gathering data." Then Cynical Cousin Dave pointed out a notice on the screen that said "Your upgrade may take several hours to complete."

I didn't think the warning applied to experienced and talented data processing wizards like me, and my drives were humming along smoothly; so my original 45-minute target still seemed reasonable. Cynical Cousin Dave asked, "Is it done yet?"

At 10:35, I hit the 69% mark for file gathering, and I remained optimistic. A dual-core Athlon should be able to accomplish a lot in the remaining ten minutes.

At 10:40, Vista was saving my settings. I was feeling really good, and aimed a "see, I told you so" smile at Cynical Cousin Dave. Then the screen went blank. Cynical Cousin Dave asked, "Is it done yet?"

At 10:49, (four minutes into overtime), my screen lit up again, and told me that my files were being expanded. It took just a few seconds to reach 23% expansion.

At 10:55, I was up to 70%, and 11 a.m. looked like a possibility. Cynical Cousin Dave asked, "Is it done yet?"

At 11:00, I was told "that's all the information we need right now." (Had my compatibility testing continued without my knowledge?)

At 11:01, Vista told me to "wait a minute while Windows prepares to start for the first time." Vista told me this with crappy white type on an ugly DOS-like black back-ground. I was not impressed. Where were all the pretty Vista colors?

At 11:05, I watched an army of dots march across my screen •• • Cynical Cousin Dave asked, "Is it done yet?"

At 11:10, 11% of the upgrade had been completed. (What the hell was Vista doing during the previous hour?) Cynical Cousin Dave asked, "Is it done yet?"

At 11:15, I reached 34%. I was a half hour past my deadline, and starting to get pissed-off. I had finished reading the good magazines in my in-box, *Jerry Springer* was a rerun, and I had nothing to do. It wasn't much fun watching the dots crawl. • • • •• • • • • • • • •• • • • • • • •• • •

At 11:26, I realized that the "several hours" warning might actually be right. Horrified, I looked for something to keep me busy. I swiveled my chair around, loaded paper in-to two printers, replaced a fading black ink cartridge, and even reconnected the USB cable for my long-dormant scanner.

The printers and scanner sit on a cabinet whose doors have been blocked for many months by a growing pile of crap. This seemed to be the right time to start my spring cleaning. I shoved the crap pile aside and pried open the sticky cabinet doors to inspect my hidden treasures.

My first prize was a bag of KitKat bars, surplus from Halloween 2005. They were individually hermetically sealed and deemed safe. I found two pieces of Riesens chocolate-covered caramels. They were of unknown vintage, and a little bit hard, and the brown was beginning to fade to gray. But Hungry Brother Marshall and I managed to ingest them without much effort or apparent harm.

At 11:31, I completed 43% of the upgrade. I also found a microwaveable Dinty Moore's chicken-and-rice meal, a Maruchan instant soup, three AA batteries, and an unopened box labeled "time sensitive" which was shipped on 8/4/04. It contained some obsolete business cards. I also found some Werther's Original caramel candies, two dollar bills, an old passport, some embarrassing pictures, and my 2003 appointment book. Cynical Cousin Dave asked, "Is it done yet?"

At 11:39, Vista noted it reached 50% of the upgrade. I found a box of Zwieback, a Costco statement, an obsolete Sirius channel guide, an ancient party invitation list, and a menu from Buffalo Wild Wings. The menu was the first thing that made Cynical Cousin Dave happy.

At 11:44, the upgrade had reached an impressive 53%, and I found a directory of Connecticut hospitals, an open bag of Tostito Scoops (my favorite variety of tortilla chips), and a Simply Asia sesame teriyaki noodle bowl. Cynical Cousin Dave asked, "Is it done yet?"

At 11:45, Vista hit 57%. I read that the Scoops were guaranteed fresh until 12/20/05, but I tasted them anyway. They were pretty good for an opened bag more than a year past its prime, but at the urging of Cynical Cousin Dave, I put the Scoops in the trash can.

At 11:47, my new operating system reached an impressive 64%. Cynical Cousin Dave asked, "Is it done yet?" I found unopened sauce pods from KFC, Taco Bell, and Arby's; plus soy sauce and duck sauce from unknown Chinese restaurants. I took a break from my cleaning and I glanced through a Vista preview magazine, and learned about applying thermal grease to a CPU. I've never used thermal grease before. I wonder how it compares to Arby's Sauce. I then went back to the cabinet, and found a charger for a long-gone Motorola cellphone, a broken telephone headset, and broken sunglasses.

At 11:51, the screen still showed 64%. I replaced a light bulb, made sure my UPS was alive, and went to the fridge for a Devil Dog. Cynical Cousin Dave asked, "Is it done yet?"

At noon, two hours into the ordeal, we were still at 64%. Ignoring the warnings of Cynical Cousin Dave, I tried some Cheetos from an open bag marked "guaranteed fresh until 1/24/06." They were still pretty crunchy, and (IMPORTANT REVELATION) old Cheetos didn't mess my hands nearly as much as fresh Cheetos.

At 12:02, we were *way* past my 45-minute estimate, but the completion percentage jumped to 73. I found a bag of dog treats. Cynical Cousin Dave asked, "Is it done yet?" Three minutes later, Vista hit an impressive 78% completion.

At 12:08, the PC restarted all by itself. The screen was blank, and the LED on my DVD drive was flashing frantically. Cynical Cousin Dave asked, "Is it done yet?"

At 12:10, I was asked to choose an operating system to start my PC. Since I had invested $259.99 plus tax, plus two hours and ten minutes of my valuable time, I chose Vista. My next decision was whether to order food from the outside, or open one of my new discoveries. I decided to play it safe, and get something freshly cooked.

At 12:12, I had the opportunity to verify the time and date, and tell Microsoft that I would be using this PC at work, not at home. Microsoft thanked me. An ethereal turquoise screen with a white horizontal line appeared. This looked vaguely Vista-ish, and I was encouraged. Cynical Cousin Dave asked, "Is it done yet?"

At 12:18, nothing on my screen had changed. I was tempted to move my mouse or press Enter, but Cynical Cousin Dave warned me not to. I checked the weather report on another PC, and decided to try to take a nap.

At 12:24, I was still awake. Nothing had changed on my screen. I started looking through the take-out menus.

At 12:26, I answered a wrong number call. My screen was unchanged, but I did dare to move my mouse. My screen didn't change. I picked a menu, and read lustily about the "Big Manny Burger."

At 12:31, I was excited — and relieved — to see some words: "Please wait while Windows checks your performance." Oh shit, am I in danger of having my compatibility canceled? Apparently I still met the standards, and I was encouraged to "Connect, Play, Have Fun."

At 12:42, my screen went black. I didn't connect, play or have fun, but I did hear the first Vista sound from my speakers. Cynical Cousin Dave asked, "Is it done yet?"

At 12:45, exactly two hours beyond my estimated completion time, my screen looked normal. Vista seemed to be alive and well, I got a pop-up message from Yahoo urging me to refinance my mortgage. Is this what I got for my $259.99 plus tax? Cynical Cousin Dave asked, "Is it done yet?" I said that I thought so.

At 1:00, we hit the three-hour mark since I first tried to open the Vista package. My screen showed that the new Windows Mail program was transferring accounts and messages from the ancient, archaic and obsolete Outlook Express (which had worked just fine). I had 18,483 messages in my deleted file, so I was prepared to wait.

At 1:20, I could finally tell Cynical Cousin Dave that the installation was officially finished. The screen was gorgeous.

(but maybe not until they're adults)

Translucent windows are impressive. The WAIT hourglass has been replaced by an animated light spiral. A movie demo was amazingly crisp, with lots of possible visual enhancements to compensate for the viewing environment. A year-old graphics problem that made diagonal letters look ragged was miraculously fixed. There are a bunch of new sound effects, including some really annoying aquarium sounds. The preview of opened files was a real crowd pleaser.

We could even see a miniature moving version of Jon Stewart interviewing Bill Gates at the same time we watched the full-size YouTube video. Program windows open with a zooming expansion, and zoom down to close. It feels Stark-Trekish, even though there's no whoosh sound (I'm sure someone's working on the add-on). A new feature, called just "computer," replaces the old "my computer." It shows the PCs on your local network, and the space on your drives, and favorite links, in one window. The "all pro-grams" list is in alphabetical order — ten years overdue.

At 1:31, after poking around, sampling, and experimenting, I checked my email for the first time in 214 minutes.

Windows Mail has a new "Junk" file that collects evil email. The very first email that Micro-soft decided was junk, had been sent to me from the folks at *Apple*.

Yup, Vista sure has some amazing tech-nology.

Upgrade Update: In 2009, it took even longer to upgrade from Vista to Windows 7.

Chapter 80
Diary of a couch
(This may piss-off Macy's.)

Oct 1	8:15 p.m.	Wife and I start looking at couches at a Macy's store in New York.
Oct 1	8:40 p.m.	We find one we like (two-piece sectional marked down from $1200 to $799), and start looking for a salesman
Oct 1	8:55 p.m.	We finally find one. He starts writing out a sales ticket. A buzzer signals 9 p.m. and he tells us to come back tomorrow. We are almost stampeded by salespeople heading for the exits. Where were they hiding 20 minutes earlier?

Oct 2	9:30 a.m.	We return to the store and complete the transaction with a different salesman.
Oct 5	11:00 a.m.	Truck arrives at our apartment, but with only one half of the two-piece sectional. Wife calls Macy's and Mr. P tells her that the other half will be delivered tomorrow.
Oct 6	3:15 p.m.	Second half has not arrived. Wife calls Macy's. Mr. P is not available, but "he'll call you back in a day or two."
Oct 11	10:15 a.m.	Wife calls Macy's and is told that Mr. P no longer works at Macy's but someone else is now working on the case and we will have our missing furniture in a couple of days.
Oct 19	2:00 p.m.	Still no complete couch. I call Macy's. After 84 rings I finally reach customer service. They put me on hold, and after seven minutes I am disconnected.
Oct 19	2:30 p.m.	I call again and reach Miss F. She can't find any record of the transaction so I give her all of the numbers from my sales ticket and she promises to call me back.
Oct 26	4:20 p.m.	I have not heard from Miss F so I call again. This time I speak to Mrs. M, who can't find any record of my sale or complaints. She says the couch half was probably lost or damaged and promises to call me back in the morning.

Oct 29	10:00 a.m.	Mrs. M has not called back so I call Macy's. After 108 rings I reach Mrs. T. She can't find any record of my sale or complaints, so I give her all of the numbers from my sales ticket and she promises to call me back in the afternoon. She doesn't.
Nov 1	10:00 a.m.	I call, and after merely 44 rings I reach Mrs. N. I tell her I have given up and am cancelling the order and want the half couch picked up and my account credited. She promises to call me back within a few days with a pickup date.
Nov 10	3:00 p.m.	Mrs. N has not called, so I call. After 82 rings and four minutes on hold I reach Mrs. M (not the same Mrs. M from before). She says I should "give it a few more days; these things take some time." I tell her I would and I know.
Nov 15	12:15 p.m.	Nothing has happened in a few more days. I call, and after 204 rings I reach Mrs. D. She says the manager will call me back.
Nov 16	11:00 a.m.	The manager has not called me, but I receive a note requesting a copy of my sales ticket, which I immediately mail.
Nov 18	3:40 p.m.	I have been living with an extra half-couch in my living room for 44 days. No one can sit on it for fear it might become soiled and not be returnable. It is blocking my other couch and chair, so my living room is completely unusable. I call Macy's and after 92

rings, a disconnect, 34 rings and a four-minute hold, I reach Mrs. H. She says an "adjuster" is working on my case. I ask why Macy's needs an adjuster to schedule a truck trip. She says she doesn't know.

Nov 22   10:30 a.m.   I have not heard from the adjuster. I call again. I speak to Mrs. M who has no record of our 11/10 conversation or of any of my other calls. She says she will "put a rush on it" and that supervisor will call me back in a few minutes.

Nov 22   11:55 a.m.   The supervisor, as expected, has not called back, so I call again. This time I speak to a third Mrs. M who promises that her boss will call me after lunch

Nov 22   2:15 p.m.   This is an historic moment: Macy's keeps its first promise! Supervisor Mr. A calls and apologizes for my difficulty but says he has no record of my purchase or any of my 14 complaints. I suggest that he fire everyone in his department. He says that they're "really good girls, but they sometimes get confused." I tell him that I am expecting guests for Thanksgiving and want the couch half picked up tomorrow. He says that's not possible. I tell him that if Macy's can't pick it up tomorrow, I will call Goodwill, the Salvation Army and the Sanitation Department, and it will go on the first truck that shows up. He agrees to a

		pickup the next day.
Nov 23	11:45 a.m.	The Macy's truck arrives but the driver expects to get two pieces. My wife explains that if there were two pieces, he wouldn't have to pick up anything. The driver is confused and calls his boss to get permission to make a "partial pick-up."
Nov 23	1:30 p.m.	I try to reach Mr. A to make sure we get full credit, not just for half a couch. He's not there, but the second Mrs. M says he'll call back. He does not call back.
Nov 24	3:00 p.m.	I call again and Mrs. N promises to send a credit memo for the full amount.
Nov 30	11:30 a.m.	I have not received the credit. I call and speak to Mrs. H (a different Mrs. H), who promises to have Mrs. N call me back.
Dec 1	11:00 a.m.	Mrs. N has not called. I reach Mrs. H who denies speaking to me yesterday. She again promises to have Mrs. N call.
Dec 2	10:40 a.m.	Mrs. N has not called, so I call and, amazingly, she answers. She says my problem is a "complicated matter," but she is working on it, and I'll get my credit memo soon.
Dec 3	4:00 p.m.	We are planning on charging over $2,000 in carpeting tonight and I want to be sure the couch problem will not interfere with our credit status. After more than seven minutes of ringing I reach Mrs. H. She can't find any rec-

		ord of my purchase, pickup or credit. She connects me to Mrs. K who says it can take up to six weeks to receive the credit memo.
Feb 8	11:30 a.m.	I receive a past-due notice and call to complain. Mrs. F says she'll stop the dunning procedure.
Feb 22	11:30 a.m.	I receive a note from Mrs. S requesting a second copy of my sales ticket. I call to ask why she needs a second copy, but she is on vacation. I speak to Mrs. W who wants to know if the couch was "tag merchandise." We determine that it was, and she feels that his new information will solve all of my problems. Somehow, I don't feel any better.
Feb 23	11:30 a.m.	Apparently the revelation about "tag merchandise" did not solve all of my problems, because I receive a second overdue notice. I call to complain and reach yet another Mrs. M who says I shouldn't worry and won't receive any more past-due notices.
Mar 23	11:30 a.m.	My third past-due notice arrives.
Apr 11	11:15 a.m. and 3:30 p.m.	During an all-day shopping excursion, over six months after we started trying to buy a couch, we again see both sections of "our" couch. One piece is in the Macy's furniture clearance center in White Plains in Westchester County and the other is in Garden City, Long Island. We don't dare try to buy them again.

Chapter 81
Low tech and no tech
(This may piss-off Walmart.)

A while ago, I returned something to a Walmart store in Middletown, New York. I did not have a sales receipt, so they said they would send me a check.

After 30 days, I got nothing and called the store. The customer service lady said she couldn't find any record of my return. I offered to read the numbers off the return receipt, but she needed to see the numbers, not hear them.

Silly; but no big deal, I thought.

I then uttered one of the most common contemporary four-word phrases: "What's your fax number?"

I was shocked at the reply: "We don't have one."

Yuck!

I like Walmart, but this was absurd. They'll sell me a fax machine but won't let me send them a fax.

Walmart is the world's retailing giant, a nearly-$400 billion-per-year behemoth that brags about its efficiency and technology. It's a success-story that sells zillions of pieces of merchandise each year — including fax machines — and they didn't have a fax machine for use by their own staff or customers.

And, no, I couldn't send a fax to a demo machine in the electronics department. And, no, I couldn't send it to the fax machine in the garden department. And, no, I couldn't send it to sibling Sam's Club in the same building.

I even offered to give them my credit card number so they could sell me a fax machine, set it up, receive my fax, and then pack up the fax machine and issue a credit to my credit card.

But no dice.

The grand temple of technology, the world-beater and Sears-beater, the company that sells almost everything to almost everyone, the biggest retail business in the universe, insisted that I *mail* them a copy of my receipt.

I never mail anything. I hate the mail. Mail doesn't work for me. I can't cope with mail. If something can't be phoned, faxed, e-mailed, FedEx'd, or UPS'd, it just doesn't go. I send electronic birthday cards, not paper ones. My desks have stacks of stuff that should have been mailed weeks, months or even years ago.

My wife has learned not to ask me to mail anything. I pump out faxes and e-mail all day long; but things she asked me to put in the mailbox are still stuffed above the visor in my car. They'll stay there until she reads this.

C'mon Walmart. Get connected. I know where you can get a good deal on a fax machine. Try aisle seven.

But wait; there's more! When Walmart was finally ready to send me the refund, an employee had to make a trip to the local post office to purchase a money order, because the store didn't have a checkbook!

Chapter 82
A little bit about the family, my classic first name, weirdo middle name, and my classic and useful last name

It's customary in many Jewish families to name a baby after a deceased relative. The new kid usually gets a similar name or sometimes just a name with the same initial. There are very few Jewish juniors, seconds or thirds.

I was named after two relatives. My first name Michael was adapted from Meyer Polaner, my maternal grandmother's uncle, who was not connected to the Polaner jelly company. (The name just means "someone from Poland," and lots of people came from Poland.) My lack of connection to the jelly people doesn't bother me because I don't like jelly and I'm not looking for freebies or discounts.

Meyer Polaner's children, Helen and Nat, lived together as adults. I assumed they were husband and wife and I didn't learn that they were siblings until I was a teenager. (That's not so bad. According to *Time* magazine, half of American high school seniors think Sodom and Gomorrah were married.) Their apartment in the Bronx later became my first marital home. They were nice people, but eccentric. It's unlikely that anyone else will ever write about them, so I'll give them some paragraphs here.

Helen's favorite hobby was hypochondria, and she enriched many doctors, hospitals and pharmacies. After about age 50, Helen used a wheelchair, but there was some doubt as to whether it was a medical necessity or merely for convenience. Her cousin, my cynical and sharp-tongued Grandma Del, insisted that in a fire Helen would stand up and run, and be the first one out of a burning building. Grandma disliked Helen's frequent and disgusting medical reports, and often responded, "Spare me the gruesome details."

When Helen died, I went to her funeral, expecting to be one of maybe three mourners. I was shocked to find that the place was packed. Apparently her money had helped scores of World War II refugees move from Europe to the United States and start new lives here. Helen lived frugally but was a very good investor with a very good heart.

Nat was overshadowed and overwhelmed by his sister and seldom spoke in her presence. Others in the family jokingly referred to him as "gnat" and pronounced the "g," like "guh-nat," to emphasize his insignificance, despite his large size. His huge pants almost reached his nipples.

Nat never became a confident driver and Grandma Del said he drove at two speeds: "slow and stop." Like Rodney Dangerfield, Nat Polaner got no respect.

Helen died first, and for a few years Nat's personality bloomed. He actually spoke, and he told interesting stories. It's intriguing to speculate how his life might have been if he didn't live with Helen, and how many others live in similar stifling relationships. When Nat died, I went through his things and found love letters written shortly after World War II. From 1947 on he was somber and almost speechless.

Michael has been the first or second most-popular male name in America since the mid-20th century. In a supermarket if a woman yells, "Michael!" half of the male population instantly turns around and says, "Yes, Mommy."

Michael comes from an ancient Hebrew name. It means "Who is like God." It's probably a question, but sometimes when I'm in the mood for self-flattery I assume my folks picked the name because I was Godlike prenatally. I like my full name, and don't like being called Mike. I hate Mickey.

I am no expert on Christian theology, but I know there was a Saint Michael who was painted by Raphael slaying Satan, and an archangel named Michael. (Actually the saint and the angel may have been the same Michael. I haven't quite figured it out.) Strangely, there has never been a Pope Michael, but there was a Pope Marcus in 336, and he became a saint! I think he looks like me.

Michaels have ruled the Byzantine Empire, Bulgaria, Poland, Portugal, Romania and Russia. Michael Dukakis failed to become U.S. president in 1988.

The name Marcus was derived from Mars, the Roman god of war, and there were *lots* of us in ancient Rome.

Marcus Cicero (106 – 43 BCE) was a Roman statesman, linguist, lawyer, political theorist and philosopher. He is considered to be one of Rome's greatest orators and writers, and introduced the Romans to Greek philosophy. During the dictatorship of Julius Caesar, Cicero favored freer republican government.

Marcus "the wise" Aurelius (121 - 180) was the Roman Emperor from 161 to his death. He looks like Dr. Jack Hodgins on *Bones*. This Marcus was the last of the "Five Good Emperors," and is also considered to be one of the most important Stoic philosophers. He was emperor during wars in Asia and with Germanic tribes. His *Meditations* stressed discipline, virtue and tranquility.

290

On the other hand, evil **Marcus** Crassus (115 – 53 BCE) was a Roman general, politician and slave dealer who suppressed the slave revolt led by Spartacus. He made the Top 10 List of richest historical figures and helped Julius Caesar start his political career. Gen. Crassus was such a greedy SOB that it's said that he was executed by having molten gold poured down his throat. COOL CONNECTIONS: In the 1960 *Spartacus* movie Kirk Douglas played Spartacus, who fought **Marcus** Crassus. In 1966, Douglas played Colonel David **Marcus** in *Cast a Giant Shadow*. Kirk's actor son **Michael** Douglas had a bit part in the movie.

Marcus Brutus (85–42 BCE) is best known for leading the assassination conspiracy against Julius Caesar. "*Et tu, Brute?*" ("You too, Brutus?") was said to a Marcus. Those words were supposedly Caesar's last words, as Brutus stabbed him on the Ides of March (March 15th) in 44 BCE. March 15th was the original income tax day in the United States. Later it was moved a month to April 15th, my birthday. That's another cool connection. We Marcuses are all connected.

Marcus Antonius, a.k.a. "Mark Anthony" or "Marc Antony" (83–30 BCE) was "Master of the Horse" under Julius Caesar and Caesar's cousin, so he probably could call him Julius, not Caesar. He identified his cousin's killers during a dramatic funeral eulogy. Shakespeare wrote his lines: "Friends, Romans, countrymen, lend me your ears. I come to bury Caesar, not to praise him. The evil that men do lives after them. The good is oft interred with their bones." This Marcus was played by Richard Burton in the 1963 *Cleopatra* movie (opposite Liz Taylor) and by Marlon Brando in the 1953 *Julius Caesar* movie. My mother used to say I look like Brando. Marcus/Mark

Antony is immortalized in the names of countless beauty parlors and pizzerias.

Siegfried **Marcus** was a prolific German inventor who spent most of his life in Austria. He invented the internal combustion engine in 1864, installed it on a cart and successfully drove it, as the precursor to the automobile. Because he was Jewish, Nazis destroyed most of the records of his work. His second car, finished in 1889, was rediscovered in 1950 and it could still be driven. The car had been stored behind a false wall in the cellar of a Vienna museum to hide it from the Nazis.

For better or worse, I'm not related to any of them. Our family name has only been Marcus for a little over 100 years. It used to start with "Dzm" and end with "ski" and had many more consonants than vowels.

We originated not in Rome but nearly 1,000 miles northeast in Sopotskin. Or Sopotkin, Sopochkinye, Sopokotzky, Sopockinski, Sopochani, or any of many variations of the name.

Sopotskin was in an area called Suwalki Guberniya. "Guberniya" is a Russian word that means "governorate." It's similar to a state. In 1897 the population was 52% Lithuanian, 23% Polish, 10% Jewish, and there were smaller percentages of other ethnic groups.

Sopotskin's location changed a lot, although the town didn't physically move. Since 1991, it's been in Belarus, near the borders with Poland and Lithuania. When my paternal grandfather's family left town, Sopotskin was in Poland.

It's also been in Lithuania, the Belarusian People's Republic, White Russia, the Byelorussian Soviet Socialist Republic, the Lithuanian-Byelorussian Soviet Socialist Republic, and the Union of Soviet Socialist Republics. It depended on who had the most powerful army or who made the map.

292

When Grandpa Walter was in grade school, in Poland, there was a picture of Russian Czar Nicholas II on the wall. Walter's father Isaac was in the leather business, supplying the Czar through Christian intermediaries because the Czar would not do business with Jews. Sopotskin was becoming a lousy place for Jews to live, so Isaac moved the family to the U.S. in 1906 and chose our fine American-Roman name.

The Czar had a Russian-Roman name: Romanov. Nicholas Romanov abdicated in 1917 at the start of the Bolshevik (Communist) Revolution and was shot in 1918.

The killing was ordered by Vladimir Lenin and Yakov Sverdlov. Yak was Jewish. Vlad had a Jewish grandfather. Russian anti-Semites *play down* the Jewish origins of Communism. American anti-Semites *play it up*. Anti-Semites also complain about Jewish capitalists. Our tribe gets blamed for *everything*. Except for Jesus. It seems very strange that so many anti-Semites think God had a Jewish son, and pray to him. No Christian anti-Semite calls Jesus a "kike."

Romanov was a busy guy. He hurt lots of Jews and non-Jews and his nickname was Bloody Nicholas. His official titles were Emperor and Autocrat of All the Russias, King of Poland, and

Grand Duke of Finland. Bloody Nick is now the Russian Orthodox "Saint Nicholas the Passion Bearer."

I find it ironic that the first name of Mikhail Poopy-Head Gorbachev, last leader of the officially atheist USSR, is pronounced so closely to the original Hebrew mee-chai-ail, which means "Who is like God." I wonder if he knows or cares. (I'm talking about the real Russian pronunciation, not the lame Americanized "mee-kale.")

My middle name, Neuman, has been a major burden for me. Neuman is only a teeny bit less alien than its source, Neumann — the first name of my mother's father's father, my great grandfather Neumann Jacobs.

Neumann Jacobs was born in Germany and came to the U. S. around 1870. His son Julius, later renamed Jay, was born in upstate New York in 1896 (the same year Grandpa Walter was born in Sopotskin). He married my grandmother Adele ("Grandma Del") Schwartz who was born in Hell's Kitchen in Manhattan in 1900. My paternal grandmother Genevieve ("Grandma Gee") Goldstein Marcus was born on Long Island in 1898.

Now that I've typed this, for the first time I've realized that my lineage is mostly Germanic. Maybe that explains why I get so pissed-off at people who are always late, like my Italo-Czech-Jewish wife.

I was unusual among my friends that all of my grandparents were alive when I was in college, and three out of four of them were born in the USA. Grandma Del was the most Yankee-like of them, with little tolerance for immigrants. She frequently criticized those with accents as "speaking with a heavy handwriting." She claimed her ancestry was high-class Austrian. My father said her people were Polish, just like his. It all depends on what year the map was made.

I was the first grandchild on both sides of the family and as a novelty I enjoyed special status for a while. Grandma Del made me feel I was her favorite grandchild, but it's possible she made my siblings and cousins feel that way too.

When I was a little child, maybe four years old, I remember sitting next to Grandma Del in the back seat of a car and she would hold my hand and fondle my fingers. It was weird and creepy and bothered me. It seemed to go beyond a normal grandmotherly gesture, but I don't remember if I asked her to stop. A great many years later there was a reprise, after both my grandfather and her later boyfriend had died. Whenever I visited her, she'd kiss me on my lips. My special status with Grandma Del lasted until she died.

I often wished my parents spelled "Neuman" as "Newman," or had given me a good American middle name like Paul. My sister Meryl's middle name sounds normal but it's spelled weird: Carin. Youngest sibling Marshall escaped the curse. His middle name is David.

All of our first names begin with "M" and end with "L." Allegedly Meryl and I were a coincidence and then Marshall made it a tradition. My parents didn't like Mitchell, Mendel, Muriel or Muttel so they stopped at three. I'm sure Sarah Palin could come up with more, like Moosetestical.

I was taught in junior high school that there is no improper way to spell a proper name. I disagree. "Michael" is the only right way to spell "Michael." It's a perfect Anglicized representation of the ancient Hebrew name.

Anyone who spells it "Micheal" is an idiot and deserves an F. Anyone who spells it "Mykul" is being innovative and denying history, but not making a spelling error. At least there's no doubt about how it's pronounced. My first name is certainly not pronounced like the letters M-I-C-H-A-E-L seem to indicate. I'll allow Mykl, Mykul and Mikal to exist, but not MiQuale, M'quil, Miquail, Mykell or Mykale.

Now there are even females named Michael. I don't like it and I want it stopped. What's wrong with Michelle or Michaela? Why do parents give their kids confusing names?

The parents of basketball player Isiah Thomas should have paid more attention in church. They left out an "a," but their kid pronounces his first name as if the letter *is* there.

For the first quarter-century of my life I hated and hid my unconventional and un-American middle name. I was so detached from the name that I misspelled it as "Numan" on a school registration form in second grade. Any kid who discovered my secret name compared me to Alfred E. Neuman from MAD magazine. *Time* magazine once misspelled his name as "Newman." For a while, when people

What, me worry? asked what my middle initial "N" stood for, I'd say that it stood for "None of your fucking business."

As a little kid, I was sometimes affectionately called "Noony" by Grandma Del. I loved her but hated the nickname.

In fifth grade an obnoxious girl who lived near me heard about it and used to follow me to school chanting "Michael Noony Marcus." In college I lived with Indian students who told me that noony is the Hindi word for "penis," which made me feel a bit better. I recently read that noony is slang for "vagina." I'm not sure about it now.

I like the look and sound of "Michael N. Marcus" and it helps distinguish me from all of the other Michael Marcuses out there so it's easy to Google me. My use of the "N" may be an unconscious homage to my grandfather Dr. Jay N. Jacobs, who used the initial to break up the alliteration. (By the way, did you notice the weird plural of Marcus? *Microsoft Word* thinks it's wrong, but it's right. *Word* accepts "buses" but not "Marcuses."

"Busses" is also an accepted plural of bus, but *I* don't accept "Marcusses.")

I used to be amazed when I learned of another Michael Marcus. But in reality, it's more likely that a male Marcus would be Michael, not Bill. Cosmetics maker Michael Marcus pissed me off when he registered www.michaelmarcus.com first. However, I did get www.michaelmarc.us.

For a few years when I stopped hating my middle name I sometimes used the pretentious pen name "M. Neuman Marcus." That label became very useful when the classy department store Neiman Marcus opened a branch near me. I opened an account and my credit card had the name "M. Neuman Marcus" on it. During my annual visits to buy a few jars of Neiman's Texas Chili, I was taken *very* good care of.

My last name has been useful while shopping, too. One time I stopped at Marcus Dairy for a newspaper and a milkshake. When it was time to pay, I playfully showed my driver's license and asked if I get the family discount.

The cashier said, "Sure, Mr. Marcus. Everything in the store is free." Actually, I paid the full bill and left a big tip. I didn't want to be a cheapskate and embarrass the family.

Chapter 83
This beard's for you

Our high school assistant principal was George Kennedy, a mean SOB with a short haircut that made him look like he had just recently left the Marines. "Granny" glasses made him seem very old fashioned — the exact opposite of the image that John Lennon would give to the same eyeglass style a few years later.

He seemed to break balls just for the sheer joy of it.

Kennedy rode a bicycle to school each day and students dreamed of flattening his tires, or shoving a stick between his spokes and knocking him off the bike and on his ass.

During my junior year, one day I was at my friend Howie's house after school, and I left a little rubber alligator there. The next day, Howie brought it to school, and when he saw me in the hallway near my locker, he tossed it to me so I could put it away.

Some busybody teacher with too much time on her hands reported the episode to Kennedy and I was called down to his office to be prosecuted and sentenced.

Kennedy informed me that I had violated Board of Education Rule 7,934, 726,422,079 subsection B revision 7.02 paragraph 9, that banned rubber alligators from school property without a permit, and he confiscated my artificial reptile.

The SOB kept the gator until the last day of school. He may have performed voodoo or satanic rituals with it.

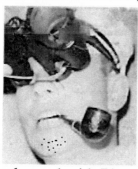

In 1963, in the fall of my senior year, I was out of school with mononucleosis ("the kissing disease') for about six weeks. I didn't have much else to do, so I grew a beard. It was a little beard, but it was pretty good for a 17-year-old. Some other kids in my class didn't even shave yet.

On my first day back to school, another busybody teacher spotted my new growth and sent me to Kennedy for a chin and cheek check. (The picture was taken on 10/11/63 with my beginner's beard enhanced with Photoshop). Kennedy was able to see the fuzz and he insisted that it was against the rules for students to have beards.

I asked him to show me the rule and he frowned. He flipped through the pages of several notebooks. He couldn't find the rule, but he came up with another solution. The evil prick said that if I didn't shave off the beard, he'd shave it off for me, but without shaving cream. I caved and I shaved.

I've had a beard since 1965. My wife and my dog have never seen my chin.

Around 1972 I happened to be in New Haven at the time of an important football game between my high school and its traditional rival. I stopped by the stadium to see who else might show up. I couldn't find any of my old classmates but I did see George Kennedy, and I couldn't resist showing off my beard. This time he said it looked good, and he couldn't send me home to shave it off.

I think he was jealous. He probably can't grow one.

Chapter 84
It didn't matter to anyone but him

I had a very good friend in high school. I'll call him "Stevie Edison" here. It's not his real name, but I don't want to embarrass him. I haven't seen him since a couple of years after we graduated. I hope he's alive and well.

Stevie was extremely smart and witty and articulate. His last name was just as famous as "Edison," and he claimed to be a descendent of an equally famous American inventor, someone every kid learns about in school.

He also claimed to be related to Jackie Kennedy's sister, Princess Lee Radziwill. Stevie's home, he wanted us to believe, was a mansion on "Edison Avenue," which was named after an earlier generation of his famed family.

The phone book showed his address in a much shabbier part of town. He explained that the discrepancy was due to his parents' need for privacy and security.

Similarly, the kids from school were never allowed to visit the mansion. He did come to my house after school a few times; and was driven home in an old car. He said the woman driving was his maid, but because of the affection she showed to Stevie, it was obvious that she was his mother.

Everyone liked Stevie, but no one understood his need to fake his family history. It was almost like a witness protection program. His friends all knew where Stevie really lived, but no one said anything to him or blew his cover to outsiders.

Hillhouse High School was a public school — not a blueblood private school — despite our principal's petty and pretentious dress code.

Hillhouse students were drawn from neighborhoods all over New Haven. Those neighborhoods ranged from glamorous to ghetto and the citizens ranged from wealthy to welfare. There was an equally wide range in students' intellect and aspiration.

Some of my classmates earned MDs and PhDs in the Ivy League; others would become soldiers, chefs, thieves, mechanics, secretaries and hairdressers.

In school, if there were cliques, the dividing lines were based much more on brain power than on income or race or religion. Although most of the kids in Hillhouse who were headed for college were white and Jewish, some who were neither "crossed over."

Billy Priestly was probably the first black guest at one all-white and mostly Jewish country club, and many of his friends joked that he was an "honorary Jew." Stevie Edison was a guest there, too. Most of his friends were Jewish kids from affluent Westville. He was a Catholic from "the Hill." I think his father drove a cab.

I was never aware of any snobbery at Hillhouse, but a classmate who remembers Stevie said, "Who knows what subtle cues he might have picked up, or imagined." Another student said, "No one ever busted him over his back-story; we had some kind of weird live and let live policy. How tolerant we were."

Perhaps the snobbism was more obvious for girls than for boys. My father owned clothing stores. But like most of the boys, I wore the bare minimum necessary to comply with the principal's "collegiate" dress code. Two of my classmates — with the same initials! — seemed to wear the same grungy sweaters every day.

Stevie, on the other hand, always wore very preppy sport-coats and blazers, and he never complained about the dress code that his classmates regarded as oppressive.

I don't know how Stevie's secrets first leaked out, but the truth was pretty well known. Some of us wanted to help him, to let him know that we didn't care where his father worked or how much money his family had.

His father was not the only cab driver in town. Stevie's friends didn't think cab drivers were bad people or bad parents, but he was obviously embarrassed.

But it's tough to start a conversation with a friend by saying, "I know you've been lying to me, but..."

I once tried to get professional help for Stevie.

When I got to college I described the situation to a guidance counselor, but he assumed I was describing *my own* situation, not a friend's invented life. Nothing I could say would convince the counselor that I really was describing Stevie, and he recommended psychotherapy for *me*.

It was like a sitcom.

I hope that Stevie eventually got the help he needed and was able to "come out."

On the other hand, maybe he did just fine.

Maybe good friends were all the help he needed.

Chapter 85
The return of Daddy Demon

At a high school reunion, I was approached by another old man.

Years earlier, when his hair was darker and greasier, Rick was known as *Daddy Demon*. In our high school yearbook, for his future, it says "uncertain."

Rick smiled, said "Hi, howya been?" and he raised his right hand to shake mine.

I kept my right hand at my side.

I reminded Rick that in the fall of 1958, when we were both in the seventh grade, he and a couple of other 12-year-old hoods ambushed me for no discernable reason. Rick used a knife to poke holes in both of my bicycle tires and then he snuffed out a cigarette on my head.

And a few months later, Rick's posse held me down on the ground with my mouth forced open so they could spit into it.

I did not shake Rick's hand.

I did tell Rick to go fuck himself.

I still remember a lot.

Epilogue
What was, and what if?

While writing this book I spent a lot of time reading old love letters, appointment books, term papers, "little black books," yearbooks and autograph books and looking at old pictures.

I Googled a lot of names and sent a lot of email. I joined Classmates.com and Reunion.com and used Facebook and Myspace and Zoominfo and online newspapers trying to find out what happened to friends, enemies and lovers from the past half century. Some people are still missing. Some stories were not written. Sometimes when I Googled, I found *my own words*, but nothing new.

Looking backwards can be fun, surprising, revealing and intriguing. But playing "what if" can also be unproductive, addictive or even dangerous.

Historians do it all the time. They get paid to ponder.

They contemplate how different life would be if the South had won the Civil War, if Germany had won World War II, if JFK and RFK and MLK had not been killed, and if one Supreme Court Justice hadn't awarded the presidency to George W. Bush.

But personal retro-speculation can cause trouble. If you spend too much time rearranging the past in your mind, you can neglect the present and hurt your future.

I n assessing my own life, I had to wonder about some decisions, indecisions and missed opportunities.

A few weeks into my first semester in college, it was obvious that I was at the wrong college and headed for the wrong career. I didn't make either choice. Elizabeth Clifford, my high school guidance counselor, picked both.

She decided I should go to Lehigh University and prepare to become an electrical engineer. She strangely ignored the facts that my math College Board scores kept going down and my "verbal" scores kept going up. She knew I liked electronics. But the electronics that I liked centered on soldering irons and screwdrivers; and engineers used slide rules. I never figured out how to use the slide rule properly. Now I use computers.

This guidance counselor — who was entrusted to guide teenagers in some of the most important decisions of their lives — really didn't know what engineers did; but she had decided that I should do what they do.

In an effort to guide me, Miss Clifford gave me an aptitude test that revealed I had a "99th percentile commonality" with chemical engineering students at Penn State.

I *hated* chemistry class. I resented memorizing the atomic numbers of the elements. The chemistry lab in every sci-fi movie I'd ever seen had a huge "periodic table of the elements" on the wall that the mad scientist could easily consult if he needed the atomic number for Bohrium.

If important professional scientists could look at the big wall chart, why couldn't high school students?

The best mark I got in chemistry was during the marking period when I stayed home with mononucleosis. The most fun I had with chemistry was mixing water with sodium bicarbonate and filling our basement with foam.

After one semester in college, I switched from electrical engineering to Lehigh's tiny but excellent journalism department — a spot that neither my guidance counselor nor I would have selected in advance.

But looking back from 2009 to 1965 it seems to have been a great place to be. It even made this book possible.

Who knew? Miss Clifford certainly didn't.

Sure, we all know that "shit happens." But so does serendipity. Lots of good things happen by accident. Even great people are born without planning.

Teenagers are expected to choose their life path, and often their life mate, with very little information and very little experience.

My junior high school expected me to decide if I would start on the path to college or not, based on five-month courses in Spanish (called "Language Exploratory") and typing ("Business Exploratory").

But learning to say "Mas salsa por favor, Señor Gomez" with an authentic accent does not mean a 15-year-old is either qualified or destined to become a doctor.

And being able to type 40 words per minute without peeking at the keys or making too many mistakes does not mean a 15-year-old will become a good manicurist.

But that's what our school system assumed.

How can a 15-, 16-, or 17-year-old pick a career that will be right at age 30, 40, 50 or 60?

Or pick a spouse that will be right at those ages?

I'm amazed at people who marry their high school sweethearts. I'm more amazed if they are still married 20 or 40 years later. How can a 16-year-old choose a 60-year-old spouse?

Strangely, it seems to work.

The divorce rate for people married when they're under 20 is much lower than those who get married when they're between 20 and 24. Sadly, my high school classmates have had lots of divorces. But many married again.

Eighteenth Century writer Samuel Johnson declared that second marriages are "the triumph of hope over experience."

The more often you've married, the more likely you are to have a divorce. The divorce rate for third marriages in the United States is over 70%.

(but maybe not until they're adults)

While writing this book, it was inevitable that I thought about, fantasized about and played the "what-if" game about some of the high school sweethearts whom I didn't marry.

One time, as the book progressed, I nearly blacked out during a medical procedure. In my mind, I reached out and held the hand of a beautiful 16-year-old girl.

I later found a current picture of her. She's a wrinkled old lady now, and one fantasy has been destroyed forever.

THE THREE BIG DON'TS

(After writing these rules, I disobeyed them. It was a disaster. Do as I say. Don't do as I did.)

❶ Don't focus on what could have been. Deal with what is. You probably can't change much anyway.

❷ Don't try to manipulate the space-time continuum. You're not Dr. Emmett Brown. You probably don't have a DeLorean with a 1.21 gigawatt plutonium-powered flux capacitor. You might not be able to come back to the future.

❸ Don't seek a lot of information. The reality of the present can disrupt the memories and fantasies of the past.

Enjoy your dreams.

MNM

Personal messages:

(Some of the women's last names are different now.)

To Joey, Scott and Fang from the Wight Reign band in Bethlehem: Please send me an email. I have the band's savings account book, and you're entitled to share $10 plus interest since 1968. Pizza or burgers?

To Barbara Anderson, a great girl friend while I was in college: Unfortunately you were too good a friend to become a girlfriend. I've learned that this particular transition never works out.

To Susan Blumenthal, the object of my unrequited love from first grade through sixth grade: I still remember your phone number, even though I never had the guts to call you. I should have. Hi!

To Donna Calechman, whom I used to visit while she babysat when I was around 15 years old: I'd sit next to you on the couch with my arm around you when we watched TV, but I never had the guts to kiss you. I should have.

To Virginia whose-last-name-I-don't-remember, who worked a few flights down from me at *Rolling Stone:* One time you stripped down to your underwear and had me paint a flower with a long stem and leaves on your side, but I skipped the part where the plant would have passed beneath your panties. Maybe you wanted me to complete the painting. I should have found out.

To Beverly, my first slightly older woman: I was a virgin then, too. I think we did pretty well for beginners. The second time was even better. So was the third time.

To Nancy Kinsley, whom I dated in college and afterward: There is a good story about you in the book. I changed your name and some of the details. Can you find yourself?

To Anthony Accurso, a junior high school science teacher: The photograph I brought to school that showed rocket ships heading from the moon to the Earth was a fake. I'm sorry.

To Marilyn Kaplan, whom I dated in high school: Around 1963, we ate in the College Spa in New Haven. You ordered a roast beef sandwich and it came with butter on it, which you didn't want. I was too much of a wimp to send it back. It was disgusting, and I should not have expected you to eat it. I'm sorry.

To (name withheld), whom I dated in college: I set you up on a date with (name withheld) because I hoped you'd go to bed with him and I was looking for an excuse to break up with you. I'm a little bit sorry.

To Rosemary Garcia, whom I dated in high school and college, and who grew up faster than I did: You told me a joke, "What if someone hosted an orgy, but no one came?" I laughed, but I didn't really understand it until a few months later. That may be the first time someone faked laughing about orgasm.

To Janice Wasserman, whom I dated in high school and who visited me for a weekend when I was a freshman at Lehigh: We missed an exit and got lost in Newark. We couldn't get tickets for the wrestling match and had to watch it on a giant projection screen. I had a nosebleed. I acted like a jerk. I'm sorry.

To Vicky Emery, who lived in New York when I lived in Bethlehem and lived in Bethlehem when I lived in New York: I wish we were better synchronized. I still see your smile. Your mother made the best non-Jewish chicken soup I ever tasted.

To Alan Melnick, who in junior high school used to tell me an ongoing daily dirty story about "Grand Pee-Prick:" I knew you were adapting *The Mouse That Roared* that took place in "Grand Fenwick" but your stories were good and I didn't want to ruin it.

To Marilyn Marcus, my wife since 1971: Don't be jealous about the other women I've mentioned. You'll share the profits if they see their names and buy books.

To my mother: When I was around 16 I was secretly attending the do-it-yourself driving school. I once made a minor miscalculation while trying to get your Plymouth out of the garage and bumped into the side of the garage. The damage to the fender and the wall were minor, but visible. Since you and Dad couldn't imagine that *I* had driven the car, Dad blamed you for the damage, and you accepted responsibility. Only a woman driver could crash and not know it, or think she crashed when she didn't. Sorry, Mom. Sorry, Plymouth.

My literary gods

I thank them for entertainment, stimulation and setting very high standards.

Dave Barry is a Pulitzer Prize-winning humor columnist and author, and the funniest writer I know of. Dave is so funny that I had to stop reading his column because I got so jealous. No one packs more laughs into a paragraph than Dave does. He used a picture of my dog Hunter in one of his books. It's called *Dave Barry's Money Secrets*. Here's a Dave Barry money secret: Dave didn't pay me any money for the picture, but I did get a free book. I'll let Dave read my book for free, too.

Jean Shepherd (1921-1999) was a radio and TV raconteur, and he probably ties with Mark Twain for story-telling ability. Shep's books include *In God We Trust - All Others Pay Cash*, *Wanda Hickey's Night of Golden Memories*, and *A Fistful of Fig Newtons*. Twain was a great writer, but Shep was much funnier.

Jack Douglas (1908-1989) was an Emmy Award-winning comedy writer on *The Jack Paar Show*, *The George Gobel Show*, *Laugh-In* and other programs. I remember him most for his book titles, including *My Brother Was an Only Child, Shut Up and Eat Your Snowshoes,* and *Never Trust a Naked Bus Driver*.

Michael Solomon and David Hirshey edited and did the headlines for the annual *Esquire* magazine Dubious Achievement Awards in the 1990s. Why *is* this man laughing?

Don Martin (1931-2000) was an extraordinary cartoonist best known for his work in *MAD* magazine. Don created such notable characters as Fester Bestertester and Freenbean Fonebone, and *printed* sound effects like "FAGROON klubble klubble." Don's books are available from Amazon.com. Buy them!

(but maybe not until they're adults)

"Uncle" Tom McCahill (1907-1975) was an automotive journalist who wrote for *Mechanix Illustrated* magazine in the 1950s and 60s. He rated car trunks by the number of dogs they could hold, and described the ride of a 1957 Pontiac as "smooth as a prom queen's thighs." Tom was a Yale graduate, and knew classic literature as well as cars. When a reader asked how to pronounce "Porsche," Tom answered, "Portia." Some of us understood. Another reader asked, "How much is the parts cost and how much do the car?" Tom answered, "Sure."

Tom Lehrer claims he "went from adolescence to senility, trying to bypass maturity." Tom graduated from Harvard Magna Cum Laude at age 18 and made Phi Beta Kappa. He taught at MIT, Harvard, Wellesley and the University of California, but is best known for hilarious songwriting, much of it political satire in the 1950s and 60s. His musical career was powerful but brief. He said he performed a mere 109 shows and wrote only 37 songs over 20 years. Britain's Princess Margaret was a fan, and so am I. I can still sing Tom Lehrer lyrics I first heard in seventh grade.

Matt Groening created *The Simpsons* and *Life in Hell*. *The Simpsons* has been the longest-running comedy show in American television history. Because it's a cartoon, some people make the mistake of assuming it's for kids. It's not, but kids love it.

Jay Ward created *Rocky & Bullwinkle, Dudley Do-Right, Peabody and Sherman,* and *Crusader Rabbit*. The Rocky show was filled with literary allusions and magnificent puns (or horrible puns, depending on your outlook on such things). Unless you're an old fart who watched TV in the 1950s and know that Durward Kirby was the sidekick on *The Garry Moore Show,* you would not appreciate the pun in "Kerwood Derby," a hat that increased the intelligence of its wearer.

I had a few very good teachers

The Hillhouse High School class of 1964 was given the impressive honorary title of "the last great class" by **Emma Ruff,** who taught English to many of us, and became Hillhouse principal after we graduated. Mrs. Ruff told me we were the last great class when I interviewed her for an article I wrote for *The New Haven Register* on the occasion of our class's 25th year reunion in 1989. Mrs. Ruff made history. She was said to be New Haven's first black teacher and Connecticut's first female high school principal. Mrs. Ruff could mix grammar with humor and sex to impress teenagers.

Ruth Leighton was my English teacher in my senior year in high school. She was probably my first teacher who regarded high school students as semi-adults, and not just tall children. Mrs. Leighton treated us with respect, and the respect was returned. She was more like a guide, not a dictator. We were clients, not prisoners. She was working for us, and with us. Our class was interrupted by lunch, and discussions were often continued in the hallways and cafeteria. Hers was one of very few classes where kids didn't watch the hands move around the clock, count the holes in the ceiling tiles, or run for the door when the bell rang.

Suellen Farrington taught me math in either my sophomore or junior year in high school. I'm embarrassed that I don't remember which year it was, or even one tiny detail about what made her a good teacher. But that fact that I do remember that she was a good teacher is enough to put her on this unfortunately short list. I had two other math teachers in high school. One is hated. One is forgotten.

Cullen Hodge was my high school physics teacher. See chapter 14.

Lawrence DePalma taught me history in junior high school around 1959, and was not afraid to ignore the Board of Education's plans if he thought he knew a better way to teach. Instead of using the latest slick and simplified textbooks, Mr. DePalma distributed tattered copies of *Morey's Ancient Peoples* that he had diverted from a trip to the dump and guarded carefully year after year. He regarded their intellectual content as more important than their physical appearance. That itself was a valuable lesson. Rev. Martin Luther King said something similar a few years later in his "I have a dream" speech.

Annette O'Brasky taught science in the same junior high school. "Annie Obsky" was tough, but unlike some other tough teachers, she had a *good* reason to be that way: high standards, not sadism. Most kids in our class were headed for college, so she said we may as well get used to doing college-level work when we were 14. Some kids were upset to find that a teacher would deduct points for spelling errors and sloppiness on term papers for science class, not English class. Mrs. O'Brasky wisely pointed out that form and content were inextricably linked, years before Marshall McLuhan declared that "The medium is the message."

Molly Nuht, my second grade teacher, had an excellent way of making abstract numbers seem real, so arithmetic would make more sense to little children. On a table by the window were ten paper plates, and each plate had a number from one to ten on it. Plate #3 held three paint brushes. Plate #6 held six horseshoe magnets. It was very real and very effective, and I've remembered the lesson for 57 years.

Ceil Gold was my grandmotherly first grade teacher in New Haven at a time of traumatic transition when I moved from New York. I got lost the first day I walked to school. A cop rescued me and I got a ride to school in his police car. When I arrived, Mrs. Gold gave me a much-needed hug. That might be illegal now. She recognized my interest in technology and called me "The Inventor." She even let me keep my "inventor's kit" at school. It was a cardboard soda six-pack filled with tools, wire, batteries, and parts rescued from radios, clocks, flashlights and a cap gun. I built some cool stuff in first grade. I still do. And sometimes I still get lost.

Elizabeth Tracy was the warm and wonderful Hillhouse High School librarian who often provided me with a much needed shelter from the storm.

Elizabeth Clifford was my high school guidance counselor who directed me to what turned out to be the right college, even though it was for the wrong reason.

Joseph McFadden was a journalism professor at Lehigh University. "Mack" was the first person who told me I could write. He taught us the important rules of reporting and encouraged us to pick our own subjects and write the way we speak. I do.

313

About the author

Michael N. Marcus is a journalist, author, advertising copywriter, and founder and president of AbleComm, Inc. ("the telecom department store").

He provides the words for about 40 websites and blogs, has been Audio-Video Editor of *Rolling Stone*, and has written for many other magazines and newspapers. Michael was one of the first writers to humanize hi-fi hardware, describing the equipment with emotion, not math.

Born in 1946, Michael's a proud member of the first cohort of the Baby Boom, along with Dolly Parton, Candy Bergen, Donny Trump, Billy Clinton and Georgie Bush.

At the urging of a misguided guidance counselor, he went to Lehigh University to become an electrical engineer, and was quickly disappointed to learn that engineering was mostly math — and slide rules were not as much fun as soldering irons.

Michael was one of a few literate people in his engineer-filled freshman dormitory and made money editing term papers. While in college he co-owned a band management company. One of their groups turned down the chance to record *Yummy Yummy Yummy, I Have Love in My Tummy*, which later became a hit for Ohio Express.

His college apartment had an elaborate and illegal multi-line phone system, a phone booth with a toilet in it, and an invisible phone activated by two hand claps.

Michael lives in Connecticut with his wife Marilyn, Hunter the Golden Retriever, and a lot of stuff— including both indoor and outdoor telephone booths, a "Lily Tomlin" switchboard, lots of books, CDs and DVDs, and many black boxes with flashing lights. Marilyn is very tolerant.

More about Michael: www.MichaelMarc.us

Text for my gravestone:

When I was in my 20s, I had delusions of immortality. I honestly thought that if I was on a plane with 393 other people and the plane crashed, I would be the sole survivor. It was probably a combination of innocence, ignorance, egomania and utter lack of confidence in others.

I also felt that if I went into a jungle alone and had to face hostile tigers, alligators or Viet Cong I would survive; but if I was part of a huge army, someone else would fuck up, and we would all get killed. I didn't like teamwork.

Now, decades later, I have a more realistic assessment of my future. I know I won't live forever. And since I don't want someone else to mess up my epitaph, here it is.

> # Michael N. Marcus
> # 1946 – 2xxx
> # "OK, what's next?"

I like "Rockwell Bold" for the type face. Someone just has to fill in the final date and pick a nice piece of rock.

As for the words, yes, I'm an incurable optimist. I've always been resilient. I recover quickly from setbacks and disappointments and I'm always looking ahead. On freezing days in January I know that the Earth gets more sunlight each day and is warming up. Spring is coming. Soon my dog and I will be in the pool and my ancient Fiat Spider will be out of the garage.

Someone, *please* make sure my stone is done right. My words are important to me. If you fuck up my stone, I'm gonna come back and bite your neck. Thanks very much. *MNM*

Colophon (why the book looks the way it does)
Breaking and starting traditions

Normally the first few pages of a book have no numbers printed on them, and then come pages with Roman numerals, and finally there are pages with standard "Arabic" numbers. This system has always seemed silly and unnecessarily complicated to me. **In this book, we start with Arabic numbers and skip the Romans.** It was much easier to put the book together this way, and I encourage others to do it, too. Even Romans don't use Roman numerals any more.

Book chapters traditionally begin on right-hand pages (called "recto" in the book business); but chapters don't always conveniently end on left-hand "verso" pages. That's why lots of books have blank left pages or left pages with just cute little pictures or quotes. That's a waste of paper, trees, energy and money; so this book ignores that tradition. **My chapters start on the page after the previous chapter ends. Some start recto and some start verso**, whatever comes naturally. We saved over 30 pages this way. That could add up to a lot of paper, and maybe save a few trees. If other publishers would do this, they would probably save lots of trees, energy and money. With concern about the depletion of forests, and the high cost of energy, that's more important than following tradition.

I don't have my name in the "header" at the top of every other page. If you're on page 178 and have a sudden urge to figure out the name of the author, you can look at the cover.

I realize that you could also easily look at the cover if you have a sudden urge to know the name of the book you've been reading. I really didn't need to put the book title all over the place like on most books. However, if I didn't put anything up there, the empty space would look silly. **I decided to put the main title on the verso pages and the sub-title on the recto pages.** I saw no need to leave headers off chapter title pages as is the custom. I can start my own custom. I like the way the book looks, and the style doesn't hurt the stories.

I put a space before and after each *em* — *dash* when dashes indicate parenthetical remarks. It seems to unite thoughts, not just words. I like it this way. Some purists don't. *The New York Times* agrees with me. The Oxford University Press disagrees. **Fuck 'em. It's my book.**

(but maybe not until they're adults)

Photo & illustration credits

Graphic images are licensed, public domain, produced by the author, used with permission, or believed to qualify as "fair use" under U.S. copyright law and do not compete with the copyright holder. If the owner of any copyrighted image wants it removed from future editions, please contact the publisher.

Front cover photo by Michael Kempf , Photoshopped by Carina Ruotolo ◆Back cover photos by H. Tarr, Edward Malley Studio, Stratford Studios and Cloe Poisson. Cloe took the 2008 picture. It's ©2008 *The Hartford Courant*, and used with permission. ◆Larry David photo from HBO ◆ Bad teeth photo by Andriy Goncharenko ◆Whoopie Cushion photo from SillyJokes.co.uk ◆Tie photo from Absolute Ties ◆Heart-beat photo from Argus ◆ "Wayward Comrade" book cover from Signet Books ◆ Bus photo from Thaut Images ◆*Wheel of Fortune* photo from Merv Griffin Enterprises ◆Health book photo from Pearson ◆Dexedrine photo from HealthCentral.com ◆Bronx photo from New Yorkl Public Library. ◆ Nun photo by Patrick Hermans ◆Police cap photo from America Wear ◆Bikini photo from Dash ◆Microscope photo from Nikon ◆ Odd Couple photo from ABC Television ◆Elton John photo from eltonjohn.com ◆Stalactite photo from Piotr Sikora ◆Clam photo from NOAA ◆Klingon mask from Halloween Express ◆Lunch counter photo by Meghan Woodhouse ◆ Gorilla arm photo by Eric Isselée ◆Dan Ackroyd as Beldar photo from NBC ◆Bill Gates photo from Microsoft ◆Lehigh River photo from Pennsylvania State Archives ◆My Mother The Car photo from United Artists Television ◆Hotdog photo from Aga & Miko ◆New Merchants Hotel photo from the Bill Weiner Collection, via Lehigh Univ. ◆Taylor photo from U.S. Army ◆Ed Sullivan photo from CBS ◆Bra photo from Germes ◆Dome photo by Alexandr Loskutov ◆Church bell photo by Harvey Hudson ◆Bob Grant photo from WABC radio ◆Inflatable life vest photo from Stearns ◆Swim fin photo from U.S. Divers ◆Eton suit from Adorable Baby Clothing ◆Jockstrap photo from Go Softwear ◆Hand photo by Anna Sinyaeva ◆Teeth photo from Monkey Business ◆Spear gun photo from SCUBA.com ◆Crayfish photo from Antti Karppinen ◆Fish photo from Vladyslav Danilin ◆Horse photo by Zygimantas Cepaitis ◆Long John Nebel photo from WOR ◆Handcuffs photo by James Steidl ◆Hillbilly photo from Summers Graphics ◆Birds photo by Domefb ◆Antenna photo from Mosley ◆Scarsdale photo from Scarsdale Schools website ◆Plunger photo from Supply Line Direct ◆Marcus Cicero statue photo from Museo Capitolino, photographer unknown ◆Marcus Aurelius statue photo from Metropolitan Museum of Art, photographer unknown ◆Marcus Crassus statue from Musée du Louvre, photographer unknown ◆Marcus Brutus statue photo by Jastrow ◆Marcus Antonius statue photo from Vatican Museum, photographer unknown ◆Marcus car photo from Unique Cars and Parts ◆Gorbachev photo from Reagan Library ◆Alfred E. Neuman picture from *MAD* magazine ◆Indian photo by Diorgi ◆DeLorean photo from DiecastMuscle.com ◆Fangs photo by Chris Harvey ◆Crutch photo from kmit ◆Graduation cap photo from Stephen Coburn ◆Baseball player image from siam images ◆Frog photo from alle ◆Breast feeding photo from NiDerLander ◆Electric chair image from AlienCat ◆Too-big jeans photo from Marin Conic ◆Skull photo from AlienCat ◆Jail bars photo from Giovanni Cardinali ◆Sisters photo from Monkey Business

317

Breinigsville, PA USA
27 November 2009

228218BV00001B/15/P